April 24, 1990

For Todd,

With affection & my
Thanks for helping
me teach my class

Best wishes,

Eddie

DISCARD

Johnson, *Rasselas*, and the Choice of Criticism

Johnson, *Rasselas*, and the Choice of Criticism

EDWARD TOMARKEN

THE UNIVERSITY PRESS OF KENTUCKY

Library of Congress Cataloging-in-Publication Data

Tomarken, Edward, 1938-
    Johnson, Rasselas, and the choice of criticism / Edward Tomarken.
        p.   cm.
    Bibliography: p.
    Includes index.
    ISBN 0-8131-1689-9 :
    1. Johnson, Samuel, 1709-1784—Criticism and interpretation.
2. Johnson, Samuel, 1709-1784. Rasselas. 3. Criticism. I. Title.
PR3534.T66   1989   89-32518
823'.6—dc20

Dedicated to the memory of
PEARL AND BARNEY TOMARKEN

Contents

Acknowledgments

I wish to express my thanks to my colleagues at Princeton University, the City College of New York, the Centre Universitaire in Luxembourg, and Miami University who listened and responded helpfully to my longtime obsession with the writings of Johnson. In particular, Professors David Mann, John Parks, Frank Jordan, William Pratt, Patricia Harkin, James Sosnoski, Britton Harwood, Thomas Idinopulos, Sasson Pearl, and Barry Chabot made suggestions on various drafts of parts of the manuscript. I wish also to thank Professors John J. Burke, Jr., and Donald Kay for their early encouragement of my work and inclusion of an earlier version of chapter 7 in *The Unknown Samuel Johnson;* Gerhard Charles Rump for his help with the publication of an earlier version of chapter 2; and Professor Paul Korshin for including a previous version of chapter 3 in volume 2 of *The Age of Johnson*. I am grateful to the University of Wisconsin Press, Dr. Rudolf Habelt, and the AMS Press for permission to reprint portions of those essays. The research for this book could not have been completed without the help of the staff at the Miami University Library, the William Andrews Clark Memorial Library, the British Library, the University of Kent at Canterbury Library, and without various grants from the Miami University research fund.

For their editorial assistance in seeing the book smoothly and efficiently through to publication, I wish to thank Karen Orchard of the University of Georgia Press and the staff of the University Press of Kentucky. I was particularly fortunate in having two careful and sympathetic readings of the manuscript. My thanks to Professors Leopold Damrosch, Jr., and John Vance for their constructive suggestions.

It has been my privilege to be the student of two of the best teachers and finest minds in our field, Ralph Cohen and Northrop Frye. Professor Frye directed my doctoral dissertation on Johnson's writings and tolerated difference before the term became fashion-able. Professor Cohen introduced me as an undergraduate to *Rasselas* and read the manuscript at various stages, always making valuable suggestions. From these scholars I gained a commitment to the interfusion of literary criticism and literary theory.

But no book would ever be written without the aid of family and friends, and this book is no exception. Stephanie and Michael Shea have contributed so much to our daily happiness as a family that they could qualify as patrons of this book. My brothers, Pete and Jim, have helped in ways that would surprise them, ways that are a natural part of their personalities. The family of Bernard and Monique Labbé enabled me to write portions of the book in the beautiful setting of Le Moana. Mrs. Pamela Porter gave her assistance as a proofreader and impromptu provider of two-egg omelets. But my greatest debt is to my wife, Annette, who miraculously managed to finish her own book while never stinting in helping with mine, and to my daughter Emma, who was patient and numbered the pages.

Abbreviations Used

Dict   Samuel Johnson. *A Dictionary of the English Language*. London, 1773.

DTS   Followed by line number from Dryden's "Third Satire" in *The Imitations of John Dryden,* London, 1693.

DSX   Followed by line number from Dryden's "Tenth Satire" in *The Imitations of John Dryden,* London, 1693.

Irene   Act, scene, and line numbers from *The Poems of Samuel Johnson,* ed. D.N. Smith and E.L. McAdam. Oxford: Clarendon Press, 1974.

JSX   Followed by line number from Juvenal's "Satura X" in *Juvenal and Persius,* ed. G.G. Ramsey. Cambridge: Harvard UP, 1952.

JTS   Followed by line number from Juvenal's third satire in *Juvenal and Persius,* ed. G.G. Ramsey. Cambridge: Harvard UP, 1952.

JTH   Followed by page number from *A Journal of a Tour of the Hebrides* in James Boswell's *Life of Johnson,* vol. 5, ed. L.F. Powell. Oxford: Clarendon Press, 1964.

JWI   Followed by page number from *A Journey to the Western Islands of Scotland,* ed. J.D. Fleeman. Oxford: Clarendon Press, 1985.

London   Followed by line number from *The Poems of Samuel Johnson,* ed. D.N. Smith and E.L. McAdam. Oxford: Clarendon Press, 1974.

LP   Followed by page number from *The Life of Pope,* in *Lives of the English Poets,* vol. 3, ed. G.B. Hill. Oxford: Clarendon Press, 1905.

OTS   Followed by page number in *The Works of John Oldham,* vol. 3. London, 1684.

Poems   Followed by page and/or line number from *The Poems of Samuel Johnson,* ed. D.N. Smith and E.L. McAdam. Oxford: Clarendon Press, 1974.

R   Followed by chapter and page number in *The History of Rasselas, Prince of Abissinia,* ed. G. Tillotson and B. Jenkins. London: Oxford UP, 1971.

VHW   Followed by line number from "The Vanity of Human Wishes," in *The Poems of Samuel Johnson,* ed. D.N. Smith and E.L. McAdam. Oxford: Clarendon Press, 1974.

Works   Followed by volume and page number from *The Complete Works of Samuel Johnson.* 2 vols. London, 1825.

           All references to the *Rambler, Adventurer,* and *Idler* essays are followed by the original number and then the volume and page number in *The Yale Edition of the Works of Samuel Johnson,* ed. W.J. Bate, J.M. Bullitt, L.F. Powell, and A. Strauss. New Haven: Yale UP, 1963, 1969.

Introduction

THIS BOOK focuses on *Rasselas:* the analysis of other works by Johnson applies a method derived from the story of the Prince of Abyssinia. In that sense, this book is the first full-length study of *Rasselas*. Yet a brief glance at the standard critical bibliography reveals that, with the possible exception of the *Dictionary, Rasselas* has received more commentary than any other work in the canon. Why have so many essays been written about a tale that has never been the subject of a book? A preliminary analysis of these critical essays reveals that the narrative has been subjected to almost every kind of critical approach during the last two centuries. Furthermore, like a critical prism, *Rasselas* displays these various methods in a new light, eliciting new kinds of insights and raising new sorts of problems. Never neglected, *Rasselas* has remained resistant in different ways to all available critical approaches of the eighteenth, nineteenth, and twentieth centuries.

The critical significance of *Rasselas* thus becomes apparent: by examining the history of commentary on this tale, it is possible to illustrate the uses and limitations of every major literary approach since the middle of the eighteenth century. Chapter One is devoted to this task. It concludes by demonstrating that critical assumptions of the past have been either predominantly mimetic or formalistic and that *Rasselas* has not been adequately understood because it requires a critical theory that can include both kinds of assumptions. Chapters 2 and 3 demonstrate how at the very outset, while the prince is still in the happy valley, *Rasselas* evokes first mimetic and then formalistic viewpoints. Chapter 4 then provides a new way of reading *Rasselas* based upon a dialectical relationship between the motifs of the two previous chapters. Part I concludes with the recognition that the theoretical assumptions which form the basis for my interpretation of *Rasselas* were not available to Johnson or his contemporaries.

Part II goes back in time from 1759, the date of *Rasselas,* to the beginning of Johnson's writing career, 1738-49, in order to demonstrate that the dialectic of perspectives was arrived at by a process of trial and error. As a practicing author, Johnson achieves insights that are beyond the scope of his own literary criticism and that of his age. Chapter 5 considers Johnson's two earliest literary works, *Irene* and *London,* in order to demonstrate that each work suffers from a lack of equilibrium, the drama enclosing itself in its own form and the poem separating its referent from its radical of presentation. Chapter 6 shows that in *The Vanity of Human Wishes* Johnson first achieves a balance between form and referent, but that an understanding of that fact requires a new kind of reading of the poem. Chapter 7 applies this innovative approach to *A Journey to the Western Islands of Scotland* and concludes with an analysis that explains why historians and literary critics feel uneasy about this work that eludes inclusion in either category exclusively.

Because the aesthetic that develops in my reading of Johnson's literature operates most successfully on the margins between the literary and the extraliterary, the question addressed in my conclusion is how the literary is to be distinguished from the extraliterary. Using the *Life of Pope,* I demonstrate that Johnson accuses Pope of attempting to live a life of poetry, and dying, as a result, a friendless man. Here Johnson, near the end of his own life, consciously employs the dialectic of perspectives, but he only applies it consistently in the biographical, not the critical, section of the *Life of Pope.* Indeed, in the theoretical conclusion, I point out that a critical theory which can accommodate both formalism and mimeticism goes beyond the theories of our own day as well as that of Johnson. Such an aesthetic of perspectivism involves the intermingling of hermeneutics or reader-response criticism and structuralism and its various poststructuralist descendants.

PART I

Rasselas and the Critics

1

A History of *Rasselas* Criticism
1759-1986

RASSELAS HAS been the most widely read and continuously commented upon of all of Johnson's writings. Since its publication in 1759
hardly a year has gone by that has not produced a new edition of or
essay upon the text.[1] Even during the nineteenth century, when
Johnson's own writings were neglected in favor of Boswell's *Life,*
Rasselas continued to be reissued and analyzed. In fact, because of the
Victorian neglect of the Johnson canon, *Rasselas* is the only one of
Johnson's literary works with a continuous critical history. As a *locus
criticus, Rasselas* has been the subject of a controversy that began
when it first appeared and that has continued to the present. The
nature of this critical disagreement is fundamental: at issue is what
kind of work it is and whether or not it achieves its purported goal.
After nearly two and a half centuries of almost continuous dispute,
critics are still unable to decide whether *Rasselas* is a novel, oriental
tale, or apologue and whether its conclusion is to be seen in religious
or secular terms.

This controversy concerns both the meaning of the text and
whether or not it is a successful work of art. *Rasselas* has been
regularly attacked since it first appeared. In 1759 one reviewer characterized it as trite and threadbare, and in 1970 a critic described it as
marked by equivocation.[2] Instead of taking sides in this debate, I
propose to adopt a new perspective, one that will help explain how
Rasselas established itself as a "classic" of English Literature—that
is, continued to be read and discussed—while critics disagreed about
its genre and conclusion. In this chapter I argue that *Rasselas* exposes
the limitations of methods from the past because it cannot be circumscribed within the traditional literary-critical categories of literature, language, or written discourse. *Rasselas* concludes by suggesting how its literary structures apply to the extraliterary, to the arena,
not of words, but of action. Chapters 2, 3, and 4 are concerned with
formulating a kind of approach that can comprehend this Janus-faced

aesthetic. But first it is necessary to turn to the critical continuum: *Rasselas* has interested critics and readers of the past two and a quarter centuries because it throws new light on old questions or raises important new issues. A survey of this criticism permits an analysis of the developing literary-critical process of *Rasselas*. Giving particular attention to the interaction between different methodologies and new readings of the text, I shall demonstrate that *Rasselas* is most fruitfully approached on the level of literary process. My own method will be seen in chapters 5, 6, and 7, to have application to other writings by Johnson leading, in chapter 8, to a discussion of the limitations of literary process.

This history is to be distinguished from ordinary accounts of past criticism in that it concerns theory as well as practice, critical approach as well as conclusions derived from that approach. The decision to employ this perspective is related to my own interpretation of *Rasselas*. Subsequent chapters will make clear how my reading differs from those of the past. But it is important to establish at the outset that this survey of *Rasselas* criticism, like all literary critical enterprises, is conducted within a hermeneutic circle. My point of departure is that *Rasselas* is an educational tale about the nature of aesthetic understanding. The religious question (for Johnson, the quest for paradise on earth) is the driving force, the impulse toward that understanding.

This survey also departs from customary practice in proceeding by way of historical principles. I select those critics from the past who exemplify the nature of the historical continuum, the critical tradition of *Rasselas* commentary, in order to show that during the two and a half century old debate, some issues have been resolved, others have arisen as new problems or as reformulated old ones, and still others have remained unresolved or neglected.

Although most of the critics mentioned refer to some of their predecessors, no comprehensive survey of *Rasselas* criticism has been attempted before. In fact, some of the critical material considered here is not included in the critical bibliography published in 1970 by James Clifford and Donald Greene and updated in 1987 by John Vance and Donald Greene. An appendix contains a chronologically arranged checklist of all the critical material on *Rasselas* available to me, with an asterisk beside those entries not found in this bibliography: it is offered, not as an exhaustive survey, but as a contribution toward a comprehensive account of Johnson criticism.

In the year of its first publication, *Rasselas* was reviewed, according to Gwin Kolb in his essay of 1984, in at least fourteen different periodicals.[3] Most of the reviews were complimentary. The *Gentlemen's Magazine* praised the author for his "striking pictures of life and nature" which served as happy illustrations "of most important truths."[4] Similarly, the *London Magazine* pointed to the "most important Truths" of the "moral Tale" as well as the "agreeable and enchanting Manner" in which it was told.[5] The *Critical Review* applauded the choice of fiction as a means of moral instruction but faulted the lack of "plot, incident, character or contrivance" necessary to "beguile the imagination." The tale was seen as a "beautiful epitome of practical Ethics," but its author's talents were considered better suited to the essay or dialogue than to fiction.[6] Sharing this negative assessment of the manner of presentation, Owen Ruffhead, in the *Monthly Review*, went one step further to launch the first full-scale attack on the tale. This "romantic way of writing required a sprightliness of imagination" which Johnson lacked. The style of *Rasselas* was labeled "tumid and pompous," and the characters were said to lack variety and a distinct manner of speaking. The narrative lacked "invention in the plan" and "utility in the design" because the topics were trite and threadbare and the conclusion did not further any good end in society. The goal of Johnson's narrative, Ruffhead concluded, was to show that "discontent prevails among men of all ranks and conditions," a truth, he pointed out, that can be learned without traveling to Ethiopia.[7]

Ruffhead is not questioning the truth of the message of *Rasselas*. Rather, he believes that the manner of presentation is so abstract and gloomy as to encourage in the young and impressionable reader—and most critics of the day, Johnson included, assumed that fiction or romances were designed for such a reader—despair.[8] As we shall see, the question of the tone of the conclusion of the narrative was contested throughout the nineteenth and into the twentieth century, but during this latter period the issue has become whether or not the end is marked by a religious resolution. This alteration in the terms of the debate involves a shift in assumptions about the genre of *Rasselas*. It is generally assumed that the charge of gloom against *Rasselas* is synonymous with an attack on the religion of the narrative. But the eighteenth-century concept of the narrative and of the religious resolve appropriate to it was different from that of the Victorians and Moderns. The nature of this difference is made clear by considering an alternative to Ruffhead's position that was also published in 1759. An anonymous defender of *Rasselas* pointed out in the *Annual Register* that whereas most novels and romances of the day used superficial morality to lend a respectable appearance to an adventure story, Johnson had employed the popular story form in order to convey important ethical doctrines in a pleasurable manner.[9]

The point of contention for these first reviewers of *Rasselas* concerned not the religion of the text but whether or not the "beauties" of the story provided sufficient interest in and compensation for a gloomy, although accurate, picture of the futility of earthly endeavors. These critics shared the assumption that the doctrine of Ecclesiastes, the vanity of human wishes, need not discourage one from savoring the limited licit pleasures of the mortal world. They disagreed as to whether Johnson's romance left its young readers with as vivid an impression of the pleasures of everyday life as of the folly of man's grand designs. During the eighteenth century, two attitudes toward the doctrine of Ecclesiastes were current, the more familiar one asserting that all earthly endeavors are vain, and an alternative proposing that although all mortal wishes are ultimately vain, some wishes are to be preferred to others. It is not merely coincidental that this latter reading of Ecclesiastes was rediscovered in 1969 by Thomas Preston in an article on *Rasselas*, the details of which will be considered later in this chapter.[10] Here it should be noted that the question of genre and the assessment of the conclusion of the literary work are interrelated because generic decisions are teleological, a function of the critic's view of the goal of the literary work.

The publication of six new editions of *Rasselas* between 1759 and 1810 provided some evidence against the early view that the tale did not please or interest its readers.[11] In the decade after the death of Johnson, 1784-94, the flurry of lives of this most famous literary figure of the second half of the eighteenth century meant that both positions on *Rasselas* were presented in biographical terms. One of the earliest of Johnson's biographers, Thomas Tyers, reaffirmed that *Rasselas* was a "lamp of wisdom,"[12] a judgment shared by an anonymous editor who in 1787 felt confident enough of the appeal and wisdom of the book to recommend that young ladies should imitate the Princess of Abyssinia, a "pattern and mirror of excellence."[13] In 1787, Sir John Hawkins, however, disapproved of the tale because although "none of [Johnson's] compositions have been more applauded than this," it is a "general satire" which exposes not only follies but also "laudable affections and propensities." Hawkins is generally credited with having begun the tradition of attacking *Rasselas* as a tale of despair and hopelessness. A careful look at his position, however, will make clear that he is carrying on the tradition of Ruffhead, not accusing *Rasselas* of lack of religious resolve.

> I wish I were not warranted in saying, that this elegant work
> is rendered, by its most obvious moral, of little benefit to the
> reader. We would not indeed wish to see the rising generation
> so unprofitably employed as the prince of Abyssinia; but it is

equally impolitic to repress all hope, and he who should quit his father's house in search of a profession, and return unprovided, because he could not find any man pleased with his own, would need a better justification than that Johnson, after speculatively surveying various modes of life, had judged happiness unattainable, and choice useless.

Hawkins concluded by warning those reading *Rasselas* "in the spring of life" not to be "captivated by its author's eloquence, and convinced by his perspicacious wisdom that human life and hopes are such as he has depicted them" but to "remember that [Johnson] saw through the medium of adversity."[14] Being now familiar with the terms of Ruffhead's attack, we notice such phrases in Hawkins as "the rising generation," readers in the "spring of life," and "he who should quit his father's house in search of a profession." Clearly, Hawkins had in mind the same young, impressionable reader who might be led astray by Johnson's austere, if accurate, representation of life. Even a passing familiarity with the historical tradition of *Rasselas* criticism suffices to call into question the generally accepted belief that Hawkins began the religious attack. That accusation does not arise until the nineteenth century. In fact, Hawkins' confidence in Johnson's religious convictions is illustrated by the assertion in his biography that Johnson intended to write a sequel in which his hero was to marry and conclude in a state of "permanent felicity."

Fate visited upon Hawkins the rare, if dubious, distinction of converting speculation into fact, or nearly so. In 1790, Mrs. E.C. Knight wrote a continuation of *Rasselas* that, as she explained in her introduction, followed Hawkins' prescription. Entitled *Dinarbas*, this story concludes with the double marriage of hero and heroine. The tale is designed to show how Rasselas and his sister find what for them constitutes the choice of life.[15] Its chief critical interest resides in the fact that it has been neglected even by Johnson scholars who might have been willing to overlook its artistic inadequacies. That this sequel has never before been considered a critical document suggests that the attempt to locate a particular choice of life is misguided. Yet for the next two centuries critics continued to attack *Rasselas* for not providing a resolution for the Prince's travels, unaware that *Dinarbas* itself exemplified the inappropriateness of such a resolution.

James Boswell, writing a year later than Mrs. Knight, considered *Rasselas* on its own terms and devised a more successful reply to the accusation of inordinate gloom. Despite his awe and respect for the wisdom and "fund of thinking" of *Rasselas*, Boswell felt obliged to comment on the author's "morbid melancholy": "Notwithstanding my high admiration of Rasselas, I will not maintain that the 'morbid melancholy' in Johnson's constitution may not, perhaps, have made life appear to him more insipid and unhappy than it generally is; for I am sure that he had less enjoyment from it than I have. Yet, whatever additional shade his own particular sensations may have thrown on his representation of life, attentive observation and close inquiry have convinced me, that there is too much reality in the gloomy picture."[16]

Boswell found Johnson's picture of life not distorted but all too accurate. In response to Hawkins' attack, Boswell characterized *Rasselas* as a *Vanity of Human Wishes* in prose.[17] During the next two centuries, this phrase was regularly used by those defending the religious reading of *Rasselas*. But Boswell was not equating the conclusions of the two works; his intention was to assert, in opposition to Hawkins, that the narrative encouraged despair no more than did the poem. Here we see a vivid example of how the history of criticism is altered by reassessing the interpretive goal of the critic. Boswell's tactical move against Hawkins was transformed by later commentators. It should also be noted here that Boswell's insistence on the accuracy of the view of reality in the narrative was the main reason why nineteenth-century readers, while neglecting most of Johnson's writings, continued to read and write about *Rasselas*. But, as we shall see, commentators of the nineteenth and twentieth centuries gradually distorted Boswell's position until eventually his name was attached to a view opposite to his own.

In 1802, William Mudford began the process of turning the biographical defense of *Rasselas* against the text. That the tale had been written at a time when the author was having to support a dying mother might excuse its "imperfect picture" of life but for the fact that the same pessimistic tone was found elsewhere in Johnson's writings, especially in *The Rambler*. This predominant melancholy was seen to produce a flawed view of reality. Mudford concluded that in illustrating his concept of the vanity of human wishes, Johnson produced "disquisitions" which have "few admirers" because they excite "no tumultuous sensations, nor awaken any sympathy."[18]

In 1807, Leigh Hunt took Mudford's position one step further by asserting that the author's melancholy constitution resulted in some distortion of the truth. The author of *Rasselas* reminded Hunt of the astronomer who accurately perceived discrete facts but combined them into a whole which was fanciful.[19] Here begins the tradition, which continues throughout the nineteenth and into the twentieth century, of characterizing *Rasselas* as lacking in religious consolation because of the author's distorted view of reality. Coming to Johnson's defense, Mrs. Barbauld, in 1810, developed another aspect of Mudford's position, the abstract, almost unreal quality of *Rasselas*. The dominant motif of the tale, the search for a choice of life, was seen as artificial because most of us "will seldom hesitate upon a choice of life." Barbauld suggested that the proper, less trite moral to be drawn from the artificiality of the choice of life theme was a preference for what subsequent critics were to call, using the words of the princess, the "choice of eternity."[20] The melancholy that the reader experienced was, according to Barbauld, directed at the search for happiness in this world, not the next. The choice of eternity, for Barbauld, provided hope for the reader, thus enabling Johnson to present a balanced, not a distorted, view of reality.

A subtle but significant alteration has occurred in the debate. In the eighteenth century, most commentators disagreed as to whether or not the licit pleasures of this world received sufficient emphasis. Nineteenth-century critics now began a debate concerning whether or not the gloom associated with the choice of life prevailed over the consolation provided by the choice of eternity. This shift in critical position becomes most apparent in the difference of opinion between William Hazlitt and Sir Walter Scott.

In 1819, Hazlitt referred to the tale as "the most melancholy and debilitating moral speculation that ever was put forth." "Doubtful of the faculties of his mind, Johnson trusted only to his feelings and fears"; he thus fell prey to his own "dangerous prevalence of the imagination."[21] Scott, on the other hand, defended *Rasselas*. Although manifesting the melancholy of the author, *Rasselas* put forth a "friendly grave" philosophy that promised hope in the other world. The number of editions and translations of the narrative, Scott believed, attested to the fact that reading the tale was not a debilitating but an uplifting experience.[22]

While Scott and Barbauld attempted to point to religious hope expressed in the narrative itself, Elizabeth Pope Whately, in 1835, wrote the only other continuation of *Rasselas*, consisting of a Christian pilgrimage that ends with the choice of eternity. Imlac here is replaced by a religious teacher named Everard, who leads the travelers from nominal faith to an explicit Christian belief. Whately's sequel seems to have received even less attention than *Dinarbas*, for modern scholars did not know of its existence until an article by Robert Metzdorf appeared in 1950.[23] Metzdorf explained that Whately was not satisfied with *Dinarbas* because in concluding with marriage it left unresolved the question of religious felicity. But Whately's tale did not, in fact, succeed in advancing the religious question. In making explicit the Christianity that was presumed to be only implicit in the original, Whately suggested that the religion of *Rasselas* was in need of further clarification. We can conclude from the neglect of Whately's narrative that Christian conversion of the characters in *Rasselas* was regarded by both defenders and attackers as inappropriate. Yet for over two centuries critics have continued to label *Rasselas* a religious apologue, unaware that Whately provided the historian of literary criticism with a prima facie case against such a categorization. Perhaps the continuations have failed to receive scholarly attention because Rasselas' choice of life is no more capable of resolution than is his choice of eternity. That the two sequels are conspicuously absent from discussions is itself a form of literary critical evidence.

Although the religious continuation of Johnson's tale was soon forgotten, Boswell's biographical account continued to be employed throughout the remainder of the nineteenth century. By the 1850s, it became commonplace to preface editions of *Rasselas* with brief biographical essays derived from Boswell. The scanty commentary written between 1834 and 1860 is to be found in the introductory material to editions intended for the general public and for use in schools. The London editions of 1823, 1838, and 1843 and the Edinburgh edition of 1824 recommended *Rasselas* for its firm moral strictures and its style. The anonymous 1823 editor proclaimed that "the moral, though not new, has, perhaps, never been before so ably, so eloquently, inculcated."[24] His Scottish counterpart explained that the "beautiful, useful tale" was one of Johnson's most "popular works."[25] The 1838 and 1843 versions, nearly identical soft-bound, small books (measuring 6 by 4 inches) prefaced the text with a three-page "Brief Notice" consisting of a very condensed version of Boswell, introduced in the following terms: "to those who look no further than this life the instruction of this sublime tale will be of no avail."[26]

Clearly, these inexpensive Victorian pocket books were intended to present to the general public proper religious and moral precepts in a fine literary style. Once the reader had been warned in the brief biographical sketch of the author's constitutional melancholy and of the circumstances under which the book was written, the gloom of the text, the editors assumed, would cease to be morally debilitating. Boswell was thus employed by Victorians to alter the view of *Rasselas*: the same argument that enabled Boswell to explain how an accurate picture of reality had been combined with Christianity was employed by many nineteenth-century editors to make allowance for the distortion of reality in what was otherwise an orthodox Christian tale. For this reason, the Reverend John Hunter, in his edition of 1860, warned his students about the "narrator's somewhat melancholy and desponding" tone but concluded that "if it darkens too deeply the scene of things temporal it at least causes thereby to shine more brightly the hope which emanates from things eternal."[27]

The Reverend William West, on the other hand, pointed out in his edition of 1869 that, although "tinged with his grief," *Rasselas* contained the religious optimism which Johnson expressed in a letter to Mrs. Thrale: "all is best as it has been, excepting the errors of our own free will." West was one of the first to attend to the exotic element of the happy valley, which he saw in relation to the *Arabian Nights, Paradise Lost*, Thomson's "Castle of Indolence," and Johnson's own translation of the Lobo-Legrand *Voyage to Abyssinia*. Johnson, he stated, was fortunate in choosing this setting because it is "invested with all the romance of history and geography, religion and superstition." This most imaginative of Johnson's works, according to West, made use of an exotic scene to unite genial pleasantry with a view of life "far from cheerful."[28]

By the second half of the nineteenth century, when it was generally accepted that the somewhat despondent tone or slightly warped view of reality was compensated for by the Christian vision, commentators began to turn their attention to other aspects of *Rasselas*—the exotic and even the humorous. In his edition of 1879, Alfred Milnes was probably the first to assert that humor was a functional part, not simply an occasional accident, in the story. For Milnes the end was still sad, although not as bitter as that of *Candide*, and the theme remained the vanity of human wishes. Nevertheless, the episodes containing the philosophy according to nature and the marriage debate were labeled comic "gems." Finally, Milnes pointed out that Johnson's tale "has been much more widely read than the far more vivacious work of Voltaire," a startling statement, however accurate or inaccurate, in an age when the man and his conversation were generally valued over his work.[29] The number of editions of *Rasselas* during this period suggests that, if not read more than *Candide*, it was at least one of the few of Johnson's works that was widely read.[30] We know, for instance, of a law case occasioned by a pirated edition of 1883, a sure sign of public interest in a text,[31] and in 1884 an anonymous reviewer in *Book-Lore* wrote that "although Samuel Johnson is generally known by his conversation and way of life as recorded by Boswell, one work [*Rasselas*] never lost its hold upon the popular mind."[32]

During the last quarter of the nineteenth century, when the religious question seemed settled by use of a distortion of Boswell, the exotic and comic elements were first carefully considered and *Rasselas* was first placed in the tradition of the novel. In 1894, Walter Raleigh included *Rasselas* in his book entitled *The English Novel*. But while referring to *Rasselas* as a novel, Raleigh also was the first to call it an "apologue," another label still used today. In fact, Raleigh characterized Johnson's achievement as the combining of these two genres: "the youth of the modern novel was a season of experiment, no rules of form had been determined, and a moral directly inculcated had never been disallowed."[33]

By the end of the nineteenth century *Rasselas* had been successfully defended against those in the early decades of the century, such as Mudford and Hunt, who asserted that the tale ended in despair. But the defense created new problems. As we have seen, hope in *Rasselas* was located in the choice of eternity theme. But the question then became how the exotic and humorous elements were related to this other-worldly motif, how the form of the tale was related to its message. Classifying *Rasselas* as a novel seemed to offer a solution to this problem, but it necessitated including within that category the apologue, a term originally applied to beast fables and then by extension to moral allegories. The problem is that during the twentieth century the novel is increasingly associated with realism and thus distinguished from moral allegory. Nevertheless, the term "apologue" is a key one for present-day critics; Gwin Kolb, for instance, in his most recent essay, which appeared in 1984, used the term freely.[34] Yet apologue was first applied to *Rasselas* in an attempt to include it *within* the tradition of the novel, while, as will soon become clear, most twentieth-century critics use the term to distinguish *Rasselas from* the novel.

Turning now to the twentieth century, we note the emergence of one issue that was to be neglected for over a quarter of a century. In 1899, Oliver Emerson had to remind his readers that his 1895 introduction to *Rasselas* used bibliographical evidence to question the universally accepted contention that Johnson wrote the tale in the evenings of one week to defray his mother's funeral expenses.[35] When Emerson's argument was finally addressed, many of his conclusions were successfully refuted, but his position was not even contested until 1927. The reason for the neglect of Emerson's argument during this period is that the tradition of the gloomy, funereal tone of the choice of life motif in *Rasselas* remained unopposed: the question of whether or not the genesis of *Rasselas* involved a literal funeral was not considered important. Moreover, the assumption of a gloomy genesis served to keep religion in the background, for any theological difficulty could be attributed to the fact that the author was mourning the death of his mother.

Instead, critics were interested in generic explanations of the tone. C.S. Fearenside, for instance, further developed Raleigh's position. Although a precursor of the novel, *Rasselas* contained more severe morality and fewer of the characteristics of narrative and story because it was an early and undeveloped example of the genre.[36] But Martha Conant, in *The Oriental Tale in England in the Eighteenth Century* (1908), placed *Rasselas* in the philosophic, not the moral, category of oriental tales. What Fearenside saw as a moralistic novel, Conant characterized as too general and abstract for the moral oriental tale. Johnson seemed to Conant to be even more abstract than Voltaire, who at least considered happiness in *Candide* in such concrete terms as a "mistress."[37]

The generic problem was thus a complicated one. Placed within the confines of the novel, *Rasselas* seemed anomalous in its lack of fully developed characters, skeletal story line and markedly open-ended conclusion. Treated as an oriental tale, *Rasselas* was typical in its philosophic quality and one-dimensional figures, but the oriental was, as Conant herself admitted, of little intrinsic import. Because Conant and Fearenside conceived of literary history in restrictive generic terms, they remained within their distinct categories, seeing no relationship between their endeavors. Attempts to explain the tone of *Rasselas* in terms of a single generic tradition revealed that the tale contained elements of both the novel and the oriental tale but could not be satisfactorily categorized as either the one or the other.

During the next few decades, a number of critics attempted to consider *Rasselas* as a novel bordering on either the philosophic oriental tale or the religious apologue. In 1910, A.J.F. Collins labeled the tale "the philosophical novel or the novel with a purpose where the story is often a mere excuse for a theory of life."[38] And in 1913, George Saintsbury described *Rasselas* as "the most remarkable example, in English, of a novel, which is to a great extent deprived of the *agremens* of its kind," while leaving behind the "carcass of a very tolerable novel." Without story, characters, or dialogue, *Rasselas*, according to Saintsbury, was a moral apologue: "Johnson used the popular form of the novel to communicate his thoughts to the general reading public."[39] Here Raleigh's notion that Johnson combined apologue and novel is made more explicit. In particular, Saintsbury explained the unique quality of *Rasselas* by describing it as a religious allegory that uses the outward trappings of the novel.

But if the novel was merely an "envelope" used by Johnson to reach the people, W.D. Howells replied that audiences in the United States needed "the truth clothed in more realism." For Howells, Johnson's irony was too subtle for the novel. Therefore, the categorization was questioned: "I call it a novel," stated the sage conversing with Howells in his Editor's Easy Chair, "but I suppose you would stickle for the term heroic romance."[40] Howells' opposition to labeling the tale a novel serves as a reminder to us that, at that time, the motive for including it in this popular genre was an attempt to account for how the reader was moved by the doctrine of the apologue, the choice of eternity. But our historical perspective will make plain that these two genres were gradually seen to point in opposite directions, the novel being realistic and secular and the apologue being allegorical and religious.

Instead of attempting to defend *Rasselas* in generic terms, Percy Houston, in 1923, focused on the basis of its moral and religious doctrine: "the pessimism of this little homily did not strike at the roots of religion and morality, but the fact of human misery was stated as something to be faced without questioning God's ultimate purposes." Johnson's avoidance of sentimentality, Houston hastened to add, "was not unfeeling."[41] *Rasselas* was thus placed at a considerable distance from the realistic novel; indeed, so much was the tale relegated to the realm of the fantastic that Russell Markland and Percy Armstrong pointed to similarities between *Rasselas* and the writings of Shelley and Emerson.[42] In 1924, Chauncey Tinker advanced Houston's position by comparing *Rasselas* to the Bible and asserting that the exotic was a "mere trapping" for the moral.[43] Here we see an important difference between the nineteenth and twentieth centuries. In the former, the demonstration that *Rasselas* contained the hope inherent in the choice of eternity accounted for its appeal. In the present century, however, when Tinker advanced a similar argument, L.F. Powell reminded his fellow critics that *Rasselas* was still the most widely printed and most generally read of Johnson's literary works.[44] For Powell the religious doctrine no longer provided a satisfactory explanation for the literary appeal of *Rasselas*.

At the beginning of the twentieth century, *Rasselas* was, for the first time, defended by being described as a novel. Although some, like Howells, rejected this argument, most commentators now sought a formal or generic explanation of the reasons *Rasselas* had earned its place among the classics of English literature. The explanation offered, that *Rasselas* was a hybrid of apologue and novel, was not widely accepted because it left undecided whether the conclusion was religious or secular. In the second quarter of the twentieth century, the genre and religious questions continued in the forefront of discussion, but the conclusions drawn in both instances differed from those of the past. The fundamental problem, however, remained how to account for *Rasselas* not as a religious text but as literature.

In 1927, Ernest Palser, in a commentary designed for school and university students, suggested that *Rasselas* was a kind of novel that soon passed out of history. Viewed in terms of its Elizabethan, seventeenth-and eighteenth-century ancestors, *Rasselas*, according to Palser, had some of the euphuistic style of Lyly and some of the elements of realism, plot, and character found in Fielding. The progress of the novel ceased temporarily after the middle of the eighteenth century, which explained why Johnson's story contained less in the way of plot, characters, and real life than had *Tom Jones*. A momentary aberration, a soon-to-be-extinct species, *Rasselas*, according to Palser, employed the euphuistic style to develop a spiritual novel that was didactic, not bitter. But the novel as a genre continued to move inexorably toward increasing realism because a picture of the unhappy side of existence could only avoid the accusation of a melancholy bias if it presented a realistic world. Palser felt that *Rasselas* appeared at a moment in history when it was possible to present a spiritual novel.[45]

Rasselas was now seen as an aberrant form of the novel—a novel, in a sense, at war with the novel. In 1932, Norman Collins suggested that as a moral genius, Johnson wrote without any sense of the novel as a form: the idea of "Dr. Johnson telling a story is rather like that of an elephant herding sheep: something much smaller could do it far better." Infusing philosophic sadness into the novel, Johnson "taught the English novel to be intellectual, a lesson that for natural reasons has rarely been applied since."[46] That Johnson maintained his intellectual integrity, refusing to bow down to the idols of the marketplace, was the reply to those like Howells who complained that *Rasselas* violated the principles of the novel, realism and the development of character. But the price paid for describing *Rasselas* as a spiritual or philosophical novel was to minimize the structural or novelistic qualities of the narrative.

For this reason, Ernest Baker, in *The History of the English Novel* (1934) defended *Rasselas* by suggesting it was a singular kind of novel because of its use of the orient. Johnson dressed up his sad philosophy in exotic ornament, approximating the novel: "thus the vogue of the pseudo-Oriental tale was bound to be transient and to leave no indelible mark upon the history of fiction."[47] *Rasselas* was for Baker a masterpiece, but because no one could duplicate Johnson's delicate oriental presentation of ideas, the exotic did not long remain a significant factor in the history of the English novel. Historians of the novel continued to account for the unrealistic by pointing to the superficial exotic ornaments, which paradoxically resulted in a more careful and scholarly treatment of the oriental aspect of the narrative. Beginning this serious investigation, Harold Jenkins, in 1940, discovered that a number of details in the happy valley did not correspond to those in Johnson's translation of Lobo's *Voyage d'Abyssinie*, the work generally assumed to be the source for Johnson's exotica. Jenkins found that the happy valley contained features from a number of Ethiopian travel books available in Johnson's day.[48]

The increased prominence accorded to the oriental is directly related to Joseph Wood Krutch's new reading of *Rasselas*, first published in 1944. Describing the book as an example of the "pseudo-oriental tale . . . familiar to [Johnson's] contemporaries as a vehicle for moral instruction," Krutch pointed out that the main theme emerges in the pyramid incident, which exemplifies the hunger of the imagination that preys on all human minds. The story concludes not with "vulgar" pessimism but with Johnson's "tragic sense of life." Specifically, Krutch asserted that although the travelers at the end of the tale return to the happy valley, the choice of eternity is "only the formal rather than the effective moral." Instead of representing opposition to the search for happiness, the return to the happy valley offers relief from the "secondary causes of distress and possessed in the largest measure the palliatives of security and pleasure."[49] Krutch emphasized that *Rasselas* differs at once from an apologue in not finally ascending to the choice of eternity and from a romance by avoiding its traditional optimistic conclusion. A masterpiece, *Rasselas* squarely faces the dilemma of man on earth.

This turning point, the first secular reading of *Rasselas*, resulted from giving due attention to the literary qualities of the narrative, specifically the oriental setting and the humor. Krutch's careful research on the exotica led to the realization that the eighteenth-century oriental tale could no more be assumed to be religious than to be romantic or fanciful. Moreover, the increasing references to the comic moments in the narrative led Krutch to characterize it not as gloomy but as tragic, because tragedy can sustain within its scope humor.[50] By the middle of this century, *Rasselas* was for the first time defended in terms that distinguished the structure of the narrative from that of *The Vanity of Human Wishes*. Krutch's methodological innovation, however, went unrecognized for some time; his position was at first inserted into the old religious controversy as if his secular reading was merely another attack on *Rasselas* for lack of religious resolution. But within a decade his influence began to be seen in the increasing interest in the formal properties of *Rasselas*.

Strangely enough, Krutch's secular reading had less effect on the religious position than on that of a group of critics who, during the next two decades, the 1950s and 1960s, avoided entirely the question of whether *Rasselas* concludes in religious or secular terms. Here again, the generally accepted notion of the critical tradition is different from the tradition itself. For over a century the dichotomy between the choice of life and the choice of eternity had been repeated and was now widely accepted as the central problem in *Rasselas*. By the middle of the twentieth century, Krutch notwithstanding, critics continued to assume that the choice of life ended in futility and that the choice of eternity provided a counterbalance against hopelessness and despair. That this dichotomy did not obtain in the eighteenth century was still to be discovered. The twentieth-century critics inherited the nineteenth-century assumptions that resulted in the following problem for them: although the choice-of-eternity coda restores hope at the end of the text, almost all of *Rasselas* is devoted to the choice-of-life motif, which was regarded as gloomy. Since the tale remained popular, critics had to account for the appeal of the body of the tale. Many mid-twentieth-century critics tried to demonstrate that the form or structure of *Rasselas* provides an aesthetic pleasure to counterbalance the gloom of the main theme. Krutch's position brought these choice-of-life features into new prominence.

In the 1950s, the comedy of *Rasselas* was for the first time pointed to not, as in the past, as a sign of Christian hope but as a principle of literary structure. This comic view of structure added a new dimension to the controversy. In 1950, when Robert Metzdorf unearthed Mrs. Whately's happy and distinctly religious continuation of *Rasselas*,[51] Clarence Tracy claimed that the need to alter or add to Johnson's conclusion was founded on a false view derived from Boswell. "Not a grim invective against life," *Rasselas* was, for Tracy, the "most sustained and most characteristic of [Johnson's] humorous compositions." Opposing Krutch's description of the tale as "tragic," Tracy called the Prince "a silly ass, seeking obstinately for absolutes in a world where only relative values are to be found, and forever knocking at an unlocked door." Even at the conclusion of the tale, the Prince, according to Tracy, "is a fool [who] never learns his lesson," an addict of "pure reason" who returns to a fool's paradise.[52]

Although, as we have seen, some earlier critics had shown sensitivity to the comedy of the tale, Tracy was the first to present a complete position based on the humor of the narrative. His formulation revealed a misunderstanding of the critical tradition. Boswell, as we know, had defended *Rasselas* against the need for a continuation on the basis of exactly the same literary theme as that of Tracy, namely, the vanity of human wishes. What, one may well ask, was the function of comedy for Tracy if it resulted in a notion identical to that of the somber view of Boswell? It is instructive that Tracy was attacked in just these terms by his contemporaries who, in various ways, unconsciously played the part of a critical ghost.

In 1951, Mary Lascelles and Gwin Kolb each opposed Tracy's position, but in different terms. For Lascelles, the humor of *Rasselas,* definitely an important factor, was of a delicate sort; the satire applied to those whom the main characters visited on their travels, not to the main characters themselves. At the end of their journey, the travelers were, according to Lascelles, not fools but people who, as a result of their lengthy journey, developed "a kind of philosophic love" that evokes our empathy.[53]

Gwin Kolb, on the other hand, accused Tracy of treating *Rasselas* as if it were a string of *Rambler* essays; as an alternative, he put forward a religious reading, which he has maintained to the present day. The tale was seen to have a distinct structure, one that serves not a comic but a serious purpose, namely, that all searches for permanent happiness on earth are doomed to failure. Having decided to write a narrative on the theme of *The Vanity of Human Wishes,* Johnson, according to Kolb, found a vehicle for the "paucity of happiness" notion, which was considered under three headings: those who, like the inhabitants of the happy valley, had all material goods; those who, like the young men of spirit and gaiety, followed particular schemes; and those who, like the Bassa, occupied positions of power.[54] Tracy was opposed in two different ways. Kolb accepted Tracy's theme, the vanity of human wishes, but characterized it, like Boswell, as somber, not comic. Lascelles accepted the comedy but did not agree that the choice-of-life search was a puerile endeavor.

The old terms now came to serve a new purpose. Gloom that in the past had been key for those attacking *Rasselas* for its lack of hope is now used by Kolb to advance a religious reading. Comedy that in the past had been pointed to as a sign of the hope present in the narrative is now used to characterize literary structure in terms neither distinctly religious nor secular. It should now be clear that formalist arguments permitted for the first time assimilation of the full range of tone, from comedy to tragedy, but, as will be demonstrated, the tone debate continued for another twenty years until gradually the two sides came to a compromise.

Meanwhile, the generic discussion continued, but now with a more direct bearing upon the question of literary structure. In 1952, F.R. Leavis claimed that the tragic theme of *Rasselas* accounted for its "moral centrality and profound commonsense,"[55] and, in the same year, John Robert Moore pointed out that although "generally regarded as a philosophical romance so devoid of action . . . that one who read it for the story would hang himself,"[56] *Rasselas* had provided some elements of plot construction for Conan Doyle. Viewing *Rasselas* as a novel now meant that the gloom could be seen as invested in a

tragic or realistic literary form that was not designed to produce in
the reader despair or hopelessness.

While these generic, structural, and tonal questions continued to
be debated, a psychological question was raised, one that was not exclusively biographical. In 1954, Richard Hovey examined the relationship between Johnson and the astronomer. But unlike previous
commentators, Hovey characterized not merely Johnson or his age
but the kind of neurosis exemplified by the astronomer/author: "the
mental illness" of the astronomer suggests "our own age rather than
the Age of Reason." Like the astronomer's anxiety, Johnson's guilt
combined with melancholy to take the form of self-mutilation and ag-
gression against the self. Using biographical evidence from Boswell
and Katherine Balderston, Hovey suggested that Johnson felt guilt
with regard to his mother, and that he recovered, like the astronomer,
by way of the company of other people.[57] Maintaining that such a
view of *Rasselas* was not Freudian but Burtonian, Hovey nonetheless
claimed that his reading revealed the modernity of Johnson's story.

Psychological readings of this kind were completely ignored by
those debating matters of genre, structure, and tone, so much so that
thirty years later, as we shall see, this position was, in a number of
respects, repeated without any acknowledgment of Hovey. The nature
of this modern psychological position will become clearer when we
examine Kathleen Grange's essay, a fuller formulation that appeared
five years later. At this point it should be noted that during this period
Boswell's psychological explanation was as neglected as that of Hovey.
Most critics in the 1950s believed that the problems of *Rasselas* could
be resolved by recourse to a more careful study of the form of the tale.
When this project failed, it again became permissible to consider
psychological questions.

In 1956 Alvin Whitley, aware of the objections to Tracy's position,
modified the comic view into a reading that avoided commitment on
the religious question. Whitley's point of departure was that both
Tracy and Kolb had been too negative in characterizing *Rasselas* as a
prose version of *The Vanity of Human Wishes*. Instead, the narrative
comically satirizes "the illusioned view of life." In the first two-thirds
of the story, naive pilgrims examine foolish choices of life; although
the last third of the book, comprised of the visits to the astronomer
and the old man, does "skirt tragedy," the manner remains comic. In
the end, the travelers "return to the Happy Valley," a conclusion that
gives the text its circular form.[58] Whitley's comic circle showed the
illusion inherent in the choice-of-life quest. Since the tale ended with
the characters coming to an awareness of this fact, it was not necessary to consider an alternative, such as the choice of eternity.

Whitley was nevertheless attacked by those who opposed the attempt to use the comedy of *Rasselas* to avoid the religious issues of *The Vanity of Human Wishes*. William Kenney, in 1957, argued that the comic reading neglected the tragic aspect of the tale. Admitting that he derived this notion from Krutch, Kenney adapted it to a Christian reading.[59] Two years later, Agostino Lombardo extended this view by asserting that the hero of *Rasselas* was not Rasselas but Imlac. By virtue of his sober, pious bearing and his tale about his disillusionment with the world outside of the happy valley, the latter clearly exemplifies a tragic Christian position.[60] This formulation, however, raised a new problem: Imlac retires from the world to the happy valley while the prince travels in the opposite direction. Kenney, in a second article, pointed out that both characters eventually end in the happy valley and explained how the valley provides a resolution for both quests. Once the prince discovers what Imlac has previously recognized, that the choice of life can never be found, then he and his mentor both return to the happy valley, which offers the next best alternative. Kenney called this option "diversification," and Bertrand Bronson characterized it as the prince's equivalent of what "London was to Johnson. Though London is not the Happy Valley, it is the best available surrogate."[61]

Now we come to one of the most important moments in this history. In a three-paragraph reply to Kenney's essay, George Sherburn pointed out that the travelers cannot and do not return to the happy valley. This single structural fact altered almost all future interpretations of the tale. In spite of his future impact, Sherburn devoted less than a single printed page to his momentous discovery. Sherburn objected to the optimism suggested by Kenney's view that the travelers return to the diversification of the happy valley. "One may regret Dr. Johnson's pessimism," he cautioned, "but must face it." Furthermore, Sherburn continued, Imlac's return to disappointment in Abyssinia prepares us for the prince's attitude at the end of his journey: "the work ends in complete frustration. The travelers are now in the condition in which Imlac had formerly found himself before he achieved the Happy Valley, now closed to him and his companions."[62]

By this means, Sherburn reaffirmed the nineteenth-century position that *Rasselas* is exemplary of its historical period; that the travelers cannot return to the happy valley is viewed as consistent with the pessimism of Johnson and his era. Such a notion, for Sherburn, is not innovative and can hardly be said to constitute a textual discovery. Nevertheless, Sherburn's three paragraphs had a profound effect upon the commentary of the 1960s and 1970s, for it altered the conception of the structure of the text. Both the religion and tone debaters had to reformulate their positions. For the former, Imlac and his history present a problem. The sage, who had been seen by these critics as the spokesman for the religious point of view, now told a tale, his history, having a different structure from that of the prince. Imlac ends his story with his decision to enter the happy valley, but Rasselas cannot return to the vale. How does one account for this difference? For those who focused on tone, the conclusion raised a new question: "The conclusion, in which nothing is concluded" could not be neatly folded into the beginning. Abyssinia was not synonymous with the happy valley, so the tale could no longer be viewed as circular in structure. But because Sherburn presented his position in traditional terms, it took some time before the ramifications of his discovery were fully recognized.

In 1961 John Aden advanced the secular element in the comic view. Comparing *The Vanity of Human Wishes* to *Rasselas*, Aden suggested that the poem delineated the "instinctive determinants" to self-deception, that is, hope, fear, or hate, while the prose work presented the "self-imposed or psychological determinants," such as fancy and eagerness, foibles which, unlike those in the poem, were "avoidable by a healthy and sound mind." One could learn how to overcome the limitations caused by credulity or naiveté in *Rasselas* but not those of fate in *The Vanity of Human Wishes*. The fatalism of the poem explained its distinct tone; its sobriety contrasted with the wry, ironic, playful attitude of the tale. Indeed, the terms "Christian" and "stoic" applied to the poem but not to the tale. The "choice of eternity," Nekayah's one passing reference to Christian doctrine, was a brief remark not identified as Johnson's final point. Moreover, the conclusion of the tale—and here Aden, presumably unaware of Sherburn, assumed a return to the happy valley—is "as pathetic as it is tragic," returning its spiritually weary characters to an infantile paradise. In so doing, *Rasselas* "seems rather a repudiation of the pessimistic and melancholy doctrine of the poem."[63]

Robert Voitle shared Aden's doubts about the Christian message; when Nekayah remarks on the choice of eternity "we are more struck by the opportunity Johnson missed to dwell on the *de contemptu mundi* theme than by his passing reference to it."[64] Aden and Voitle were moving toward the application of the philosophic notion of *l'absurde* that was first presented explicitly by Ellen Leyburn. Comparing *Rasselas* to Albert Camus's *La Peste*, Leyburn asserted that both works advance the belief that although life is largely misery, commitment to an active life helps combat suffering. The main difference between the two tales, according to Leyburn, is that Camus used an allegorical structure and particularized individuals while Johnson employed oriental trappings appropriate to grand generalizations. Leyburn insisted that Johnson's narrative not be seen as a "doleful book" because, like Camus's narrative, it encouraged activity, not passive despair. Indeed, Camus's atheism was not considered as alien to Johnson, for whom religion provided not comfort but a dread of annihilation and damnation. Finding Johnson's position in *Rasselas* comparable to Camus's atheism, Leyburn made quite obvious the threat posed to the religious position by the satiric secular interpretation, even though her own strategy was not to deny the religion of *Rasselas* but to highlight the similarity between it and *La Peste*.[65]

During this same period, Kathleen Grange continued the psychoanalytic reading of *Rasselas* begun eight years earlier by Richard Hovey. Without mentioning her predecessor, Grange, like Hovey, focused on the astronomer, characterizing him as schizoid and emphasizing that the travelers showed varying degrees of understanding of this mental disease. Johnson was applauded for realizing that fulfilling the astronomer's needs—"desire for friendship, usefulness and ego-satisfaction"—was a more effective therapy than rational explanation.[66] At this point, the psychological tradition divides into two separate but related strands. Hovey explained the astronomer in terms of the relationship between Johnson and his mother. Grange restricted herself to the text, focusing on the manner in which the scientist regains his sanity. I shall have occasion to return to this distinction between the textual and the biographical aspects of the psychological tradition. Here it is important to note that the other textual critics ignored Grange as they had Hovey. Psychological criticism was at this time almost completely neglected only to erupt, as Freud would have predicted, in the next generation.

The centrality of structural considerations is evidenced by Donald Lockhart's *PMLA* essay of 1963, which remains the most comprehensive study of the exotic background material for the happy valley. The previous scholarship in this field was divided by Lockhart into two categories, the literary school, favoring such traditional, unrealistic sources as Milton's "suppos'd true paradise," and the historical school, emphasizing Johnson's translation of Lobo and other travelers' accounts of Ethiopia. But Lockhart found a number of specific elements of the happy valley that could not be accounted for by either of these two kinds of sources. He therefore turned to a number of works available to Johnson that combined the paradise-on-earth convention with actual accounts of the exotic retreat set up for the children of the emperor of Abyssinia.[67] Lockhart concluded that Johnson had done careful research for his happy valley well before the death of his mother, an assertion that prompted W.K. Wimsatt to refer to this article as the "PMLAization of Johnson's working habits."[68]

Nevertheless, Lockhart succeeded in documenting the fact that both historical and literary materials were pertinent to the happy valley.

That the secular and religious critics shared a commitment to the importance of form and were thus beginning to influence one another is attested by F.W. Hilles' attempt to mediate between them in 1965. In place of Kolb's two-part structure, Hilles offered a triune form, the result of subdividing the world beyond the mountains that Kolb had considered as one unit. The abduction of Pekuah marks the beginning of a new section because, according to Hilles, the travelers who up to this point have been only observers are now participants. Having restructured the tale, Hilles characterized the tone of the story as that of a "sad smile": "modern commentators . . . overstress the comic elements . . . as orthodox critics have dwelt overmuch on the tragic." But the words and structure "suggest a balance."[69] Hilles offered this alternative organic structure in an attempt to encompass both comedy and tragedy, the religious and the secular. Although beneath surface similarities ultimate and irreconcilable contradictions remained, Hilles did succeed in demonstrating that the abduction of Pekuah marked a new stage in the tale. The pyramid episode was seen as an event because it involved action, not merely conversation. And subsequent commentators felt obliged to come to terms with this structural phenomenon.

In 1967 Emrys Jones modified Hilles' structure by extending the first part through chapter 16 and treating the last chapter as a separate "coda." In his conception of the conclusion, however, Jones was the first to develop the full implications of Sherburn's discovery. The last chapter functions, according to Jones, like the end of *Love's Labours Lost*, to remind us that life is a critique of art, that is, the artistic form itself is "broken because the flow of life cannot be checked."[70] A part of the structure, the coda was seen to undermine artistic structuring; *Rasselas* was for Jones a form designed to break open its own form. This important insight was, however, not adequately explained. The truism that life does not obey the laws of art explains little about why a carefully structured work of art concludes with reference to this fact.

Nonetheless, Jones was the first critic to suggest that the inability to reenter the happy valley indicated that the humor at the end of *Rasselas* was directed at the form of all human wishes and therefore applied to the form of *Rasselas* as well. That the quest for organic form resulted in the discovery of a formal technique in *Rasselas* which satirized such a quest testifies to the vitality of the enterprise of literary criticism and provides a vivid example of why the discipline must be seen to exert its own special kind of historical force while being inscribed in history. Indeed, most of the commentary of the next decade can be seen as an attempt to account for Jones' coda.

In 1968, William K. Wimsatt, Jr., gave two reasons for his doubt as to the significance of structure in *Rasselas*. First, the tale had been written in haste, a fact indicated by Johnson's "absentmindedness, his slight inconsistencies of time and setting which suggest additions." For instance, in the first edition, Pekuah is not referred to by name until chapter 30; in the second edition, her name is added in chapter 16. Wimsatt surmised that Johnson had introduced the abduction of Pekuah in the middle of the tale to increase the action and in revising the text had hurriedly patched up the earlier section. Although not "serious aesthetic deficiencies," these lapses produced a "lumpy, bumpy structure." Second, the divisions suggested by Kolb and Hilles could have been as suitably realized in an essay as in a narrative. After tentatively proposing his own six-part division, Wimsatt admitted that all such divisions were of "little aesthetic moment" because, lacking the structure of a novel by Fielding or Austen, *Rasselas* had only the form necessary to meet its modest requirements—"a quasi-dramatic narrative—not a beginning, middle and end but one of accumulation." Yet *Rasselas* was not considered to be an oriental tale in any profound sense: "the deliberate simplification, even complacent ignorance about the actual colors of life in the supposed locale of Johnson's story, is a kind of counterpart and symbol of the general human truth he would be getting at."

Nonetheless, Wimsatt did discuss the function of the exotic. "What are we to make of the fact that the obvious element of morality is cast in the shape of an oriental tale?" Having given up on any attempt at finding an "organistic" structure, Wimsatt turned to style. The "moderate exoticism" of the style of *The Rambler* "did not find its ideal setting until Johnson wrote *Rasselas*." Producing a "sad grim smile"—here Wimsatt, like Hilles, combined the somber school of Kolb and that of comedy articulated by Whitley—the style of *Rasselas* enabled Johnson to conclude with a view of absurdity suggestive of that of Samuel Beckett but at a higher level, where the choice of eternity still means something, where eloquence remains—"an eloquence profound and moving."[71] Wimsatt implied that Johnson's moderately exotic style enabled him to look down into but remain above the abyss of absurdity. The perception of structure evoked by *Rasselas* was the result of Johnson's style, an achievement, for Wimsatt, more important than the fact that one could not find an "objective correlative" for this structure in the text. Hence, form became less significant than the perception of it, or the perspective which permitted such a perception. Accounting for the rupture in the textual circle discovered by Jones, Wimsatt suggested that the structure was completed by the reader, who was guided by what one of Wimsatt's students, Stanley Fish, has called "affective stylistics."

The difficulty involved in the sundering of organic form to bolster a religious reading of *Rasselas* is evidenced in the position of John Hardy, who combined the views of Wimsatt and Jones. In an informative and up-to-date introduction to his 1968 edition of *Rasselas*, Hardy applied Jones' final insight, that life breaks open the circle of art, to indicate that Johnson's story was an eastern tale and a romance "in appearance only." The arbitrary and uncertain elements of life were used by Johnson, according to Hardy, to satirize "happiness-ever-after" assumptions inherent in the romance and the oriental tale. A *Vanity of Human Wishes* in prose, the narrative had for Hardy as its central irony that "in setting out to observe life, one risks letting life slip through one's fingers." The conclusion, he continued, is not pessimistic because the prince, "Johnson's hero," has "the last word," expressing his hopes. Furthermore, that the travelers do not return to the happy valley gives the story the configuration of a "parabola" rather than a circle, "for experience tempers but does not nullify naiveté."[72]

The difficulty presented by this position is formidable: if, as Hardy believed, *Rasselas* is in the form of a parabola because it concludes outside of the happy valley and this side of the realm of eternity, how can the tale be a *Vanity of Human Wishes* in prose when the poem clearly concludes with the consolation of Christianity? Moreover, if the central irony of *Rasselas* is that "in seeking a choice of life you neglect to live," how does the irony apply to Imlac, especially when he utters this phrase? Hardy's attempt to demonstrate that the satirical puncturing of all human hopes and aspirations served a religious purpose meant that Imlac, the prophet of the tale, had unaccountably to be excluded from the satire. Yet Hardy made clear that, for him, the prince, not Imlac, was the hero of the story.

In 1969, when Kolb's religious form had been questioned, Thomas Preston made an important contribution toward a religious reading. Studying the two schools of interpretation of the Book of Ecclesiastes, one cautioning us to despise this world and the other encouraging a limited enjoyment of earthly pleasures, Preston applied the latter to *Rasselas*. The reformed interpretation of Ecclesiastes maintained that although the only realm of total bliss is eternity, this life, where the prince pursues the choice of life, offers the possibility of partial contentment. As interpreted by Bishops Lowth and Patrick in the eighteenth century, this view insisted that some modes of life offer less unhappiness than others and that one of man's duties is to search for such a state of limited but lawful pleasure. *Rasselas* was thus seen as a religious apologue with a commitment to life as well as to eternity. Not surprisingly, Preston's historical findings reinforce the literary-critical research articulated in the present survey: as I pointed out earlier, a number of eighteenth-century critics assumed that the vanity-of-human-wishes theme did not preclude the possibility of some licit mortal pleasure.[73] It has taken Johnsonians two centuries to rediscover this fact because of their tacit assumption that literary criticism and historical scholarship need not be concerned with the history of literary criticism.

Nevertheless, as in the eighteenth so too in the twentieth century, this notion did not resolve the religious question: commentators still disagreed as to whether in the end *Rasselas* recommends the pursuit of some vain endeavors or concludes that all such quests are equally futile. But the 1960s marked one important achievement. The tone debate came to an end. The comic secularists admitted to an element of gloom related to the notion of *l'absurde*. And those who favored a somber religious reading recognized an element of humor in the story. The larger differences between the religious and secular readers remained, but tone ceased to be referred to as evidence for one or the other position because most commentators now recognized the presence of comedy and tragedy, laughter and irony. New problems, however, arose. Careful formal analysis revealed that Pekuah's adventure is unique and that the final chapter is aptly entitled "The conclusion, in which nothing is concluded."

In 1970, the religious debate was continued by Patrick O'Flaherty, who attacked *Rasselas* in an article entitled "Dr. Johnson as Equivocator: The Meaning of *Rasselas*." For O'Flaherty, the irony of *Rasselas* is all-pervasive; in opposition to Lascelles, he argued that the satire applies to the pilgrims as well as to those whom they visit. In addition to the specific episodes poking fun at one or another main character, the journey itself satirizes the pursuit of a choice of life. Moreover, "the world as depicted in *Rasselas* is bleak and forbidding," for the religion of the narrative offers no comfort, no resolution. Lascelles' concept of hope was rejected because the search encourages neither despair nor hope but is a "species of folly," and hope itself is presented as a neutral drive, neither good nor bad, simply persistent. Kenney's notion that comfort is provided by diversification was questioned because Imlac remains unhappy, as evidenced in his escape with the pilgrims from the happy valley.

Insisting that religion is present in *Rasselas* even though there are references to chance, O'Flaherty returned to what he characterized as Boswell's belief that the "paradox of *Rasselas* is that in it an absurdist view . . . is not irreconcilable with the idea of a supervising

Divinity." Since Christianity "does not teach utter absurdity and futility," O'Flaherty agreed with the Victorians who were "disturbed" by the religion of *Rasselas*, which does not finally ascend above absurdity but remains on the same level in a state of contradiction to it. Johnson presents us with "two fundamentally opposite interpretations of human existence lying side by side as if there was no reason for conflict." His religion, according to O'Flaherty, comes to be marked more by fear than by faith, and in *Rasselas* we have a kind of "catharsis; a purgation of sorrow in absurd comedy, and of doubt in a grimly deterministic philosophy of life which is revealed, on close analysis, as equivocation."[74]

Although following in the tradition of the Victorian religious attack on *Rasselas*, O'Flaherty also appropriated the modern existentialist doctrine of *l'absurde* articulated, in very different ways, by both Leyburn and Wimsatt. Johnson is accused of equivocation because the notion of absurdity, while present in *Rasselas*, cannot be reconciled with the doctrine of Christianity in the story. These two doctrines, according to O'Flaherty, negate one another. Here we confront a new stage in the religious debate. The notion of *l'absurde* which had been rejected as secular by most of those advancing a religious reading, was here accepted but seen to result in equivocation. Furthermore, O'Flaherty used Boswell in an attempt to counter the suggestion by Wimsatt that *Rasselas* provided a religious perspective upon life's absurdity. But Boswell, as we know, had not accused Johnson of equivocation. On the contrary, he asserted that *Rasselas* faced reality fully and that those who experienced a questioning of faith in the tale were unable to face Johnson's unflinching view of the truth. O'Flaherty saw equivocation because he recognized that the satire in *Rasselas* undermines all attempts at formal closure; the choice of eternity, like the choice of life, is never achieved. Because the religious question is raised but never answered, O'Flaherty believed that *Rasselas* ends with equivocation, not resolution.

Mary Lascelles, in a second article on *Rasselas*, pursued an alternative inference from O'Flaherty's argument, namely, that the religious question remains unanswered because Johnson was interested in a secular problem. For Lascelles, the question was "whether *Rasselas* is a profound essay in moral philosophy or a satire on the moralist's search for a clue to the riddle of life." Favoring the latter view, Lascelles believed that the religious reading must dismiss the oriental aspects of the tale as mere ornaments. She proposed a four-part structure, incorporating Jones' coda within the astronomer incident. Labeled as "dreadful," chapter 45, the conversation with the old man, was dismissed as a later addition and certainly out of place. "So everything turns on our reading of the final episode [the astronomer] and its central character." Denying Raleigh's assertion that this incident supplied "the picture with a shade darker than death itself," Lascelles saw hope here because the astronomer, unlike other exemplars of folly visited by the travelers, is cured of his delusion. The episode also has formal significance in transcending "the limitations of contemporary allegory and drawing on an older and greater tradition." As the astronomer develops from an allegorical character into one who comes to life, is cured, and joins the traveling party, *Rasselas* moves beyond the oriental allegory common in the periodical essays to develop the final theme of "the function, not in art but in life, of the imagination."[75]

But since life, as Lascelles herself admitted, does not enter until the end of the story, this notion left out of account most of the narrative, where imagination presumably could only operate in the context of art. In the same year as that of Lascelles' essay, Donald Greene also proposed a four-part structure, but one that ended in ambiguity. The conclusion of *Rasselas* was seen as similar to that of *Candide*; the larger issues remain unresolved, and one simply returns to one's garden.[76] Influenced by Jones' innovative idea of a coda, Lascelles and Greene both advanced readings that sought to avoid the religious question, yet they arrived at diametrically opposite conceptions of the reader's final response.

Harold Pagliaro attempted to incorporate this polarity within a dialectical reading of *Rasselas*. Employing a notion of time and timelessness that Geoffrey Tillotson first advanced in 1959,[77] Pagliaro approached *Rasselas* as a novel. Ironically, this essay appeared in 1971, the same year that Tillotson published an introduction to the tale from which he omitted any reference to his own previous ideas on time. While Tillotson now believed that there was no important difference in form between *Rasselas* and a religious or moral essay, Pagliaro used Tillotson's earlier notion to forward his case for the story as a novel.

But the problem of how to include timelessness within the fabric of the novel was to prove a formidable one. The prince and Imlac are, according to Pagliaro, poles in a dialectic representing youth and age that finally become interfused; their opposition and eventual linking "define the fictional world" of *Rasselas*. By the end of the tale the two points of view become one; the "Imlac-Rasselas axis is an eternal one, yet changing, as Rasselas journeys toward Imlac." The reader, however, "identifies wholly with neither" of the characters. At the end, the Imlac-Rasselas axis is transformed into the choice-of-life/choice-of-eternity or time/eternity axis: "the reader, unlike the characters who turn heavenward, may turn to the novel—its collection of mediated pairs of forces—both their antagonism and their interpenetration, in perpetuity."[78] The characters turn to heaven, and the reader is left with the form of the novel. Pagliaro had accepted O'Flaherty's belief that the religious and secular quests are irreconcilable; he differed from O'Flaherty in urging the reader to focus upon the secular novelistic structure. But that structure can no longer claim wholeness if it leaves out of account the characters' final decisions.

In the 1970s, the brief respite from attack that *Rasselas* had enjoyed during the 1950s and 1960s ended. The attempt to avoid the religious question by disclosing the holistic form of the choice-of-life journey was doomed to failure once it was seen that the narrative is not circular in design. Those favoring the religious reading could thus either attack the structure of the tale, as did O'Flaherty, or, like Wimsatt, argue that the lack of closure for the choice-of-life motif was itself a means of pointing to the choice of eternity. The early 1970s also produced a dramatic development concerning the difference between the end of the prince's journey and that of the history of Imlac. Now seen as a part of the larger context, Imlac was no longer assumed to be Johnson's spokesman, and his views were discussed in relation to those of the other characters in the tale. For example, in 1971, only seven years after Tillotson and Kallich assumed that Imlac's poetic principles were synonymous with those of Johnson, Howard Weinbrot documented the function of the irony directed against Imlac in his "dissertation upon poetry." He demonstrated that some of the poetic principles in this chapter do and others do not coincide with Johnson's own beliefs.[79]

The debate that followed the appearance of Weinbrot's article concerned the extent and kind of modification of the poetic doctrines implied by the satire: most participants, however, accepted the fact that humor was present and functioned in part to distinguish Imlac's poetics from those of Johnson. Paradoxically, the recognition that *Rasselas* is not an organic whole highlighted the limitations of the circular aspect of Imlac's history, which was now seen as inscribed within a larger but open-ended kind of structure.

In 1973, Ian White argued that *Rasselas* could be seen to have as its final goal education. A "novel in miniature in which each chapter break and title has a function," *Rasselas*, according to White, catches the reader up in the story from the first sentence because Johnson wrote "beyond his usual statements, in a kind of sublime which calls new powers into being." This sublime style distances the reader so that the characters and locations of the story can be perceived as "intellectual types" going through the stages of an educational process.[80] But the same process that White found to be contained in a novelistic form, Thomas Curley, also writing in 1973, described as allegorical: *Pilgrim's Progress* provided "a thematic blueprint for the creation of *Rasselas*" that arrived at the choice of eternity.[81] The question that remains unanswered is whether the educational procedure is secular or religious.

Carey McIntosh suggested that the two need not be viewed as mutually exclusive. Developing the notion of a paradox between the gloom of the choice-of-life motif and the hope inherent in the choice of eternity, McIntosh speculated about how the travelers, after making the choice of eternity, could continue seeking the choice of life.[82] But this all-embracing formulation raises a question about the nature of the relationship between the two quests. How is the choice-of-life quest altered after the choice of eternity has been made?

The nature of the problem now facing criticism was aptly illustrated by William Holtz's tribute, in 1974, to Joseph Wood Krutch. Explaining that Krutch had "recalled discovering an identity of mood between *The Modern Temper* and the somber note of Johnson's work, particularly his *Rasselas*," Holtz pointed out that "the story of Rasselas has no religious component and the prince's question hangs over this purely sublunary narrative unanswered." But, according to Holtz, Krutch differed from Johnson in being unable to maintain the balance between secular and theological. "Krutch's study is consistent" with modern emphasis on Johnson's skepticism "in all matters but religious ones . . . and his conflict between religion and experience."

In his own life, Krutch finally opposed the "radical discontent" of *Rasselas*.[83] We have already seen, in our earlier discussion, that in 1944, when Krutch advanced his "tragic" secular reading of *Rasselas*, he did not express his personal dissatisfaction with such a notion; Holtz drew this inference from an admission Krutch made in his autobiography. But the dilemma that Holtz located in Krutch's personal life became a literary-critical one, that is, had a bearing on the *Rasselas* commentary of the mid-1970s. Once the structural configuration is seen to reside in the reader, not the text, the attitude of an important reader such as Krutch has critical significance. For the question now becomes what sort of critical posture is appropriate for the reader of *Rasselas*.

In 1975, Earl Wasserman responded to this question by attempting to demonstrate that the text itself directed the reader by way of what he called an "implicit context." According to Wasserman, *Rasselas* refers the reader to material outside of the text that points toward the proper response to *Rasselas*. Specifically, the choice of Prodicus and the tablet of Cebes, archetypal stories known to schoolboys of the eighteenth century, are the models for the structure of *Rasselas*. The former was molded into the choice-of-life motif, and the latter became the basis for the journey or quest theme. Both, however, were markedly transformed by Johnson; the choice of life is never found, and the journey ends inconclusively. The consequence is *"formal absurdity,"* which explains the "quiet" comedy and final functional ambiguity.[84] Although for Wasserman the formal subversion operates against the choice of life in favor of the choice of eternity, it is not clear from his argument why another reader could not perceive it operating in the opposite direction.

In fact, because of his emphasis on the subversive element in *Rasselas*, Wasserman was placed in the company of doubters by a critic forwarding an orthodox Christian position. Arguing that *Rasselas* is a proof for the immortality of the soul, Robert Walker described Wasserman's view that the choice of eternity was only "the implicit theme of the book" as a position that "sounds like" the secular reading of Joseph Wood Krutch.[85]

Here we see more explicitly what has been implicit throughout this survey: *Rasselas* evokes the deeply personal spiritual beliefs of critics, whether of a religious or a secular kind. This survey of these views suggests that in avoiding final commitment on the religious issue, *Rasselas* encompasses the various aspects of its own controversy.

But the battle within continued. A new stage in our history, however, is signaled by the fact that the religious position based upon reader response is now seen by a more traditional critic as equally suited to a secular reading. Also, it now ceases to be customary to refer to *Rasselas* as a *Vanity of Human Wishes* in prose because, on the one hand, religion, if seen to be present in the narrative, is characterized as less overtly present than in the poem and, on the other hand, the comic and exotic elements of the tale are clearly accepted as unique to it. In short, the religious debate now concerns a narrower issue and is placed in sharper focus.

An instance of this new focus is provided by the difference between William Vesterman and Walter Jackson Bate, both writing on Johnson the man. For Vesterman, the style of *Rasselas* gradually changes from that of the early chapters, which are marked by a detached and admonitory view of imagination—"ye who listen with credulity"—to that of the conclusion, where the characters are allowed the pleasure of creating imagined worlds, knowing that they cannot be "fixed": "so different is the last chapter from the first that the only hope finally deluded is the author's intention. As he deals artistically with the implications of the intentions, the imaginative effort involved brings out Johnson's greatest power, and the result for us is the history of a week in the life of the imagination."[86] Vesterman believed that Johnson began with the intention of judging the travels from a religious perspective, but that his artistic integrity led him into a sublunary context, where he concluded.

Bate, on the other hand, after admitting to the presence of many secular literary "archetypal forms," including the fairy story, the eastern tale, the pilgrimage idea, satire manqué, and the *Bildungs-roman*, found an implicit religious conclusion, which is never made explicit because of "Johnson's own inner taboo . . . against specific religious discussion on his own part in his writing."[87] The difference here concerns only the final impression left on the reader; both agreed that the body of the text contains religious and secular elements as well as comic and tragic moments.

But perhaps the best illustration that the debate about tone, a term which had been seminal for the "New Criticism," has passed out of history while the religious question remains can be seen from the summary of *Rasselas* offered by the 1979 installment of that stalwart of standard opinion, the *Oxford History of English Literature:* compared now not to the *Vanity of Human Wishes* but to *The Rambler,* *Rasselas* is distinguished from the latter by virtue of its "fresh perspective," "intensity and compendiousness." The end of the tale, although "exceedingly austere," was seen as "far from despairing."[88] Thus, the religious question remains unresolved while the tone is characterized by combining the schools of gloom and grim smiles. The tone debate was thus brought to an end.

During the latter part of the eighteenth century, throughout the nineteenth century, and in the first part of the twentieth century, tone was discussed in direct relationship to religion, the shared assumption being that Christianity contained in its essence some form of hope. For a few decades in the middle of the twentieth century, a number of critics argued that the tone of *Rasselas* was a function of its literary structure, not of theological commitment. But when many recognized that the form of *Rasselas* was deliberately open-ended, religion was displaced from the text to the reader. Tone at that point ceased to be a decisive factor because the attitude inherent in one's religious convictions was seen to be individual and highly subjective. The tone debate was not resolved but abandoned because new critical assumptions rendered the entire matter moot.

Turning now to the early 1980s, we can understand the critical concerns of the present decade by analyzing two essays which represent contrasting approaches to *Rasselas.* In 1981, Irvin Ehrenpreis published an article in *Novel* which is devoted to delineating the structure of *Rasselas.* In a section of the essay entitled "Theory," Ehrenpreis explained that structure can only be a term of use if it refers to "a design conceptually prior to the completion of the work under examination, and established in such a way that both the author and the reader may know it." "In this sense," he continued, "structure is inseparable from literary genre."

In the following section of the essay, Ehrenpreis sought to define the genre of *Rasselas*. He began by explaining that it is not a novel but a "proto-novel," then proceeded to classify it as a "philosophical romance" before deciding that it is an "oriental tale." Yet his concluding paragraph contains the following sentence: "A critic might notice that the features I have been examining appear in works by Johnson which in no way refer to oriental tales."[89] Clearly, Ehrenpreis' struggle with the generic problem makes evident that Johnson includes elements from most of the narrative genres available to him but does not permit the reader to rest with one prevailing genre.

Alan Liu, on the other hand, avoided the entire question of genre by use of discourse analysis and psychoanalytic theory. One result of the move from text to reader, it should be noted, is the rise to legitimacy of psychological criticism. Furthermore, Liu's use of terminology derived from the works of Jacques Derrida and Jacques Lacan indicates that *Rasselas* has not lost its ability to attract new methods. Writing in 1984, Liu began with O'Flaherty's notion of the equivocation between the choice of life and the choice of eternity. But instead of concluding, like O'Flaherty, that the religion of *Rasselas* is therefore flawed, Liu adopted a deconstructive strategy, focusing upon the equivocation. "The 'moral' of Johnson's first paragraph which tells us not to wish, is undermined by its own hidden wistfulness," that is, we are directed simultaneously to wish and not to wish. The result for Liu is a sort of hollow desire which produces the "embalmed signifier," the catacombs.

Since the reader is here seen as at once the observer of the embalming process and that which is embalmed, instead of selecting either a religious choice of eternity or a secular choice of life, we are taken by Liu on a Lacanian journey in search of the psychological significance of the embalmed signifier. The "missing link" is Johnson's mother, a discovery which, according to Liu, gives added resonance to the term used in the catacombs episode, "mummy." Johnson's "guilt" about his mother is found buried in the text of *Rasselas*; Liu concluded that this "embalmed signifier, compelling such a complex wake of public denial and private hunger, is the central structure of Johnson's thought."[90]

Although his terminology is contemporary, Liu's position was in the tradition begun by Hawkins in the eighteenth century and continued in our century by Hovey. This position locates fissures and flaws in the text that it attributes to Johnson's feelings toward his mother. But, as we have seen, there is another psychological tradition begun by Boswell and continued by Grange that seeks to explain Johnson's anxiety concerning his mother by recourse to an analysis of the structural and generic conventions of *Rasselas*. In ignoring the history of criticism, particularly the psychological and generic traditions, and restricting his deconstructive method to discourse, Liu is deconstructed by history. The historical perspective employed for this survey suggests that we in the 1980s can no more escape from the dilemma of the genre and structure of *Rasselas* than resolve the matter by selecting one strand of the history, one prevailing genre that will settle the question of structure.

In conclusion, what do we learn from this history of *Rasselas* criticism that will affect subsequent analysis of the narrative? First and most important, the religious question cannot be resolved; I must account for its function as a question, as a driving force. Second, in addition to being, like most literary works, a mixture of genres, including the novel, apologue, romance, oriental tale, and many others, *Rasselas* makes clear that it cannot be positively labeled or generically essentialized. Critics must recognize that they make decisions about which genres prevail on the basis of their interpretation of the text. I need to explain why *Rasselas* calls attention to this process. Third, although not circular in structure, *Rasselas* has functional formal properties. The abduction of Pekuah differs in kind from the conversational nature of episodes previous to it. And the astronomer incident is unique in a number of respects, not the least of which is the fact that the astronomer is cured and becomes a member of the traveling party.

These three points correspond to the three ages of criticism in our analysis, the eighteenth, nineteenth, and twentieth centuries. I am proposing that elements of the different methodologies from these three centuries must be combined. The mimetic critics of the eighteenth century recognized that Johnson was not attempting to resolve the religious question but to represent it. The impulse to find paradise on earth, what Rasselas calls the search for the choice of life, cannot be circumscribed in a literary world; it can only be adequately understood as being ultimately referential, gesturing beyond itself to the realm of the extraliterary. The prince's escape from the happy valley must be seen to represent a move from a "supposed True Paradise" to a world subject to contingency, not merely a shift from one kind of discourse to another. Nevertheless, the world inside, like that outside the happy valley, has its literary properties. It is governed by generic and formal conventions. And here we can make use of the work done by our nineteenth-and twentieth-century predecessors.

The nineteenth-century commentators realized that *Rasselas* stretched generic conventions to their limits. I conclude from their findings that Johnson thwarts the reader's generic expectations at the same time that he manipulates the fictive characters' expectations in an educational context to point to the knowledge that derives from the horizon of expectations. But only in the twentieth century has it been demonstrated that the literary quality of *Rasselas* is bound up with its structural properties. This structure comprises the movement from the happy valley to the world represented by the pyramids, followed by the denouement, which involves the astronomer and the return to Abyssinia, not the happy valley. The text unfolds as a literary form that reaches out beyond the bounds of the literary. I conclude from this twentieth-century commentary that the narrative process of *Rasselas* is a form of human understanding.

The belief that there is a dialectical relationship between mimeticism and formalism has provided the enabling concept of my commentary. It derives from *Rasselas*, and here Johnson's practice, as is often the case, goes beyond his theory and that of his age. For *Rasselas* demonstrates how the religious impulse in man, the desire for paradise on earth, involves the interaction of the formal and mimetic capacities of man. The concept of paradise is an imaginary idea, a form of forms. The ability to conceive of it realized on earth requires a mimetic mode of thought, referring us beyond the imaginary. The happy valley fosters in the young prince both of these capacities, which he formulates in his decision to seek not *a* choice of life but *the* choice of life. At the conclusion of the story, Rasselas knows that his wish cannot be obtained but continues looking for it in Abyssinia. "The conclusion, in which nothing is concluded" signals to the reader that the procedure of *Rasselas*, that of the reader and the characters in the tale, has achieved the level of principle. The quest for the choice of life finally arrives at awareness of its own procedure, that is, the recontextualization, by means of the altering of the horizon of expectations, of the choice-of-life search.

Thus, Johnson's little story book, as he called it, manipulates generic and formal literary characteristics—notions that only come into criticism in the nineteenth and twentieth centuries—to show how man's religious impulse leads to an understanding of how the literary process applies to the human world. I conclude that the theoretical dilemma posed by *Rasselas* can only be resolved when the hermeneutic and structuralist conceptions are seen in dialectical relationship to one another.

2

Prison-Paradise

Preparation for Entry into the World

THE SOURCE of the two-century-old religious controversy concerning *Rasselas* is evident in the first sentence of the tale. "Ye who listen with credulity to the whispers of fancy, and pursue with eagerness the phantoms of hope; who expect that age will perform the promises of youth, and that the deficiencies of the present day will be supplied by the morrow; attend to the history of Rasselas prince of Abissinia." In its diction, cadence, and rhythm, this invocation is reminiscent of the Book of Ecclesiastes, and accordingly, a number of commentators have labeled *Rasselas* an apologue. But, as we have already had occasion to point out, this generic category leads to many difficulties, not the least of which concerns the end of the tale, "The conclusion, in which nothing is concluded."

Moreover, this first sentence contains other generic suggestions. The phrase "the history of Rasselas prince of Abissinia" is familiar to those who have consulted the title page of almost any work of eighteenth-century fiction, as in the "History" of *Moll Flanders, Clarissa Harlowe,* and *Tom Jones*, to mention but a few. In using this term in his title and again in his first sentence, Johnson must have recognized that he was clearly associating his story with this tradition, which is referred to by modern scholars as that of the novel and which is generally seen as "realistic" and secular. Before even beginning to pursue other generic allusions, such as the moral or oriental tale and others to be discussed subsequently, we thus come upon the two-sided quality of *Rasselas* that has troubled critics for so long; the choice-of-life motif, appropriate to eighteenth-century fiction, versus the choice of eternity, suggestive of the apologue. Having evoked this dualism in the opening sentence, Johnson does not pursue or attempt to resolve it; instead he turns to a description of the happy valley.

This chapter will follow the narrative procedure of *Rasselas* to explain why Johnson begins by placing the choice-of-life/choice-of-eternity axis in the happy valley. My contention is that Johnson uses the exotic paradise as a point of departure because it evokes literary and extraliterary traditions that enable him to suggest how the literary procedure can be applied to the extraliterary realm.

The literary process involves an interaction between two traditions that are themselves mixtures. The literary paradise convention, a combination of oriental paradise and *beatus ille* allusions, is shown in relation to an extraliterary amalgam consisting of the travel accounts of Abyssinia and of the orientalized British garden.

The happy valley is different from any other location in *Rasselas*. Here "all the diversities of the world were brought together, the blessings of nature were collected, and its evils extracted and excluded" (*R* 1.2). The Prince of Abyssinia, however, is not content in this bower. He has ceased to find pleasure in its amusements or tranquillity in its repose. The reader knows at the outset that the protagonist will not remain in the happy valley. The Prince's departure also signals a change in fictional mode; after the escape from the prison-paradise, the exotic characteristics of *Rasselas* become less prominent and less important. Arthur Weitzman, who found that some of the episodes outside the happy valley make reference to staples of "Oriental fiction of the eighteenth century," believed, nonetheless, that these later eastern elements are less "romantic" than those located in the happy valley.[1]

Yet from the outset the royal retreat is portrayed as an ideal sullied by the real, a fragile paradise from which anxiety and mistrust can never be wholly excluded. Protected from all beasts of prey, the vale is subject to the floods of the Nile; it contains more kinds of exotic plants and herbs than any normal climate could sustain, but its inhabitants are not immune to boredom. The most famous Abyssinian literary paradise is that mentioned in *Paradise Lost* when, in describing a foil to Eden, a terrestrial paradise located "under the Ethiop line . . . where Abassin kings their issue guard," Milton refers to a "supposed True Paradise."[2] Johnson further develops the tradition of the earthly aspect of the Abyssinian paradise by detailing the limitations of the happy valley. But Maren-Sofie Røstvig has demonstrated, in *The Happy Man,* that there was another literary tradition of retirement to a garden paradise, which began with the English translations of the Polish Jesuit Mathius Casimire Sarbiewski's Horatian odes of the 1640s and 1650s. In Sarbiewski's poetry "we first find a suggestive fusion between the classical *beatus ille* themes, the Christian theme of the solitary joys of the *hortus conclusus*, and the Hermetic theme of the sentient landscape which yearns for god and the stars, and which serves man out of love for the divine spark in him."[3] One of Johnson's first poems was a "Translation of Horace's

'Epode the 2ᵈ' (Beatus ille)." This rendering of Horace displays not merely Johnson's early interest in the retirement motif but also an ironical attitude toward some desires similar to those found in the description of the happy valley. Consider, for example, the conclusion of the translation:

> Thus did the Us'rer Alphius praise,
> With transports kindled, rural ease,
> His money he collected strait,
> Resolv'd to purchase a retreat.
> But still desires of sordid gain
> Fix'd in his Canker'd breast remain:
> Next Month he sets it out again.   [*Poems* 16.73-79]

Although the usurer first brings to mind the hermit of chapter 21 (to be discussed later), he also reminds us of the prince in the happy valley, particularly when we recall his being described as suffering from "the wants of him that wants nothing." The irony in *Rasselas,* however, is more complex. The prince's heart is not "canker'd" by any single obsession; instead, he is driven by a series of desires that correspond to a number of generic conventions to be explained in detail later in this chapter.

But first we need to analyze the allusions to the two extraliterary traditions, the "oriental" garden and the travel accounts of Abyssinia. Johnson began his literary career in 1735 by translating one of these accounts, Jerome Legrand's French version of Father Lobo's *Relation d'Abissinie.* This text interested Johnson because it consistently contrasted the expectations of the missionary, derived mainly from hearsay and legends, with what he actually found in Abyssinia. In the preface to the *Voyage to Abyssinia,* Johnson applauds Father Lobo's respect for historical fact: "he appears by his modest and unaffected Narration to have described Things as he saw them, to have copied Nature from the Life, and to have consulted his Senses not his Imagination; He meets with no Basilisks that destroy with their Eyes, his Crocodiles devour their Prey without Tears, and his Cataracts fall from the Rock without Deafening the Neighboring Inhabitants."[4] Legrand, however, is scolded by the British translator for his bias against the Portuguese, as evidenced in some of the dissertations the Frenchman added to the original text: "He has made no scruple of preferring the Testimony of Father du Bernat, to the Writings of all the Portuguese Jesuits, to whom he allows great Zeal, but little Learning, without giving any other Reason than that his Favourite was a Frenchman. This is writing only to Frenchmen and to Papists: A Protestant would be desirous to know why he must imagine that Father du Bernat had a cooler Head or more Knowledge: and why one Man whose account is singular, is not more likely to be mistaken than many agreeing in the same Account."[5]

For this reason, Johnson, as Joel Gold has demonstrated, took great liberties in selecting and abridging the French text, thereby revealing his own attitudes and beliefs concerning the history of the exotic.[6] One of these attitudes is an interest in the contrast between the expectation engendered by the imagination and the actual as experienced by the senses. For instance, in discussing the path of the Nile, Lobo meticulously demonstrates how the geographical facts call into question secular and scriptural legends. After describing in matter-of-fact terms the beginning of the Nile, Johnson renders Lobo's conclusion as follows: "Many interpreters of the Holy Scriptures pretend that *Gibon* mention'd in *Genesis*, is no other than the *Nile*, which encompasseth all *Aethopia*; but as the *Gibon* had its source from the terrestrial Paradise, and we know that the *Nile* rises in the Country of the *Agaus*, it will be found I believe no small Difficulty to conceive how the same River could arise from two Sources so distant from each other . . ."[7]

Terrestrial paradises are subject to the laws of geography, asserts the missionary, and we are reminded of how the residents of the happy valley are forced to retreat to higher ground at the flooding of the Nile. But more characteristic of the *Relation* than the undermining of legend is the intermingling of religious mystery with historical fact. Lost in the "Field of Salt," fainting with "Heat and Weariness," Lobo and his companions find a well:

> The *Moors* who had arrived at the Well, rightly guessing that we were lost, sent one of their Company to look [for] us, whom we heard shouting in the Woods, but durst make no Answer, for fear of the *Galles*. At length he found us, and conducted us to the rest, we instantly forgot our past Calamities, and had no other Care than to recover the Patriarch's Attendants. We did not give them a full draught at first, but poured in the Water by Drops, to moisten their Mouths and Throats, which were extreamly swell'd, by this Caution they were soon well. We then fell to Eating and Drinking, and though we had nothing but our ordinary repast of Honey and dry'd Flesh, thought we never had regal'd more pleasantly in our Lives.[8]

This episode exemplifies the combination of religious mystery and historical fact that clearly fascinated Johnson. In the exotic setting, an Ethiopian Field of Salt, the hand of God is present, but His gift, life-sustaining water, must be administered carefully drop by drop. Moreover, the divine miracle accentuates the limitations of man: the food and drink may taste especially pleasant, but under such circumstances, even the most ordinary provisions would seem extraordinary. The incident in *Rasselas* which comes to mind is that in which the prince and his fellow pilgrims first emerge from the happy valley: "In the morning they found some shepherds in the field, who set milk and fruits before them . . . being faint and hungry, she drank the milk and eat the fruits, and thought them of a higher flavour than the products of the valley" (*R* 15.42). Since the prince and his sister have struggled through a tunnel in the course of escaping from the happy valley, the superior taste of the meal is more likely to be the result of their physical exercise than of the special flavor of the food and drink. The princess, having until this moment resided in the happy valley, has uninformed expectations about the world outside, as did Father Lobo before traveling in Abyssinia.

   That *Rasselas* alludes to both the legendary/religious and the historical aspect of Abyssinian paradise literature is borne out by Donald Lockhart's research on the sources for the happy valley.[9] Johnson was from early on in his career interested in those who "consulted" their "Senses" as well as those who drew on their "Imagination" concerning the Ethiopian paradise on earth. My point, however, is to demonstrate how these kinds of expectations function in an educational journey that arrives at human understanding. In this regard, we must turn to still another aspect of the allusive happy valley, that of the orientalized eighteenth-century garden.

Early in the century, gardeners began to turn away from the symmetrical geometric shapes fashionable in the seventeenth century to what was characterized as a more natural look. Many examples could be cited, ranging from the plans of aristocratic landowners, like those of Sir William Temple or Lord Shaftesbury, to the manuals of practicing gardeners such as Timothy Nourse and John Lawrence. Addison and Pope were instrumental in bringing about this change in landscape design. Morris Brownell believes that Pope was probably consulted about the alterations to the garden at Chiswick that took place during the 1720s: "Oriental was added to classical authority for the development of the landscape garden at Chiswick by Burlington's protégé, the architect Robert Castell. . . . Thus Burlington and his circle were able to visualize Chinese 'Sharawadgi' (a generation before William Chambers returned from his visit to China) at precisely the moment the setting for the classical villa at Chiswick was being planned, and sanctions were found for iregularity in gardening."

   Brownell explains that by 1730 "Pope had established his reputation as a garden designer in a large number of important places including Cirencester, Richmond Lodge, Down Hall, Wimpole, Rousham, Stowe, and others."[10] By the time Johnson wrote *Rasselas*, one would not need to be a gardening enthusiast to be aware of the important change in landscape design that had been realized in many British gardens. So close was the relationship between literature and gardening at this time that scholars have demonstrated that the influence even worked in the opposite direction, some eighteenth-century gardens being designed in imitation of literature.[11]

Moreover, a number of studies appeared in the early 1750s indicating that the change in horticultural fashion was largely the result of oriental influence. Father Attiret's account of the emperor of China's garden near "Pekin," a description first available in England in 1752, stressed the new basic principle of "natural artificiality," of "ordered disorder." Instead of the immaculate hedges, gravel walks, and trim straight lines of seventeenth-century European gardens, Attiret told his friends back home about the serpentine curves, the huge rocks and cascades, and the delightful pleasure-houses built with "a beautiful disorder." Discussing a palace built at great expense by the emperor for the "Princes of the blood," he explained that such buildings "look almost like those fabulous Palaces, which are said to be raised by Inchantment, all at once, in some beautiful Valley, or on the Brow of some Hill."[12] He described the complex of houses and small palaces, with their intercommunicating, often hidden or secret, doors and passages, some destined for ladies, others for eunuchs or servants, and yet others for the emperor himself. The following lines from the first chapter of *Rasselas* might have found a place in Attiret's letter: "This house . . . was built as if suspicion herself had dictated the plan. To every room there was an open and secret passage, every square had a communication with the rest, either from the upper stories by private galleries, or by subterranean passages from the lower apartments. Many of the columns had unsuspected cavities, in which a long race of monarchs had reposited their treasures" (*R* 1.3-4).

One of the most famous eighteenth-century writers on Chinese gardening was Sir William Chambers. In his *Dissertation on Oriental Gardening*, first published in 1757, he mentioned Attiret and explained far more fully what his predecessor had noted but briefly. For the Chinese gardeners, "nature is their pattern," he declared firmly, "and their aim is to imitate all her beautiful irregularities." Chinese gardeners, according to Chambers, believed that there were three categories of "scenes" that the true artistic gardener could seek to create according to the natural materials, the scenery, and, of course, the finances at his disposal: "the pleasing, the horrid, and the enchanted." The "horrid" and the "enchanted," in which numerous devices, from gibbets to wild beasts, were used to create fear and amazement in the beholder, are of little relevance to *Rasselas*, but

Chambers' description of the "pleasing" might have been an inspiration for Johnson's garden: "When there is sufficient supply of water, and proper ground, the Chinese never fail to form cascades in their gardens. They avoid all regularity in these works, observing nature according to her operations in that mountainous country. The waters burst out from among the caverns, and windings of the rocks. In some places a large and impetuous cataract appears; in others are seen many lesser falls. Sometimes the view of the cascade is intercepted by trees, whose leaves and branches only leave room to discover the waters, in some places, as they fall down the sides of the mountain."[13] The happy valley, it will be recalled, contains rivulets descending from mountainsides covered with every sort of herb, flower, and fruit; these rivulets drain into a cascade that leads into a lake filled with all species of fish and fowl.

Landscape gardens in England at the time contained elements remiscent of those mentioned by Attiret or Chambers that are relevant to the happy valley. Many travelers of the day attested to this fact. In 1754, Richard Pococke described St. Giles Wimborn in the following terms: "The Gardens are very beautifully laid out, in a serpentine river, pieces of water, Lawns, &c: & very gracefully adorn'd with wood. One first comes to an Island in which there is a Castle, then near the water is a Gateway with a tower on each side, & passing between two waters, there is a fine Cascade from the one to the other. . . . There is a pavilion between the waters, and both a Chinese and stone-bridge over them."[14] The rage for oriental gardens reached such proportions that in 1753 Francis Coventry, writing in *The World*, burlesqued the entire fashion. Beginning with the observation that the taste had turned away from the old symmetrical garden, Coventry remarked that while an old mathematician would refuse "to go to heaven in any path not triangular" the gardener of the mid-eighteenth century would probably refuse if the path were not serpentine. He then described a house and garden designed by a parvenu landowner named "Squire Mushroom."[15] After constructing a Gothic mansion, the squire turns the full force of his genius to the garden:

> At your first entrance, the eye is saluted with a yellow serpentine river, stagnating through a beautiful valley, which extends near twenty yards in length. Over the river is thrown a bridge, *partly in the chinese manner*, and a little ship with sails spread and streamers flying, floats in the midst of it. When you have passed this bridge, you enter into a grove perplexed with errors and crooked walks; where having trod the same ground over and over again, through a labyrinth of horn-beam hedges, you are led into an old hermitage built

with roots of trees, which the squire is pleased to call St. Austin's cave.[16]

It is particularly important to recognize that gardening allusions in the happy valley refer not merely to landscape texts but also and more importantly to actual horticultural practice. We know that Johnson liked to retire to a summer house at Streatham and that he visited Shenstone's garden, the Leasowes, which was a *ferme ornée* designed upon natural-artificial oriental principles.[17] In fact, by the middle of the eighteenth century no well-informed person could have been unaware of the rage for orientalized gardening. Of course, the motivations for and the designs of these gardens must have varied considerably. Few frequenters of these landscapes would have realized that the principles of design were related to the long-standing tradition of paradise on earth and to the *beatus ille* literature.[18] Fewer still would have understood why Pope included in his garden a monument to the memory of his mother, thus emphasizing the distinction between terrestrial and celestial paradise.

But Johnson recognized that for most people—albeit unknown to them—part of the appeal of the oriental garden lay in the desire for a paradise on earth. This desire unites the religious/legendary and the literary/Ethiopian material and joins together the *beatus ille* tradition and the fashion for *sharawadgi* in the mid-eighteenth-century English garden. Johnson's strategy of allusions in his description of the happy valley involves the deliberate crossing over from the literary to the extraliterary. The initial result is to evoke the paradise-on-earth desires manifest in the very popular oriental tale and, more significantly, in Britain's green and pleasantly orientalized landscape.

But the happy valley section of the tale does more than isolate such drives; it demonstrates the function of the process of isolation. Having described the prince's place of residence and his attitude toward it, Johnson, in chapter 6, demonstrates how the expectations engendered in the reader by the allusions in the happy valley section and in the prince (by way of living in the happy valley) function in the learning procedure which will be employed during the prince's travels. The flying episode is remembered by readers who recall little else about the happy valley. It is so striking because of the comical way the unfortunate inventor fails in his attempt to fly and because it is the first moment in the story that emphasizes not a precept but an event. Previous to this episode, we have been warned of the tedium of the vale and of problems such as the flooding of the Nile, but these are natural limitations. The flyer, however, nearly drowns as a result of his own experiment, and the prince, having hoped to fly out of the happy valley, feels for the first time truly imprisoned. The flying episode is, in a literal and metaphorical sense, the Fall in Johnson's paradise on earth; the inventor's plunge into the lake prefigures Rasselas' descent from the mountain retreat to the outside world. More importantly, here we are introduced to the method of disillusionment employed throughout the remainder of *Rasselas*, one reminiscent of that found in other Johnsonian works, particularly in *The Rambler*, numbers 204 and 205.

Published in 1752, this pair of essays features Seged, the ruler of Ethiopia, who retires from his urban court for a ten-day respite to a beautiful island "cultivated only for pleasure, planted with every flower that spreads its colours to the sun, and every shrub that sheds fragrance in the air." Here he hopes to "try what it is to live without a wish unsatisfied" (5:297). During the first three days, he is beset with depression and boredom; on the fourth day, a crocodile enters the garden, and the following two days are marred by contention among his guests. On the last day, Seged's daughter, the princess Balkis, becomes ill and dies. The disappointed lord concludes by bequeathing his narrative to future generations "that no man hereafter may presume to say, 'This day shall be a day of happiness' " (5:305). Seged's project is defeated on its own terms, and it is for that reason that Johnson allows the Ethiopian ruler himself, rather than the narrator of the *Rambler* essay, to present the final moral to the reader. Seged concludes that he who attempts to escape from the corruption of the urban court to rustic simplicity will find that the countryside contains its own physical evils, breeds its own kind of human corruption, as a result of boredom, and can offer no consolation to those who lose their loved ones. The crocodile is a key image; it invades what Seged hoped would be a charmed circle. Once the bubble of retirement is burst, the Ethiopian learns never again to expect to find complete earthly happiness at a particular time or place.

The flyer in *Rasselas*, however, has already learned this lesson. Having pointed out to the prince the many pleasures that flight promises—"to survey with equal security the marts of trade, and the fields of battle; mountains infested by barbarians, and the fruitful regions gladdened by plenty, and lulled by peace"—he nevertheless insists that his invention be kept a closely guarded secret because "against an army sailing through the clouds neither walls, nor mountains, nor seas could afford any security." Moreover, the scientist in *Rasselas* has finished a number of successful projects, the most notable of which is a water wheel that provides music for the courtiers and irrigation for the garden. Even the unsuccessful attempt at flight is not a complete disaster; although "half dead with terrour and vexation," the inventor survives his ordeal. And the bathetic clue—that the wings were modeled after those of the bat—suggests that the satire is directed not at human flight *per se* but at a blind form of flight. The allusion to Icarus reinforces the impression that the topic of this chapter is not the question of human flight but the manner in which one attempts it.

My point is that Johnson wants us to see that Seged's experiment is futile and should not be attempted again in any form but that the inventor in *Rasselas* can be expected to go on experimenting. The hopes and desires of the flyer are shared by Rasselas and the reader. The failure to fly means that such expectations are frequently thwarted, not that the process of trying to achieve these goals is itself futile or self-defeating. On the contrary, because Rasselas' and the flyer's desires are in the right direction—upward and outward, rather than, like Seged's retreat, inward—even their failure will further their education.

The question then becomes what the prince and the flyer learn from the abortive attempt to fly. Because the descent from ideals to practical reality is a common device in eighteenth-century fiction, we can refine our understanding of this episode by comparing it with similar ones in works of the same period. Many commentators believe that the inventor's attempt to fly is a form of pride, for, as the prince points out to him, "every animal has his element assigned him; the birds have the air, and man and beasts the earth." Here one is reminded of the famous oriental religious allegory of the eighteenth century, Joseph Addison's "The Vision of Mirza," an essay that first appeared in *The Spectator* in 1711 and has been seen by many critics as a precursor of *Rasselas*. Mirza, who, like Rasselas, can be characterized as "high-minded," is guided up a mountainside by a "genius," a figure resembling Imlac. But this sage does not lead the way to a different part of the world; he points back to the valley from which Mirza has climbed.

Suddenly, the entire scene changes: the valley becomes a "Vale of Eternity," and the body of water is now the "great Tide of Eternity." The oracular is superimposed upon the ordinary, a transformation that is most apparent when reality returns: "I then turned again to the Vision which I had been so long contemplating, but instead of the rolling Tide, the arched Bridge, and the Happy Islands, I saw nothing but the hollow Valley of *Bagdat,* with Oxen, Sheep, and Camels grazing upon the Sides of it." The animals on the slopes take the form, in the vision, of animalized humans on the Bridge of Human Life. In the midst of "Mirth and Jollity," they unexpectedly stumble and fall into the vale of misery below. These people are as immersed in everyday life as are the animals, grazing intently, their heads lowered. Mirza, however, raises himself above mundane concerns by climbing the mountain and contemplating the "vanity of human life."[19] He is rewarded with a glimpse of the Happy Islands that represent heaven. Addison's message is clear: attend to the hereafter, not to the present. The vision of eternity is granted only to those who raise themselves above, instead of remaining enveloped within, the mortal, animal world.

But Johnson does not seem to be advising his hero to move beyond the mortal world of the flyer. In fact, when the inventor plunges into the water, it is the prince who pulls him to land. Furthermore, the experiment itself takes place in large part because Rasselas and the flyer encourage one another. The very idea of attempting human flight results from the prince's attention: "the workman was pleased to find himself so much regarded by the prince, and resolved to gain yet higher honours" by devising a means of "the swifter migration of wings." Having ignited the inventor's ambitions, the prince himself feels rekindled hope for "passing the mountains." Rasselas, unlike Mirza, who remains apart from what he observes, is implicated from start to finish in the flyer's experiment. In this way Johnson indicates that his subject is the prince in this world, not the hereafter. And although such knowedge may be seen as belonging on Addison's bridge, this side of the Happy Islands, Johnson directs us to focus, not upon the Great Tide of Eternity but upon the educational principle that will apply to the "Vale of Misery" when the prince escapes from the happy valley.

The nature of this principle is further clarified by comparing the flying episode in *Rasselas* with a similar one in *The Citizen of the World* (first published in 1760-61) that occurs in the "valley of ignorance." Since Goldsmith and Johnson were good friends during this time, it is possible that they discussed and commented upon each other's orientalized valleys. But the question of influence is not germane to the present discussion. Rather, my goal is to explain how the flyer's mishap in *Rasselas* is related to the process of acquiring knowledge by comparing it with a similar accident in *The Citizen of the World* designed to exemplify ignorance. Goldsmith's setting resembles that of Johnson. "In this sequestered vale, bless'd with all the spontaneous productions of nature, the honey'd blossom, the refreshing breeze, the gliding brook, and the golden fruitage, the simple inhabitants seemed happy in themselves, in each other; they desired no greater pleasures, for they knew of none greater; ambition, pride, and envy were vices unknown among them."[20]

The narrator of this allegory, Zindavesta of Zoroaster—certainly one of Goldsmith's finest oriental names—begins the tale with an unhappy youth who leaves the vale in search of the "*Land of Certain-*

ty." Finding his first guide, the *"genius of Probability,"* too slow, the restless young man turns to the "genius of *Demonstration,"*[21] who, after much protestation, admits that he is unable to reach the land of Certainty and passes his ward on to the *"Daemon of Error."* This peculiar creature sets off for the *"Land of Confidence,"* warning his charge not to look down at the *"Ocean of Doubts"* below. But upon hearing strange voices, the young man does look down and falls "headlong into the subjacent *Ocean of Doubts,* from whence he was never to rise." Here the letter ends. As the genius drops the "astonished traveler," so Goldsmith thwarts the reader to emphasize that only the ignorant believe there is a fast and easy way to certainty.[22] Goldsmith's traveler makes his fatal error in turning away from the geniuses of Demonstration and Probability. The allegory tells us that one must employ these slow and painstaking means to certainty. The flyer, on the other hand, is not an impatient man. He is understandably vexed at his failure, but his previous achievements give us reason to assume that he will patiently continue to pursue the unhurried means recommended by the genius of Probability.

Unlike Goldsmith, Johnson does not drown his experimenter, because he does not want us to conclude that the flyer's failure merely manifests his ignorance. On the contrary, the flyer learns an important, if embarrassing, principle about his flying contraption: "his wings, which were of no use in the air, sustained him in the water." That the floating wings save the inventor's life is an important comic element of this episode. We laugh at the flyer, especially when we recall his remark in a previous discussion with the prince, that "he that can swim needs not despair to fly: to swim is to fly in a grosser fluid, and to fly is to swim in a subtler." Although condemned to struggle in a grosser fluid, the scientist need not despair, for he has escaped from a dangerous mishap alive and unharmed. Whether or not Johnson believed in the ability of man to fly, it is clear that the "bat-winged" contrivance represents man's inability to foresee the direction or final goal of his "flight."

The flying episode symbolizes the contingent nature of man's educational procedure, that man learns by understanding the ways in which his ideals, hopes, and expectations, when put to the test in reality, are frequently thwarted.[23] In the same year that *Rasselas* was published, Voltaire produced his *Candide*, a tale that concludes with the philosophical principle of contingency. Since the two tales have been frequently compared, we can restrict our discussion to how Johnson's educational principle in the flying episode differs from its equivalent in *Candide*. It has been remarked that Voltaire would have drowned Johnson's flyer.[24] Certainly the results of the flying episode in *Candide* are more disastrous than those in *Rasselas*. Candide can only leave Eldorado when the king has provided him with a flying balloon that enables him to pass the mountains. Although Voltaire's protagonist does fly over the mountains without mishap, he is disappointed in another and more profound sense. For Candide, Eldorado is an ideal retreat except that it lacks his Cunégonde. But having sacrificed all the paradisal qualities of Eldorado to seek his beloved, Candide finally finds Cunégonde when she is so ugly and deformed that he marries her out of obligation, not desire. Thus Voltaire presents the principle of his *conte philosophique*: man can choose from two possibilities, retreat into a garden world like Eldorado or struggle in the world at large. In the last chapter, a woman puts the following question to the protagonist:

> I should like to know which is worse, being raped a hundred times by negro pirates, having a buttock cut off, running the gauntlet in the Bulgar army, being flogged and hanged in an auto-da-fé, being dissected and rowing the galleys—experiencing, in a word, all the miseries through which we have passed—or else just sitting here and doing nothing.
> —It's a hard question, said Candide.[25]

The flight from Eldorado is emblematic of the philosophical paradox at the heart of *Candide*: any mortal retreat must by its very nature exclude some desirable elements, but the quest for happiness in the world at large results at best in the arrival at one's goals in unanticipated and usually undesirable ways. The alternative offered at the end of the tale, that of cultivating one's own garden, is exacted at the price of limiting one's desires. Candide can hope to remain protected from the hurly-burly of the contingent world by remaining in his own garden, but that choice entails giving up the quest for the ideal represented by the young and beautiful Cunégonde. Unlike the wretched and abused Cunégonde at the end of the tale, her ideal image represents for Candide the means of achieving personal contentment. In *Rasselas* the characters never cease to search for this goal, as is made clear in the next-to-last sentence of the story: "Of these wishes that they had formed they well knew that none could be obtained." Although Rasselas now recognizes that he will not find what he has called the "choice of life," he still searches for it. In this respect, it is important to remember that the travelers at the end of Johnson's tale return not to the happy valley, which can be seen as the prince's own garden, but to Abyssinia, the world where one's deepest desires are regularly thwarted.

Furthermore, Johnson's garden is different from Voltaire's Eldorado in that the flyer is not sheltered from contingent events even in the happy valley. The result is less disastrous than outcomes of similar ventures in the tales by Goldsmith and Voltaire because Johnson is not satirizing ignorance or philosophical principles. Instead, he is concerned with the gradual procedure by which one acquires practical knowledge. After the flyer's failure, the prince will perhaps in the future invest less hope in an invention that has never been tested, and the inventor may learn to include in his next experiment a plan in case of failure, what modern scientists call "a fall-back procedure." Although hardly momentous, these conclusions are important to the individuals concerned, for it is by way of such minute, quotidian forms of education that we increase our knowledge, advancing toward what the prince calls the "choice of life." And although this goal is never achieved, Imlac's history, the subject of our next chapter, makes clear that some means of approach are to be preferred to others.

But before moving on to Imlac, it is important for us to understand why Johnson's garden alludes to both a literary and an extraliterary tradition. In my view, the happy valley represents the human drive for paradise on earth: the depiction of such an impetus presents a particular problem for the literary artist because it must be rendered not merely as an ideal, a paradise, but as one that contains in the ideal its own realization, a paradise on earth. But the fictive nature of literature places it at one remove from actualization, even that of its own contents. Johnson negotiated this problem by creating a garden that intermingles literary and extraliterary allusions; the happy valley blends the literary traditions of *beatus ille* and "Abassin" Eden with the extraliterary traditions of the history of Abyssinia and the designs of actual gardens in mid-eighteenth-century England. Together, they form the paradise-on-earth concept: paradise deriving from literary allusions, and earth from historical and horticultural allusions.

But the depiction of the desire for paradise on earth itself presents a problem—how does one render the garden as a place that can never be located? To put it another way, how does one show that the desire is to realize on earth that which is unearthly? Johnson creates a happy valley presented as an actual place in the beginning when the prince is unclear about the nature of his desire. But when at the end of the tale Rasselas understands that what he wants on this earth is beyond its bounds, the happy valley ceases to be a place he can reach. Thus the reader comes, with the prince, to understand that the happy valley represents at once a place and a desire beyond any place: the paradox inherent in paradise on earth is represented by a literary process, a journey from an earthly paradise to an earthly drive toward paradise.

Johnson is interested in man's paradise-on-earth desire because it is elemental to human understanding: the quest for the choice of eternity is basic to the choice-of-life quest. And, as I shall show in chapters 3 and 4, the responses evoked by the paradise-on-earth allusions are related to what is learned about the choices of life. We can now understand why *Rasselas* has evoked over two centuries of religious controversy. The paradise-on-earth impulse is one way of formulating man's spiritual quest and is therefore usually seen as synonymous with religion. My contention is that Johnson is not interested in the religious resolution of this impulse but in the manner in which this drive contributes to Rasselas' knowledge about making choices of life. Previous commentators have assumed that the spiritual element in *Rasselas* must by its very nature conclude either in the realm of literature or in that of religion.[26] I believe that Johnson, in *Rasselas*, has devised a literary means of applying the paradise-on-earth motif to neither the literary nor the religious but to the extraliterary, to that realm of human understanding where all of us make daily decisions about our "choice of life," our individual and ultimately futile attempts to find paradise on earth. Such a reading of *Rasselas* illustrates how the literary can point to the extraliterary. The next two chapters will provide further examples supporting this claim.

3

The History of Imlac
Methodological Implications

AFTER HAVING seen how the happy valley nurtures the prince's desire to find the choice of life and, in the flying incident, how the thwarting of this expectation serves educational purposes, we meet Imlac, who tells his life story. This narrative takes up the next six chapters, about half of the happy valley section, and contains perhaps the most famous part in the book, chapter 10, Imlac's "dissertation upon poetry." This tale within a tale so inspires the young prince that he asks Imlac to be his guide in the choice-of-life quest. Imlac also guides the reader of *Rasselas*: the narrative process highlighted in the interpolated tale suggests a new kind of approach to *Rasselas*. My purpose in this chapter is to explain why "The history of Imlac," featuring a poetics, is presented before entry into the world beyond the happy valley. My argument is that "The history of Imlac" contains the procedure by which the longings bred in the happy valley can be employed in understanding the outside world.

We have seen how the religious reading of *Rasselas* leads to the view that Imlac is the conveyer of the message of the tale, a position made explicit by Agostino Lombardo,[1] who in 1959 asserted that the hero of *Rasselas* is Imlac, and by Robert Walker[2] who in 1977 argued that *Rasselas* was written to demonstrate the immortality of the soul, a notion introduced in Imlac's "history." These two modern formulations represent the culmination of a tradition that goes back to the eighteenth century when, for instance, Boswell, in his *Life of Johnson* (1791), identified Johnson with Imlac.[3] This equation of the author with a character in his story explains how Imlac's poetic principles have been taken to be those of Johnson. My method will be to treat the "history of Imlac" as a literary tale within another literary tale and to demonstrate how Imlac's poetics functions within that "double" context. In this way it will be seen that Imlac is not synonymous with the author but is a guide or "genius" for the young prince. If Rasselas can be said to be an innocent with regard to the world outside the happy valley, then Imlac represents experience. But, as we shall see, for Johnson the voice of experience is no substitute for experience.

One indication that Imlac is to be seen as part of a literary context, not as an authorial spokesman, is provided by the clear reference to the convention of the *beatus vir*.[4] This aspect of the *beatus ille* tradition discussed in the previous chapter is alluded to when Imlac gives his reason for choosing to retire to the happy valley. "Wearied at last with solicitation and repulses," he tells the prince, "I resolved to hide myself for ever from the world" (*R* 12.35). By the time *Rasselas* was published, the *beatus vir* motif had developed considerably since its emergence in the early seventeenth century. In the Renaissance, according to Røstvig, the *beatus ille* theme could be found in one of three forms: the contentment of mental retirement, the equilibrium of the golden mean, or the happiness of country life. During the Restoration, however, the mystic rapture of the poets of the early seventeenth century was transformed into a Cartesian rapture, a sort of "scientific expedition."[5] And although the retirement concept remained popular during the eighteenth century, it underwent some development: "The happiness of the eighteenth-century *beatus vir* came to depend less upon the *parva rura* and the *nil admirari* of Horace than upon the *rerum cognoscere causas* of Virgil. The intellectual analysis of the landscape of retirement became the prime duty and interest of the would-be *beatus vir*; the old quest for personal happiness became virtually identified with the search for the true knowledge of the hidden cause of things."[6]

The significance of the shift during the eighteenth century from Horace to Virgil is that the former manifested none of the intellectual curiosity found in Virgil's apostrophe to Lucretius. Keeping in mind that the seventeenth-century *beatus vir*, the "Hortulan Saint" who retired after the Civil War to find God in his garden, was transformed in the early eighteenth century into a poet-philosopher who turned to nature to comprehend the universe, we can see that Imlac is indeed derived from this tradition.[7] The primary motivation for Imlac's travels is desire for knowledge. Although his father hopes that his son will become a successful merchant, Imlac has no interest in commerce. Having begun his travels with a general curiosity, however, Imlac decides, in the course of his journey, to become a poet; it is in this capacity that he gains entry to the happy valley and attracts the attention of Rasselas.

During the rainy season, when the prince has little else to do, he reads a poem by Imlac and asks to meet the poet. The prince's interest in Imlac's poetry suggests a relationship between knowledge, curiosity, and poetry: "He commanded the poet to attend him in his apartment, and recite his verses a second time; then entering into familiar talk, he thought himself happy in having found a man who knew the world so well, and could so skilfully paint the scenes of life" (R 7.19). For Rasselas, Imlac's art as a poet resides as much in his knowledge of the world as in his skill in presenting that knowledge in poetic language. Indeed, the terms scholar and poet are used interchangeably throughout this section, indicating that the acquisition of wisdom is seen as an intimate part of the process of becoming a poet. In this respect Johnson was very much a man of his age, for the separation between aesthetics and knowledge, especially scientific knowledge, was not posited until the late eighteenth century.

A well-traveled, experienced man of the world who now turns to retirement, Imlac is certainly reminiscent of the eighteenth-century *beatus vir*, the man who turned to the natural garden in order to understand the Lucretian order of things. But the matter is complicated by the fact that Imlac retired to the happy valley not only for purposes of contemplation but also because of disappointment and disgust with the larger world. Johnson is here manipulating the retirement tradition for his own purposes: seventeenth-century "Hortulan saints" showed little interest in the world beyond their private retreat. Imlac, however, explains in detail how his hopes and desires were thwarted in the public world. Returning home after his travels in the expectation of receiving the caresses of his kinsmen and the congratulations of his friends, Imlac finds that his father is dead, his brothers have moved away, and the local nobles are not interested in his story. After an unsuccessful attempt to open a school, he proposes marriage to "a lady that was fond of my conversation," but his suit is rejected because his "father was a merchant" (R 12.35). It is primarily as a result of these difficulties and frustrations that Imlac decides to take up residence in the happy valley.

Unlike the traditional *beatus vir*, who retires for purposes of religious or philosophical contemplation, Imlac turns to the happy valley because he cannot make his way in the commercial world that has little respect for him as an intellectual. Johnson modifies the *beatus vir* convention to make Imlac's tale within a tale serve as an illustration of learning that involves the thwarting of hopes and expectations. In place of the empirical or Cartesian learning of the traditional eighteenth-century *beatus vir*, knowledge of life, Imlac's journey prepares us for knowledge about the choice of life that involves not only the acquisition of "facts" but the willingness to submit to life's battering of our desires.

For this reason, the conversation between Rasselas and Imlac involves knowledge not as a mental capacity but as a means to achieve happiness. For example, the first question the prince asks after hearing Imlac's history is as follows: "Tell me without reserve; art thou content with thy condition? or, dost thou wish to be again wandering and inquiring" (*R* 12.35). The sage replies that although knowledge does not provide the total contentment Rasselas seeks, it does make one less unhappy than those who remain ignorant:

> "Great Prince," said Imlac, "I shall speak the truth: I know not one of your attendants who does not lament the hour when he entered this retreat. I am less unhappy than the rest, because I have a mind replete with images, which I can vary and combine at pleasure. I can amuse my solitude by the renovation of the knowledge which begins to fade from my memory, and by recollection of the accidents of my past life. Yet all this ends in the sorrowful consideration, that my acquirements are now useless, and that none of my pleasures can be again enjoyed. The rest, whose minds have no impression but of the present moment, are either corroded by malignant passions, or sit stupid in the gloom of perpetual vacancy." [*R* 12.35-36]

The paradox inherent in choice-of-life knowledge is illustrated early in Imlac's history when he explains that his decision to devote himself to learning went against his father's wishes. His father, intending to have his son trained to be a merchant, sent him to a school where he first "found the delight of knowledge, and felt the pleasure of intelligence." Having thwarted his father's wishes, he now sets off on his travels to gratify his predominant desire "by drinking at the fountain of knowledge" (*R* 8.22-23) and discovers almost immediately that learning produces as much unhappiness as happiness. At Agra, Imlac explains, he conversed with the wisest men, "some of whom I found morose and reserved, and others easy and communicative; some were unwilling to teach another what they had with difficulty learned themselves; and some shewed that the end of their studies was to gain the dignity of instructing" (*R* 9.25).

In spite of recognizing that some of these scholars do not derive happiness from knowledge, Imlac continues to regard education as a desirable goal. Thus the power of the Europeans over their eastern neighbors, Imlac explains, derives from their knowledge: "They are more powerful, Sir, than we," answered Imlac, "because they are wiser; knowledge will always predominate over ignorance, as man governs the other animals" (*R* 11.30).

In the final chapter of this "history," Rasselas recognizes that the most important question elicited by Imlac's life story concerns the relationship between learning and happiness. Imlac's reply constitutes the most positive of his assertions in the entire tale:

"Knowledge is certainly one of the means of pleasure, as is confessed by the natural desire which every mind feels of increasing its ideas. Ignorance is mere privation, by which nothing can be produced: it is a vacuity in which the soul sits motionless and torpid for want of attraction; and, without knowing why, we always rejoice when we learn, and grieve when we forget. I am therefore inclined to conclude, that, if nothing counteracts the natural consequence of learning, we grow more happy as our minds take a wider range" (*R* 11.32).

Clearly, Imlac's history functions to prepare Rasselas and the reader for an educational journey. But before analyzing how the narrative process of Imlac's history is related to the travels of the prince, we need to consider one preliminary question. Because Imlac is so deeply committed to the acquisition of knowledge, Rasselas wonders how the sage can be content with the limited range of learning available in the happy valley. This question brings us to another aspect of the *beatus vir* motif, the cult of rural retirement. Johnson wrote on many aspects of this subject, some of which bear upon Imlac's "history." For instance, in *Rambler* number 6 (April 1750), Cowley's desire to retreat to a plantation in America is treated satirically: "When he was interrupted by company, or fatigued with business, he so strongly imaged to himself the happiness of leisure and retreat, that he determined to enjoy them for the future without interruption, and to exclude for ever all that could deprive him of his darling satisfaction" (*Rambler* 6,3:34).

Johnson goes on to point out that Cowley forgot "that solitude and quiet owe their pleasures to those miseries, which he was so studious to obviate." Rural retirement is seen as a manifestation of man's need for variety and desire for change, a view that explains why Imlac, who has only recently gained entrance to the happy valley, is nonetheless willing to help the prince escape and accompany him on his quest in the outside world. The sage has presumably been in the mountain retreat long enough to want to leave. Further evidence that Johnson generally conceived of the rural retirement convention as a physical manifestation of a psychological yearning is contained in his translation of Horace's Book I, *Ode xxii*, which he revised two if not three times during the period from his school days until 1757, the date of the final version. The last four lines are as follows:

Place me beneath the burning Zone,
  A Clime deny'd to human Race;
My Flame for *Lalagé* I'll own;
  Her voice and Smiles my Song shall grace. [*Poems* 10.21-24]

The heat of the narrator's rhetoric seems inseparable from that of the "Clime." Similarly, Rasselas believes that the following warning is

Imlac's projection of his own disappointments: "the world, which you figure to yourself smooth and quiet as the lake in the valley, you will find a sea foaming with tempests, and boiling with whirlpools" (*R* 12.37).

But it would be misleading to suggest that Johnson viewed retirement in wholly negative terms. On the contrary, in *Rambler* 7, he makes clear that retreat has an important purpose. "The love of Retirement," he explains, "has, in all ages, adhered closely to those minds, which have been most enlarged by knowledge, or elevated by genius." Those people who possess all the outward signs of happiness and success have, nonetheless, "felt the langours of satiety, and found themselves unable to pursue the race of life without frequent respirations of intermediate solitude" (*Rambler* 7, 3:36). Johnson goes on to argue in this essay that frequent and regular periods of solitude are essential for knowledge: "other things may be seized by might, or purchased with money, but knowledge is to be gained only by study, and study to be prosecuted only in retirement" (*Rambler* 7, 3:37).

To summarize, Johnson approves of retirement as a temporary respite for reflection, study, and meditation but warns that those who pursue it in the hope of finding the happiness that eluded them in society will be disappointed. Retreat has an educational function but cannot be expected to increase one's happiness. Imlac's view exemplifies this position. He explains to the prince that he is less unhappy than the other residents of the happy valley because his mind is full of ideas and experiences from the world without, but with each passing day he finds his memory fading and feels increasingly the need to return to society to replenish his mind with material for contemplation.

But the "history of Imlac" is to be distinguished from Johnson's other pronouncements on the retirement motif in one significant respect. Instead of narrating a *Rambler* essay, Imlac tells a story within a story; he presents a history for a fictive listener. A new dimension is thus added: the reader witnesses both the prince's response to Imlac's tale and Imlac's response to the prince. The literary context of *Rasselas* permits a dialogue between these two Johnsonian positions: the *beatus vir* conventions direct the reader to notice not merely the content of the characters' speeches but also their personal viewpoints and the interaction between those viewpoints. The most common means of calling our attention to the significance of the personal postures of Rasselas and Imlac is humor, an aspect of *Rasselas*, as we saw in chapter 1, only recently discovered and appreciated.

For instance, when the prince first sends for Imlac, his tale is interrupted: "as he [Imlac] was going to begin his narrative, Rasselas was called to a concert, and obliged to restrain his curiosity till the evening" (*R* 7.19). At this point in the story, it should be kept in mind, the prince has just had his hopes of escape dashed by the failure at flight; the irony here is that in this valley, which for the prince is ordinarily tedious, one diversion, a concert, delays another, Imlac's conversation. Significantly, the first meeting of Imlac and Rasselas involves the thwarting of expectations concerning pleasure and diversion.

But the episode grows more complex when Imlac's posture is established and the two characters begin to interact. Having been kept at the concert until midnight, Rasselas returns anxious to hear the story of Imlac's life and insists that the poet begin that evening. The prince's enthusiasm, shown in his interjections and questions, makes his presence felt throughout the history. He acts like a younger Imlac, the character from the past evoked *by* and *in* the poet's autobiography. Sensing the identification that is developing between the prince and his younger self, Imlac warns his rapt listener not to expect much glamour and excitement from his narrative: " 'Sir,' said Imlac, 'my history will not be long: the life that is devoted to knowledge passes silently away, and is very little diversified by events' " (*R* 8.20). Of course, Imlac, as ever, is being perfectly honest, but his history, instead of putting the prince to sleep, strengthens his resolve to escape and leads him finally to invite the older man to accompany him on his travels.

Although Imlac's story seems dull and ordinary to the well-traveled speaker, it proves novel and fascinating to the secluded prince. The humor is delicate and turns upon both characters. The inexperienced prince is enamored of even the most commonplace elements of the world beyond the mountains, while Imlac, in his vast experience, seems to have forgotten how new and exciting ordinary experience can appear to a novice. The comedy is delicate because it does not undermine the characters in the manner of Swift or Pope but rather calls attention to two different kinds of limitations—the prince's naiveté and Imlac's complacency. In this respect, Johnson can be placed in the tradition of eighteenth-century narrative, for his characters adopt postures ranging from those of Parson Adams to those of Uncle Toby, which often arouse laughter but not contempt.

Johnson employs this narrative convention in the early section of *Rasselas* to establish a relationship between knowledge and the dynamics of viewpoint. For instance, after issuing his warning about the dullness of his tale, Imlac describes his father as a rich merchant of "mean sentiments" who desired only to grow richer and hide his riches from the governor of the province. The prince asks why the governor would threaten wealth legally acquired and why an independently wealthy man should crave more money. In response to the first question, Imlac explains that no form of government can be perfectly just; in spite of the vigilance of the "supreme magistrate," some abuses will remain. Rasselas cannot grasp this point, but concerning the answer to the second question he shows himself to be a more promising student. The last part of the explanation offered for Imlac's father's insatiable desire for wealth is comprehensible to the prince: "some desire is necessary to keep life in motion, and he, whose real wants are supplied, must admit those of fancy," Imlac explains. Having himself already experienced the "wants of him that wants nothing" (*R* 3.7), the prince can comprehend a similar feeling in Imlac's father.

On the other hand, the assumption inherent in Imlac's previous response, that all political systems are subject to some abuses of power, lies beyond the ken of the prince whose life has been restricted to the happy valley. The point is humorously reinforced in Imlac's account of his youthful days. Sent to school by his father to "qualify for commerce," Imlac comes to "delight" in "knowledge" and "despise riches"—silently (*R* 8.22). The smile directed at the vulgar merchant outwitted by his intelligent son is like that elicited by Imlac when he assumes that the secluded prince will be able to comprehend the notion that all political power is subject to abuse. The delicate irony highlights characteristic postures of Imlac and Rasselas to show that the points of view of experience and innocence are both marked by limitations.

The interfusion of these viewpoints in *Rasselas* produces important modifications of Johnsonian notions. For instance, Imlac explains that upon arrival at Surat he first encountered envy, one of the most frequent topics of the periodical essays. Surmising that Imlac is rich, his traveling companions decide to cheat and defraud him: "they exposed me to the theft of servants, and the exaction of officers, and saw me plundered upon false pretences, without any advantage to themselves, but that of rejoicing in the superiority of their own knowledge" (*R* 9.24). The prince is astonished to find that anyone would injure another without any benefit to himself. Imlac explains that envious people do not necessarily act out of self-interest. The prince replies: "proceed, I doubt not of the facts which you relate, but imagine that you impute them to mistaken motives" (*R* 9.25). Again, two contrary points of view are manifest. The inexperienced prince cannot believe that people would want to harm another for the sheer joy of hurting someone; the seasoned traveler has met those whose actions are motivated by a kind of selfishness that does not benefit them.

Both viewpoints need to be kept in mind to understand envy, as Johnson makes clear in *Rambler* number 183 (December 1751). First, envy is distinguished from interest, which is defined as illicit or malevolent gain, a form of evil motivated by desire for material profit. But the Rambler believes that the law of mutual benevolence is less often broken by crimes motivated by interest than by envy, because the former are limited to the "narrow compass" where something tangible is to be gained, while the latter are not subject to circumstantial requirements. "Envy may always be produced by idleness and pride, and in what place will not they be found?" (*Rambler* 183, 5:197). This concept of envy can be seen to involve a tension between the points of view of Rasselas and Imlac. A form of "motiveless malignancy," envy is, as the young man points out, contradictory; nevertheless, it is true, as his elder asserts, that envy is a frequent and pervasive aspect of human existence. Each pole prevents the other from falling into contradiction or self-negation. Rasselas' attitude calls attention to the self-defeating aspect of envy, and Imlac's position shows that the vice, however inconsistent, is endemic to mankind.

Such a "stubborn weed" of the mind is envy that the narrator of this *Rambler* essay suggests the use of what he characterizes as a "dangerous and empirical morality, which cures one vice by means of another," namely, that those tempted by this vice consider that to envy another is to admit to that person's superiority. The antidote suggested for envy is a form of egotism, the reminder that to make another an object of envy is an admission of that person's superiority. In *Rasselas*, however, this attitude results not in a cure for envy but in a more depraved form of it. The people who defrauded and cheated Imlac, upon hearing shortly afterward that he has achieved some influence with the Emperor, apply to him for a recommendation at court. Surprised, Imlac reproaches them for their past behavior but is heard with a cold indifference indicative of neither shame nor sorrow: "they then urged their request with the offer of a bribe; but what I would not do for kindness I would not do for money; and refused them, not because they had injured me, but because I would not enable them to injure others; for I knew they would have made use of my credit to cheat those who should buy their wares" (*R* 9.25-26). Imlac's speech produces the opposite of its intention: far from repenting their evil, these merchants believe that since Imlac will not succumb to envy, he will surely be tempted by self-interest in the form of a bribe.

Rasselas thus moves a step beyond the *Rambler* essay. Imlac's experience makes clear that the envious merchants' acceptance of his influence at court does not prevent them from continuing to seek to demean him. Indeed, their recognition of his superiority increases their desire to bring him down to their level. The two-sided, not to say contradictory, element of envy remains unresolved in the literary tale, because each position is identified with a different character.

The younger man maintains that it makes no sense to cause others harm without benefiting oneself; the older man asserts that his experience confirms that people do act upon this "inconsistent" motivation. Johnson's concept of envy is altered in the context of *Rasselas* because the conventions of narrative commit him to consistency of character in a conversation lengthier than the discussion typical of the periodical essay.

Johnson demonstrated an interest in the relation of opposed viewpoints from early on in his literary career. One of his first surviving poems is a translation of the dialogue between Hector and Andromache in the sixth book of *The Iliad*, the famous moment when the wife castigates her husband for neglecting his family. In Johnson's rendition, Andromache warns that the town of Troy is vulnerable to attack and urges Hector to mount a defense from within the fortified walls. Hector replies that he must fight outside the walls for precisely that reason:

> She ceas'd, then Godlike Hector answer'd kind
> His various plumage sporting in the wind
>   "That post, and the rest shall be my care
> But shall I then forsake th' unfinish'd war?" [*Poems* 20.60-63]

Husband and wife propose opposite strategies, the inner defense as opposed to an outer one, to forward the same goal. Further evidence that Johnson was interested in polar viewpoints toward the same end is seen in his translation of Addison's "Battle of the Pygmies and the Cranes," a poem that J.D. Fleeman believed was written about the same time as the translation of the *Iliad*.[8] Both employ a situation of warfare to explore the clash of viewpoints, although in the latter Johnson uses irony to establish a vantage point for the reader above the fray.

In *Rasselas*, the function of the axis of viewpoints becomes most prominent in chapter 10, the dissertation on poetry, which contains one of Johnson's most famous lines, "the poet does not number the streaks of the tulip."[9] In fact, the meaning of the phrase has been the subject of a controversy that began in 1943 when Arthur Friedman disagreed with William Wimsatt, Jr. Defending the position he adopted in his book *The Prose Style of Samuel Johnson*, Wimsatt explained that Imlac is the spokesman for Johnson's position. The key phrase pointed to was "just representations of general nature"; "just" was taken to mean true or appropriate; that is, the tulip should be shown in a garden, not on Fleet Street. By general nature, Wimsatt explained, Imlac and Johnson mean that the poet should represent only so much as serves to "recall the original to every mind." This doctrine is, according to Wimsatt, "the familiar neo-classical theory found in Du Fresnoy's *Art of Painting*, in the writings of Johnson, especially in the tulip passage in *Rasselas*, and in the *Discourses* and *Idlers* of Reynolds."[10] Friedman, citing a passage from the *Preface to Shakespeare*, asserted that Johnson did not always prefer the general to the particular.[11]

But Wimsatt had already anticipated such an objection, stating that inconsistencies were bound to occur in Johnson's position because the poetic principle was self-contradictory. Here the matter rested until 1955, when Walter Jackson Bate altered his earlier position, which was in accord with Wimsatt's. "Johnson's position," Bate asserted persuasively, "in short, avoids the usual monotonous quarrel over the issue of generality versus particularity in art. It avoids this debate by subsuming it within a larger framework. What is wanted is detail—the familiar, the concrete, the vivid and sensory—for the sake of form; and what is desired in the form is the ability to apply not only to the particular details that serve as the immediate vestibule or conductor to it, in a work of art, but also others that are cousin to them."[12] But Bate did not demonstrate specifically how Johnson avoided this monotonous quarrel nor what the larger framework was that subsumed it.

Hence, in the 1960s, Martin Kallich[13] and Geoffrey Tillotson[14] continued to consider Imlac's speech in favor of the grandeur of generality as essentially that of Johnson. And, as we know, in 1971 Howard Weinbrot set out to demonstrate systematically that although Imlac and Johnson overlap on some issues, they differ on several others and clearly disagree on two.[15] But Donald T. Siebert, Jr., replied, in 1974, that the differences between Johnson and Imlac are minor, having to do with mood and style: "The point is not that Imlac is wrong but that his grandiose language has betrayed him into a state of solipsistic rapture."[16] The only difference between the position of Siebert in 1974 and that of Wimsatt in 1941 is that what had previously been attributed to the inconsistency of neo-classical aesthetics was now attributed to the comically obsessive posture of Imlac.

Clearly, the discovery that humor is employed against Imlac has not resulted in any significant alteration in our understanding of the aesthetic position presented in "A dissertation upon poetry." An approach that employs the axis of perspectives, however, can provide an alternative to the "monotonous quarrel over the issue of generality versus particularity." Imlac's aesthetic will be seen as a part of the narrative process of chapter 10, which will itself be viewed, in my next chapter, as a part of the narrative process of *Rasselas*. By this means I shall demonstrate that the reader is provided with an aesthetic procedure that alters his conception of "A dissertation upon poetry" and of *Rasselas*.

Imlac starts his dissertation by explaining that shortly after realizing that poetry was considered everywhere the highest form of learning he was struck with wonder at the fact that "in almost all countries, the most ancient poets are considered as the best" (*R* 10.26). He then speculates on three possible reasons for this universal veneration for early poetry: First, unlike other humanistic endeavors, poetry is not an ability acquired gradually but is conferred at once. Second, the ancients achieved a level of esteem for being the first, an honor no subsequent poets can hope to match. Third, since poetry describes eternal and immutable truths, the ancients left nothing new or original for the moderns to portray. After this intellectual enumeration, couched in neutral language and narrated in a distant manner, Imlac begins to use the first person pronoun, which changes the tone from that of disinterested observation to that of personal intimacy. "I was desirous to add my name to this illustrious fraternity," he tells the prince, but the training necessary for poetry entails more than the art of imitation. Explaining that knowledge of nature and mankind are also necessary, Imlac begins to grow enthusiastic about his art.

Having now reinserted himself into that period of his life when he decided to become a poet, Imlac explains that he saw everything with a "new purpose." All the details of the world are of interest. Mountains and deserts provide "images and resemblances," as do "the crags of the rock and the pinnacles of the palace," or "the mazes of the rivulet" and "the changes of the summer clouds" (*R* 10.27). During this inspired and far-ranging description, a verbal scaling of Mount Parnassus, the prince interrupts with a remark more appropriate to one looking down at the foot rather than up at the peak of Parnassus: "In so wide a survey," says the prince, "you must surely have left much unobserved. I have lived, till now, within the circuit of these mountains, and yet cannot walk abroad without the sight of something which I had never beheld before, or never heeded" (*R* 10.28). The comedy here is reinforced by the reversal of roles, the young dreamer bringing the older, typically more sober mind back to mundane reality. But Imlac relentlessly continues his ascent. Instead of pausing to reflect upon the justness of the prince's remark—that if nothing is useless to a poet, how much potential poetic material he must neglect—Imlac points to the final goals of art: " 'The business of a poet,' said Imlac, 'is to examine, not the individual, but the species; to remark general properties and large appearances: he does not number the streaks of the tulip, or describe the different shades in the verdure of the forest' " (*R* 10.28).

At this point, the poet and Imlac are indistinguishable; his business is the speaker's personal credo. The next stage is achieved when this aesthetics of ecstasy results in grand poetic generalizations. The shift here from the first to the third person pronoun is indicative: "he must be acquainted likewise with all the modes of life . . . he must divest himself of the prejudices of his age or country; he must consider right and wrong in their abstracted and invariable state . . . he must write as the interpreter of nature, and the legislator of mankind . . . he must know many languages and many sciences . . . " (*R* 10.28-29). At this juncture, the narrator interrupts Imlac's history and begins a new chapter in the following way: "Imlac now felt the enthusiastic fit, and was proceeding to aggrandize his own profession" (*R* 11.29). This signals the end of the longest passage of direct discourse in the happy valley section; in fact, only Pekuah's narration contains a passage where the teller of an interpolated tale is permitted to continue for such an extended period of time. But Pekuah is not interrupted in her tale. Imlac is interrupted in a double sense. Following the above cited observation, the prince exclaims, "Enough! Thou has convinced me, that no human being can ever be a poet" (*R* 10.29). Undeterred, Imlac resumes his discourse with, "to be a poet is indeed very difficult." " 'So difficult', returned the prince, 'that I will at present hear no more of his labours.' " Then immediately, as if in embarrassment at his own peremptory tone, he adds, "Tell me whither you went when you had seen Persia," retrieving the situation by leading Imlac away from poetry and back to his history (*R* 11.29-30).

Let us first reflect on Imlac's process before considering the reason for the narrator's interruption. Imlac began his dissertation by reassessing classical art from the point of view of one who was once a poet but now has retired from public life; from his present lofty and distant perspective, he sees that for a number of possible reasons, ancient poets were and probably always will be more esteemed than the moderns. Young would-be poets are put firmly in their place. Gradually, however, Imlac warms to his task, especially as he reminds himself of the difficulties and hurdles which "I" experienced as a struggling poet. The third stage then emerges, an enthusiastic fit about those in the profession who, like "myself," have withstood the severe tests and continue to live up to the high standards of "our" calling.

At this point, it may be helpful to pause and establish that Imlac's enthusiastic claim for poetry is to be distinguished from the traditional image of the immortality provided the artist by his art.

Johnson presented this notion in his translation of Book II of Horace's *Odes*, which concluded as follows:

> Restrain your tears and cease your cries,
> Nor grace with fading flours my Herse,
> I without fun'ral elegies
> Shall live for ever in my verse. [*Poems* 13.21-24]

That the poet lives after death in his verse is an ancient idea; Imlac's assertion that the poet should legislate to mankind is a considerably larger and, in Johnson's day, more unusual claim.

But we cannot therefore assume that Imlac is to be seen as having arrived at an absurd position. His poetics, even at the height of his enthusiastic fit, contains sensible notions worthy of serious consideration. For purposes of summary, they can be separated into three divisions. First, book learning, although necessary, is not sufficient; the poet must study life. Second, all forms of life, rural and urban, are relevant to the writer. Third, the man of letters must attend to the species, not the individual, and should be superior to the accidents of time and place in both nature and history. These three principles, however, contrast with those contained in the discussion of ancient poetry at the beginning of this dissertation on poetry. Concerning the universal veneration of the ancients, Imlac had suggested that great writers may simply be born with their talent, a "gift conferred at once"; later in the same chapter, he tells the prince that the poet must know not only literature but also life, implying a long if not endless apprenticeship. Having earlier suggested that the respect for the ancients might be attributed to the accident of their having been first, the sage now describes the poet as one who must be above random occurrences. Finally, having previously pointed out that the writers of antiquity may have achieved their superiority by being the first to articulate the eternal and unchanging truths of man and nature, Imlac, in his enthusiastic fit, now asserts that the man of letters must dedicate himself to all the details of life, that "to a poet nothing can be useless."

Whether or not it is possible to reconcile these two views of poetry, they are presented to emphasize contrasting attitudes, the poles of a process. The first part of the dissertation on poetry, based on the assumption that the oldest writers are, for one reason or another, the most venerated, would discourage the most zealous aspiring poet. But the ensuing conversation so exalts the poet, "the interpreter of nature and the legislator of mankind," that we feel, as does Rasselas, that such a being is beyond this world. The difficulty here can be resolved by reminding ourselves of the literary context.

At the beginning of the chapter, identifying himself with his present state of retirement in the happy valley, the sometime poet displays his command of his own past. The momentary and the concrete, the fabric of history and the material of poetry, are seen as random, unpredictable, and well beyond the control of the creative writer. The passage that follows starts as an individual credo but soon develops into a poetics. Now the particulars are most intimate and personal, and Imlac's tone is accordingly more hopeful. Recreating rather than surveying his past, Imlac grows enthusiastic, reinvolving himself in the world of poetic particulars, instructing his novice in the observation, digestion, and selection of the concrete. The properly trained writer can be in control: indeed, he should legislate to the world. Having become for a moment a semblance of his younger self, Imlac rekindles his belief in the poet's ability to assimilate and employ history, that realm which at the outset of the dissertation seemed so far beyond the control of any poet. The movement between these two postures or aesthetic poles represents the poetic process. Remolding the specifics of the present, the poet ascends to and re-formulates the universal. From this vantage point, he can look down upon and assess the randomness and mystery of the historical details of his past.

We can now understand why the narrator interrupts Imlac's dissertation to point out to us that the speaker in a fit of enthusiasm is aggrandizing his profession. Reinscribing Imlac within the text of *Rasselas* functions not merely to qualify Imlac's authority but, more significantly, to call the reader's attention to the place of Imlac and his history in the narrative process of *Rasselas*. The humor at this point converts a product, an aesthetic doctrine, into a process, a narrative procedure. The monotonous quarrel about whether the general or the particular predominates is replaced by a dialectical concept, a relation of polarities that cannot subsume one another. That one or the other of the two poles may *seem* more important is a manifestation of an aesthetic stage, either the immersion in par-ticulars or the emerging from them toward generalizations. This new reading of "A dissertation upon poetry" makes clear why the chapter on poetics is placed in the happy valley: the aesthetic procedure is presented in preparation for the educational travels of the prince of Abyssinia.

The extremes of the poetic process represent the range of expecta-tions one can adopt in a learning situation, and, not surprisingly, the conclusion or the kind of education that results is directly related to these expectations. Ordinarily, Imlac will ascend quickly to the level of a general truth while Rasselas will characteristically dwell longer on the particulars. Occasionally, the characters exchange roles, or other less prominent personages, such as Nekayah and Pekuah, take their place. But, as we shall see, the reader is always provided with an axis of viewpoints; indeed, one of the important reasons that permanent solitude is considered a danger is that it prevents the interplay of contrasting perspectives.

Imlac's dissertation on poetry reveals an aesthetics of understanding. His travels and the knowledge he gains from his experiences lead him to become a poet, an achievement that equips him to guide Rasselas on his educational travels into the world beyond the mountains. The poles of poetry, the particular and the general, will, as I shall demonstrate in the next chapter, form a dialectic of perspectives basic to the learning that results from the journey. In my view, Johnson selects a well-traveled poet to lead his protagonist because poetry displays the interweaving of the particular and the general, a procedure that, in the choice-of-life quest, is the key to increased human understanding. The preparation for the prince of Abyssinia's search is doubly literary. First he is placed in a literary valley, a paradise on earth, in order to nourish the desire for a choice of life. Then he is introduced to a poet who provides an aesthetic mode of perception essential to an understanding of the choices of life available in the outside world.

Johnson's own conception of the proper goal for the new kind of fiction of his day involved not merely knowledge but also understanding of virtue and decency. In all other respects, however, the happy valley exemplifies the views of narrative in *Rambler* number 4, the clearest and most often cited of Johnson's statements on this topic. Published nine years before *Rasselas*, the essay begins by labeling this new kind of writing "the comedy of romance." This phrase is employed to distinguish eighteenth-century fiction from seventeenth-century romances, the contents of which are enumerated as "a hermit and a wood, a battle and a shipwreck." Unlike these earlier writers who resorted to "incredibilities," the authors of Johnson's day require of themselves not only book learning but also "general converse and accurate observation of the living world." In combining traditional and literary with contemporary and historical Abyssinian paradise material, the happy valley aptly illustrates the Rambler's position. Moreover, Rasselas as a protagonist also fits into the Rambler framework in terms of both form and function: "But when an adventurer is levelled with the rest of the world, and acts in such scenes of the universal drama, as may be the lot of any other man; young spectators fix their eyes upon him with closer attention, and hope by observing his behaviour and success to regulate their own practices, when they shall be engaged in the like part" (*Rambler* 4,3:21).

The prince of Abyssinia's privileged social position provides him with the opportunity to seek what all young, impressionable readers would presumably hope for, the choice of life. And his final recognition that this desire cannot be fulfilled is consonant with the Rambler's belief that since the "power of example" has so great an effect upon the young reader, "the best examples only should be exhibited." In this respect, *Rasselas* certainly has stood the test of time, for as we saw in chapter 1, the keen moral eye of Victorian schoolmasters found no fault.

But the conclusion of *Rambler* number 4 raises a problem for the careful modern reader of *Rasselas*: "It is therefore to be steadily inculcated, that virtue is the highest proof of understanding, and the only solid basis of greatness; and that vice is the natural consequence of narrow thoughts, that it begins in mistake, and ends in ignominy" (4,3:25).[17] For the Rambler, understanding of the world is held as synonymous with knowledge of virtue. In the literary critical terms of the eighteenth century, the issue is that of poetic justice. In the *Life of Addison* (1779), Johnson adopted a position on this issue opposite to that implicit in this *Rambler* essay. But here my interest is in Johnson as a writer of fiction, not as a critic. And in distinguishing the narratives of his own day from seventeenth-century romances, Johnson was joined by most other eighteenth-century authors. The terminology employed by Johnson's contemporaries, however, clarifies the problem.

Most characteristic of practicing fictionalists is Samuel Richardson's exclamation in a letter to Miss Mulso, dated 5 October 1752: "What a deuce, do you think I am writing a Romance? Don't you see that I am copying Nature . . . ?" It is striking that the author whose first narrative was subtitled "Virtue Rewarded" defended his art not in the moral terms of the Rambler but on the basis of truth to nature. Of course, Richardson at other times resorted to an ethical defense, but the truth-to-nature argument was also employed by Fielding and Smollett, to mention two of many who could be cited. In *Tom Jones*, the narrator explains that he omits "elves and fairies, and other such mummery" because in relating actions of man "great care is to be taken that we do not exceed the capacity of the agent we describe" (Book VIII, chap. 1). Similarly, Smollett, in the Preface to *Roderick Random*, points out that since romance involves "most monstrous hyperboles," he prefers to follow Cervantes and "assume the sock, and point out the follies of ordinary life." Of course, Fielding and Smollett, like Richardson, also believed that their work advanced the cause of virtue. But recent critical attention addressed to the fictions of these writers has revealed that the conflict between truth and virtue is often manifested in the work and that the traditional didactic reading neglects the truth-to-nature aspect.

Johnson's literature is still seen as subordinate to his moral and religious writings. Consequently, *Rasselas* is considered, if not a *Vanity of Human Wishes* in prose, an apologue of some sort or a satire of the choice-of-life quest. In either case, the travels in the world become of secondary importance, merely serving to exemplify moral or religious views already established in the happy valley. I propose, as an alternative to this position, that the history of Imlac provides the method for pursuing education in the world beyond the mountains and that this kind of educational quest can be located within the tradition of eighteenth-century fiction as described by Johnson's contemporaries.

The natural question that now arises is, if this approach to *Rasselas* is in accord with the views of Johnson's contemporaries, why has it taken over two centuries to come to the fore? This question can only be adequately answered by turning to literary theory. Derived from critical approaches that have only become available in our time, my method combines theories usually thought to be irreconcilable, structuralism and hermeneutics. In order to clarify this position, I shall locate aspects of my analysis of chapter 10 of *Rasselas* that use ideas formulated by these two kinds of theoreticians. Specifically, Gèrard Genette and M.M. Bakhtin will represent structuralism while Lucien Dällenbach and Wolfgang Iser will exemplify hermeneutics.

The key moment for my purposes occurs when Imlac is interrupted by both the narrator *and* the prince. The humor here has been explained in the past by recourse to matters outside the context of Imlac's narrative: specifically, by pointing out that the aesthetic doctrine is inconsistent or that the rhetorical posture of the speaker must be separated from his doctrine. But it seems to me that the humorous interruption has some intrinsic import, and here Wolfgang Iser's "gap" or "blank" helps. Iser insists that the "emptiness" of the gap "cannot be filled by a single referential meaning." Instead, the critic must pursue his own reading process, which will unfold to reveal the figure in the carpet.[18] This insight enabled me to see that Johnson was presenting not a product, a poetics, but a poetic process.

The next difficulty was to explain why Imlac is interrupted in a double sense, not only by Rasselas' comical remark but also by the narrator. At this point, Lucien Dällenbach's *mise en abyme* and Gérard Genette's analysis of "metadiegetic narrative" pertain. Dällenbach's claim that the interpolated tale often functions as a mirror of the larger tale enabled me to understand how the educational method of *Rasselas* could be reflected in "The history of Imlac."[19] Genette's analysis helps explain how Imlac's history has been understood in the past. One type of metadiegesis "consists of a purely *thematic* relationship of contrast . . . or analogy; . . . regular genres, like the parable or the apologue . . . are based on that monitory effect of analogy." This concept is exemplified by the prevalent critical view that Imlac's history prefigures the futility of Rasselas' search for the choice of life, both purveying the theme of the vanity of human wishes. But Genette also points to another kind of diegesis where "it is the act of narrating itself that fulfills a function," permitting the suggestion that Imlac's history functions not merely thematically but also to reveal the narrative method of the educational quest.[20]

This mode of analysis, however, leads to a larger question: how can the narrative method implicit in *Rasselas* be different from that of Johnson's other writings, particularly when the characters in this story seem to use language and ideas from the remainder of the canon, especially the periodical essays? M.M. Bakhtin examines this phenomenon. In the context of the novel, Bakhtin maintains, the languages from other genres participate in a more complex field of discourse, where they are subject to a "dialogic" interaction with one another, an interanimation that changes them, producing what he calls "heteroglossia."[21] This insight led to the formulation of what has been referred to as the axis of perspectives.

But while my analysis is indebted to these four theoreticians, my conclusion diverges markedly from theirs. Not surprisingly, as reader-response critics, Iser and Dällenbach conclude with the reading process. The former argues that a reading that fills in the gaps without recourse to extrinsic referentiality "plays a not unimportant part in the process of 'becoming conscious,' "[22] while the latter concludes that careful attention to the *mise en abyme* restores balance to "the heart of the reading activity."[23] My own conclusion, however, concerns not merely the status of the consciousness of the reader or of the characters, but how knowledge relates to action. I believe that *Rasselas* finally refers us beyond the realm of mind to the realm of conduct. Here we find ourselves outside the boundaries of Genette, who establishes at the outset that his analysis refers exclusively to narrative discourse, "the only [level of narrative] directly available to textual analysis," not to story, which is the proper sphere of history.[24] And although Bakhtin includes within his purview "extraliterary" as well as "literary" languages, his analysis is restricted to the realm of discourse; the means for examining the relations between the two, the "chronotope," combines space and time, or history and ideology, in a linguistic unit employed as the subject of discourse analysis.[25]

In my view the method of Imlac's history must be applied to the "choice of life," a phrase Johnson originally thought of using for the title of his story. And while the "choice" involves an analysis of the person who chooses—the subject of reader-response criticism—and an understanding of the alternatives available—revealed by structuralist and poststructuralist discourse analysis—, "life" refers to more than mind and language. It points to conduct; Imlac's method suggests how an awareness of mind and language should be incorporated into the act of choosing. The informed choice involves the conscious subject discovering by way of language the possibilities open to him. Literary theory can best grasp the method implicit in Imlac's history for pursuing the choice of life by combining the insights of hermeneutics and structuralism.

The structuralist, by way of discourse analysis, discovers that metadiegesis reveals the dialogic process of diegesis, that the interpolated tale contains the method of the narrative as a whole. But explaining the significance of this discovery necessitates reflection upon the readerly process: namely, that we understand *Rasselas* by the means provided in Imlac's history. But reader-response criticism leads to self-reflexivity, precisely what caused the prince's first mentor to advise against leaving the happy valley in pursuit of the choice of life. My position is that Imlac's method points to a reflection upon the relationship between the meaning of the speakers' discourse and their behavior. This principle of human knowledge cannot be restricted either to the realm of reader-response or to that of the discourse of which Rasselas is a part. The next chapter will demonstrate how this poetics combining elements of structuralism and hermeneutics serves an educational function, how the literary method presented in the happy valley, when understood in terms of the choice-of-life travels, applies not only to the reading and structure of *Rasselas* but also beyond the confines of *Rasselas*.

4

A Journey to Understanding

THE EDUCATIONAL journey is so pervasive in eighteenth-century fiction that few narratives of the period are without it in one form or another. But the motive for Rasselas' journey is different from that of Moll Flanders, Tom Jones, or Candide. The prince of Abyssinia searches not for financial security or his beloved Sophia or Cuné-gonde but for the choice of life. This phrase, as we have seen, contains allusions to religious, historical, horticultural, and literary elements of the paradise-on-earth tradition. Johnson's educational journey is thus to be distinguished from those of Defoe, Fielding, Voltaire, and other writers of his day in that the impetus for the travels is to be understood less in terms of the protagonist's personal motives and more in terms of a general idea, the desire for paradise on earth. In my view, Johnson raises his tale to this level of generalization because he wishes to arrive at the underlying principle of the educational journey. This chapter will follow Rasselas' quest in order to demonstrate that this principle must be understood in terms of its own manner of unfolding.

For purposes of convenience, Rasselas' educational travels will be divided into four sections. This division is not offered as another structural configuration but rather as a means of describing the progression of the tale. Chapters 16-22 present various choices of life that inhibit learning. The marriage debate, chapters 23-29, differentiates opposing perspectives, innocence and experience, the particular and the general. The pyramid episode (chapters 30-39) demonstrates how this axis of perspectives functions in a contingent situation. The last ten chapters, which include the incidents concerning the astronomer, the old man, and the visit to the catacombs, clarify the nature of the educational process employed in the tale. In analyzing these sections of Rasselas' journey, certain periodical essays and others of Johnson's works will be referred to in order to show how the tale of the prince of Abyssinia employs traditional Johnsonian dicta but, by placing them in a new or more extended literary context, modifies and changes them.

The first episode outside the happy valley concerns the young men of "spirit and gaiety." Although initially attracted to the lively conversation of the café society, the prince soon becomes bored with their superficial pleasures. Before leaving "his friends," he decides it is his obligation to explain to them the error of their ways, but to his disappointment, instead of listening to his thoughtful advice, they respond with scornful laughter. In *Rambler* number 201 (February 1752), a sober young businessman is misled by a society like that in *Rasselas*. After a few nights in the company of those who enjoy "perpetual vacancy," Aliger neglects to pay his creditors and, on the day appointed for signing legal papers, rambles in the country. Yet he has not lost all sense of decency. "His benevolence draws him into the commission of a thousand crimes, which others less kind or civil, would escape." His pockets are filled with petitions and his desk with letters of request, but while having the best of intentions, he neglects to act or even to explain his lack of action. Although a compassionate moralist, the Rambler asserts that this well-meaning individual led astray by men of spirit and gaiety does more harm than an evil man. In *Rasselas,* however, the prince feels "ashamed" of such a way of life, not because it can distract him from his duties, but because it is a life without a plan: "He thought it unsuitable to a reasonable being to act without a plan, and to be sad or cheerful only by chance" (*R* 17.48). He therefore lectures his young friends not on their wrongs to others but on the personal indignity of being unable to account for their past or future: "Let us, therefore, stop, while to stop is in our power: let us live as men who are sometime to grow old, and to whom it will be the most dreadful of all evils not to count their past years but by follies, and to be reminded of their former luxuriance of health only by the maladies which riot has produced" (*R* 17.48).

That this declamatory speech produces laughter in its audience is not surprising, especially when we recall that it is delivered in the equivalent of the local tavern. Johnson was sensitive to the rhetoric appropriate to a scene of convivial drinking. In 1751 he composed the following lines to his friend Giuseppe Baretti:

Rispossa del Johnson

At sight of sparkling Bowls or beauteous Dames
When fondness melts me, or when wine inflames,
I too can feel the rapture fierce and strong
I too can pour the extemporary song;
But though the number for a moment please,
Though musick thrills, or sudden sallies seize,
Yet lay the Sonnet for an hour aside,

Its charms are fled and all its power destroy'd;
What soon is perfect, soon alike is past:
That slowly grows which must for ever last.   [*Poems* 168.1-10]

Here the traditional *carpe diem* theme is amended slightly to include, in addition to the usual wine, women, and song, the occasional poem, the extemporary "Sonnet" that, however "perfect," has only a fleeting charm. Thus Johnson suggests that poetry, like friendship, will be more likely to endure if it is realized by gradual progression. Rasselas' notion of planning for rather than running away from the future is therefore a valid concern. And by 1753, in *Adventurer* 120, Johnson articulated the danger inherent in the counterfeit happiness of café society. "The world," we are informed in *Adventurer* 120, "in its best state, is nothing more than a large assembly of beings, combining to counterfeit happiness which they do not feel, employing every art and contrivance to embellish life, and to hide their real condition from the eyes of one another." Affliction, nevertheless, strikes all people, rich and poor, although "in different proportions." The good man is no more protected from such afflictions that the idle frequenter of convivial assemblies. For he who abstains from frivolities may still be the victim of the envy of the others and is in any case subject to the "influences of natural evil"; "his house flames like others in a conflagration . . . he bears about him the seeds of disease." The essay concludes that "this general and indiscriminate distribution of misery" affords some proof of a "future state," for affliction helps us avoid temptation here by directing our hopes to the hereafter (*Adventurer* 120, 2:469).

Rasselas experiences what may be his first moment of misery when he is rejected by his laughing comrades and must collect what remains of his pride in order to continue on his journey. But the episode in *Rasselas* does not conclude on a religious note, and in this respect it resembles an *Idler* essay published five years after the *Adventurer* essay and less than one year before *Rasselas*. The anonymous correspondent writing in *Idler* number 18 (August 1758) provides numerous examples of false pleasures, explaining that this folly continues because few disturb themselves "with the detection of fallacies which do us no harm, nor willingly decline a pleasing effect to investigate its cause." The next stage is self-deception; "in time, all are deceived by the cheat to which all contribute." Finally, the Idler ends by going one step further, exposing the false pleasure involved in exposing counterfeit pleasure. All of us in our different ways are guilty of pretending to delight in that which gives us little real pleasure, including those who write "characters which expose the vanity of life" (*Idler* 18, 2:56-59). This last-named "pretended" pleasure has reference to the Idler and to the correspondent who has written the letter to the Idler. The function of this self-inclusive irony is to make clear that the distant observer of seeming social pleasures is involved in the deception and self-deception practiced by the more active participants.

But in *Rasselas* the prince is finally distinguished from the young men of spirit and gaiety, and here the narrative goes beyond the periodical essays. In addition to laughing at Rasselas, the young men "drove him away." When isolated, the prince supports himself against "the horrour of derision" by the "consciousness that his sentiments were just, and his intentions kind," thereby regaining the tranquility necessary to continue his search. Two distinct paths of pleasure are here demarcated. The prince pursues his choice-of-life quest by seeking the truth about worldly pleasures; the men of spirit and gaiety continue to laugh and enjoy themselves by removing from their presence any form of truth or reason, refusing to listen to anyone who points out that their pleasures are counterfeit.

Instead of concluding with the religious notion that all mortal pleasures are insufficient or with the satirical idea that the exposure of counterfeit pleasure is itself a form of what it reveals, Johnson has the prince of Abyssinia turn away from such societies because they prevent learning. In fact, this first section of the "outside world" portion of *Rasselas* is devoted to various choices of life that impede education, snares that the prince must avoid. Most obvious in this respect are the shepherds in chapter 19. These unhappy laborers are so mired in ignorance that even the account they give of their rustic way of life reveals only the hatred that cankers their hearts. Their inarticulate rancor prevents our knowing whether they are the victims of their landowners or of their own belligerent ignorance.

A less obvious impediment to the educational journey is provided by the incident of the stoic philosopher in chapter 18, following immediately after the episode involving the young men of spirit and gaiety. Scorning thought and reflection, these young men are counterbalanced by the stoic, who believes that thought can transcend all emotion. Johnson devoted an entire *Rambler* essay to a thorough and devastating critique of stoicism, but as we shall see, *Rasselas* again goes beyond the periodical essay.[1] The stoic creed, according to the Rambler, is marked by a contradiction; in denying that pain is an evil, the stoics deprive themselves of the only possible reason for their instruction on the bearing of pain. Moreover, the Rambler continues, "the controversy about the reality of external evils is now at an end"; the miseries of life are "now universally confessed" and therefore we must consider how they may be avoided or at least "mitigated and lightened" (*Rambler* 32, 3:175). The remainder of the essay is devoted to the means by which man can accept his difficulties with patience, the chief security against the "fruitless anguish of impatience" being faith in God.[2] Clearly, the philosopher in chapter 18 is guilty of impatience when, in consolation for the death of his daughter, Rasselas parrots the stoic's own doctrine and receives the following testy reply: "Young man, you speak like one that has never felt the pangs of separation." But the chapter concludes with reference to the philosopher's oratorical abilities, without mentioning the religious issue: "The prince, whose humanity would not suffer him to insult misery with reproof, went away convinced of the emptiness of rhetorical sound, and the inefficacy of polished periods and studied sentences" (*R* 18.51).

This episode undermines stoicism by way not of religion but of rhetoric. The prince first notices the sage at the "hall of declamation" because of his clear pronunciation and elegant diction. Marked by the skillful use of numerous tropes, the lecture is characterized as an exhortation. So habitual a rhetor is the stoic that even in a moment of despair, upon hearing that his beloved only daughter has suddenly died, his speech is marked by artful oratorical devices: "What comfort can truth and reason afford me? of what effect are they now, but to tell me, that my daughter will not be restored?" (*R* 18.51). Appropriately, the orator now uses his rhetorical abilities to explain that polished language is of little consolation in the face of death. Such scenes debunking ideal postures are common in eighteenth-century fiction, the most famous being Parson Adams' loss of temper at the reported drowning of his youngest son. But Fielding, writing in the tradition of the novel, pursues the character of Adams, who in his earnest attempt at Christian patience manifests in his conduct a subtler version of his doctrine.

Less interested in the philosopher as a character, Johnson indicates an alternative point of view on rhetoric.[3] The eloquence that captured the prince's imagination now reveals the limitations of language. It is significant that this point about the philosopher is made by Imlac in conversation with his student: "Be not too hasty to trust, or to admire, the teachers of morality: they discourse like angels, but they live like men" (*R* 18.50-51). And we know that the prince has begun to understand Imlac's point even before the end of this chapter: Rasselas "had now learned the power of money, and made his way by a piece of gold to the inner apartment, where he found the philosopher." That every moralist is also a man becomes manifest in the philosopher's behavior in mourning for his daughter. We come again to the relationship between the particular and the general, and it is instructive to note that Imlac, somewhat uncharacteristically, points to the particular lest the prince become wholly consumed with the general.[4]

The axis of perspectives is a constant in *Rasselas*, even though the spokesperson of a given point of view may change. These first chapters outside the happy valley demonstrate the perils of ignoring or avoiding the double perspective. The men of spirit and gaiety refuse to recognize that their exuberance serves to distract them from their deepest anxieties. The shepherds cannot see that the rancor, which to them is the result of the cruelty and neglect of their superiors, may appear to justify such harsh treatment. And the stoic's oration suggests to us how rhetoric may also function to reveal the limitations of rhetoric. Each of these encounters is illustrative of insensitivity to or unwillingness to profit from the learning that can result from attending to the opposite point of view. The prince of Abyssinia is protected from these errors by the presence of his traveling companions, who present another viewpoint and other observations on the relationship between the different perspectives.

Chapters 21 and 22 demonstrate that education requires contrasting viewpoints and a social situation that encourages application of both perspectives. The incident involving the hermit (chapter 21) demonstrates the difference between intellectually subsuming another viewpoint and fully appreciating the otherness of that viewpoint. Here it is well to keep in mind that we are moving to a higher level of enquiry; the hermit is a more cultivated and civilized man than those visited up to this point in the journey. His cave contains several "apartments," some of which are designed to afford "lodgings to travellers, whom darkness or tempests happened to overtake," and although he eats only fruits and water, his guests are provided with "flesh and wine."

In this respect he resembles the hermit in Johnson's brief parody of Thomas Warton's retirement poem. When a young man approaches a recluse assuming that he is a "Hermit hoar, in solemn cell / Wearing out life's evening gray" (*Poems* 207.1-2), the sage smiles at the "lad" and offers him a beer. The hermit in *Rasselas* explains that retirement for him was not a means of escaping the corruption or comforts of civilization. He became disillusioned with the military life and decided to seclude himself in a cave that he had formed into "chambers, and stored . . . with all that [he] was likely to want." But he has been for some time "unsettled and distracted": "in solitude, if I escape the example of bad men, I want likewise the counsel and conversation of the good . . . the life of a solitary man will be certainly miserable, but not certainly devout" (*R* 21.57). At this point we share in the travelers' admiration for the wisdom of this unhappy sage and are accordingly surprised by his decision to return to the city "tomorrow": "They heard his resolution with surprise, but, after a short pause, offered to conduct him to Cairo. He dug up a considerable treasure which he had hid among the rocks, and accompanied them to the city, on which, as he approached it, he gazed with rapture" (*R* 21.57).

This behavior contradicts much of the hermit's earlier advice. He had counseled the prince concerning the choice of life in the following terms: "to him that lives well, every form of life is good; nor can I give any other rule for choice, than to remove from all apparent evil" (*R* 21.56). But his own rapturous gaze upon the city certainly represents a more positive and intense desire than that of removing oneself from all apparent evil. Moreover, his high hopes concerning Cairo seem misplaced in view of the fact that one of his reasons for deciding to become a hermit was his disillusionment with urban society.

Since my second chapter included a discussion of Johnson's attitude toward retirement in the periodical essays, it will be more useful here to compare the hermit in *Rasselas* to "The Vision of Theodore, The Hermit of Teneriffe" (1748), Johnson's lengthiest piece devoted to the subject of retirement and education. A hermit for fifty-seven years, Theodore begins his overtly religious allegorical dream-vision by addressing the reader in the following terms: "I was once what thou art now, a groveller on the earth, and a gazer at the sky: I trafficked and heaped wealth together, I loved and was favoured, I wore the robe of honour and heard the musick of adulation; I was ambitious, and rose to greatness; I was unhappy, and retired" (*Works* 2:501).

After over half a century of contented seclusion, Theodore suddenly feels impelled to climb a mountain that looms above his hermitage. After first resisting this impulse, the hermit climbs part of the way, pauses for rest, falls asleep, and is addressed in a dream by a "being of more than human dignity" who suggests that the climber look down below before continuing his ascent. The remainder of the tale is a long and very detailed dream-allegory, but for our purposes only the following elements need be kept in mind. At the bottom of the mountain, the children of Innocence are placed in the hands of Education, who repeatedly warns her charges of Habit, the villain of the allegory: "those whom Habit should once subdue, had little hope of regaining their liberty" (*Works* 2:502). After leading the children to a certain point, Education hands them over to Reason, who cannot compel them but advises them to follow both Reason and Religion. Some, however, employ only their rational faculties, while others, in accordance with Reason's advice, follow the path of Reason and Religion. The former are more easily deflected from their path by Appetite and Passion than the latter, who are vulnerable only to Habit, which, if it does prevail, can be overpowered by the combined forces of Reason and Religion.

The most essential point in the allegory is that the educated person recognizes that faith requires both reason and religion. Without religion, reason is directionless, subject to the distraction of passions, appetites, and bad habits. Education has achieved its end, on the other hand, when its students have learned to use reason as a guide to the practical fulfillment of the mission of religion. Hence, Theodore has his dream at a midway point in his ascent, that point where reason and religion combine forces. Even before beginning his ascent of the mountain, Theodore used his reason to reflect upon his passion, his longing to climb the mountain, leading him to recognize that his impulses cannot be suppressed but can be channelled. At that point, religion provides the proper goal to be pursued by means of these harnessed drives.

The hermit in *Rasselas,* however, explains that his solitude has not enriched his faith: "I am sometimes ashamed to think that I could not secure myself from vice, but by retiring from the exercise of virtue, and begin to suspect that I was rather impelled by resentment, than led by devotion, into solitude" (*R* 21.57). Certainly, his concerns are far from religious when at the end of the chapter he sets off, treasure in hand, gazing with rapture upon Cairo. Yet we do not do justice to the hermit if we assume that he is irreligious, for the prince has informed us that the hermit is known in Cairo for his "wisdom," and his own account of his state shows a concern for goodness and devotion. The incident is, however, presented in secular terms: "One, who appeared more affected with the narrative than the rest, thought it likely, that the hermit would, in a few years, go back to his retreat, and, perhaps, if shame did not restrain, or death intercept him, return once more from his retreat into the world" (*R* 22.58). Doomed to shift endlessly between city and country, the hermit remains oblivious to his own pitiful but humorous public spectacle, that of a sage who having once retired in disgust from the city now returns to it with the expectations of a country youth.

The full significance of this episode can be most readily grasped by attempting to visualize the prince looking in astonishment at the hermit, who gazes longingly at the city. Thus the narrative directs the reader to notice the relationship between the postures of the two men who are each distracted from awareness of themselves. What we see that the participants do not see is significant. The hermit's decision to avoid evil has resulted in the repression of Rasselas-like positive hopes that then periodically erupt, taking here the ludicrous form of a fond gaze upon the city from which he previously fled. Experience should temper and qualify innocence, not negate it, because the adult effort to avoid all naive desires may result in moments of folly. But the hermit is too obsessed with Cairo to notice that his behavior evokes in others surprise, pity, or laughter. It is this insensitivity that is the highest price of solitude, and neither reason nor religion can help the hermit in *Rasselas*. What he needs is the society of people like those who travel with Rasselas, friends who will point out his own comical public spectacle. In fact, it would seem that the sociability of the traveling party brings about the hermit's sudden decision to return to the city. The hermit enjoys the society of Rasselas and his fellow travelers and associates this pleasure with Cairo. He is likely to be disappointed because urban society is more frequently marked by unruly crowds and anonymous gatherings than by small groups of intelligent and convivial people.

In the company of Imlac, Nekayah, and Pekuah, Rasselas has a valuable resource that he has yet to appreciate. As is customary in *Rasselas*, the prince learns gradually, usually by way of the accretion of negative examples. For instance, complementing the episode of the hermit, the philosopher of the next chapter who instructs the prince in "The happiness of a life led according to nature" is also subject to periodic eruptions of passion. Finding a humble and docile pupil in Rasselas, the philosopher expatiates fulsomely: "when he had spoken, he looked round him with a placid air, and enjoyed the consciousness of his own beneficence" (*R* 22.60). The prince soon discovers that this man is one of those "sages whom he should understand less as he heard him longer." But far from being perturbed by his pupil's response, the sage feels encouraged; the prince "bowed and was silent, and the philosopher, supposing him satisfied, and the rest vanquished, rose up and departed with the air of a man that had co-operated with the present system" (*R* 22.60). The present system is one in which empty phrases are repeated by a philosopher who cannot distinguish between tacit assent and polite but firm disagreement.

Clearly, no particular philosophic doctrine is here represented, for the speaker's trite and garbled language cannot be identified with any single school of thought. Rather, the irony is directed against a pedantic posture. Complacent and pompous, the pedagogue is encouraged by the silence of his students, who probably either sleep or listen passively, astonished at his unfounded self-confidence. Like the hermit, this philosopher is blind to his public spectacle, the one smiling benignly upon the mute but uncomprehending audience and the other rushing toward the way of life he recently abandoned in disgust. Both men lack friends like Imlac and Nekayah who care enough about them to respond with the smile that could result in the embarrassment necessary for change.

The six chapters preceding the marriage debate demonstrate how solitariness of various kinds prevents access to the opposite point of view essential to education. Although, as we have seen, polar points of view are regularly presented in the periodical essays, Rasselas has an advantage over equivalent characters in them. The other perspective is presented to the prince by friends and companions whose irony is tempered by sympathy, as is exemplified by Imlac's remark in chapter 16, "when you feel that your own gaiety is counterfeit, it may justly lead you to suspect that of your companions not to be sincere" (*R* 16.46). The *Rambler*, the *Adventurer*, and the *Idler* make similar points in almost identical terms, but the difference is that in *Rasselas* the words are spoken not by a voice but by a character in context, a fellow traveler. The marriage debate makes plain the new element added by the embodiment of viewpoints in literary characters.

Although chapters 23 to 30 are usually referred to as the marriage debate because matrimony is the topic discussed at greatest length, it should be kept in mind that this section of *Rasselas* begins with the prince and princess deciding to investigate both the public world, which for them means that of political power, and the private realm, which they believe to be epitomized by marriage. Concerning the former, Rasselas is so quickly and completely disillusioned by what he sees at the Bassa's court that most of the conversation concerns the domestic scene. Nevertheless, the prince's experience of public life helps us understand the attitude he will adopt during the marriage debate. While still awestruck by the opulence of the palace, Rasselas sees the Bassa carried away in chains; as a result, the prince begins to meditate on the "prerogative of power" but is interrupted by the succeeding Bassa's removal from his position and the murder of the Sultan who had favored both Bassas. Convinced of the radical instability of political power, Rasselas turns in desperation to the domestic scene, only to be disillusioned by Nekayah. But since the prince will in the ensuing conversation continually take the naive and inexperienced view, it is well to pause at this early point when the princess is the ingénue. In recounting his experience at court, Rasselas explains that the governor, in delegating authority, could not avoid being at times "misled" and "betrayed":

> 'The discontent,' said the princess, 'which is thus unreasonable, I hope that I shall always have spirit to despise, and you, power to repress.'
>   'Discontent,' answered Rasselas, 'will not always be without reason under the most just or vigilant administration of publick affairs.' [*R* 27.70]

This exchange is reminiscent of an earlier one between Rasselas and Imlac in chapter 8 when the prince expresses his outrage at his father for permitting injustice in his kingdom. Imlac tries to explain to the secluded young man that the ruler cannot control all crime, but at that point the prince does not understand. Now, having lived at court, Rasselas explains the same notion to his sister and receives a reply similar to his own previous one. The point is that in spite of their intelligence, Rasselas and Nekayah, at different points in the story, lack the necessary experience. In the succeeding conversation, the prince is the naïf only because he, unlike his sister, has not studied the domestic scene.

The perspectives of innocence and experience are applied to the question of whether happiness resides in the public or private realm in *Rambler* number 190 (January 1752), but, as we shall see, in *Rasselas* it has a different final effect. First among "emirs and visiers," Morad lives for many years with absolute power, prosperity, and good health, until one day suddenly he falls from power into a state of discontent, disease, and melancholy. On his deathbed, the deposed monarch summons his son Abouzaid, advising him not to aspire to "publick honours" but to content himself "with private dignity," and to "diffuse thy riches among thy friends" (*Rambler* 190, 5:231). Following the dictates of his father, Abouzaid "wisely considered that domestick happiness was the first to be secured" and therefore raises the pay of all his staff. But he is robbed by two servants jealous of the superior trust placed in another domestic. Henceforth, Abouzaid decides to live only with his equals, but familiarity among these peers leads each individual to indulge his own caprice and advance his own opinion over the other. Abouzaid, therefore, widens the circle of his acquaintances; his table is henceforth either crowded by many competing for his attention or empty because of the resentment of courtiers not preferred above others. Turning now to the "force of gratitude," he gathers about him needy scholars and artists, but soon these talented people forget their former poverty and look upon their host as a "wretch of narrow capacity." Dismissing these ingrates, Abouzaid addresses the final words of the essay to Hamet, a poet: " 'Hamet,' said he, 'thy ingratitude has put an end to my hopes and experiments; I have now learned the vanity of those labours that wish to be rewarded by human benevolence; I shall henceforth do good, and avoid evil, without respect to the opinion of men; and resolve to solicit only the approbation of that being whom alone we are sure to please by endeavouring to please him' " (*Rambler* 190, 5:233).

Concluding with one character addressing another, this *Rambler* essay anticipates the dialogic technique that Johnson perfected seven years later in *Rasselas*. But here the incomplete conversation leaves the reader with the question Hamet might have posed; namely, "If you have decided to do without the society of people like me, why are you addressing your resolution to me?" The essay also seems un-finished in that one form of private life Abouzaid has not tried is marriage.

Many *Rambler* essays, however, do discuss marriage. In fact, the Rambler announced early on, in number 18, published in May 1750, that he intended "to treat in more papers on this important article of life." These papers examine the various abuses of marriage that the Rambler had mentioned in this early essay and can therefore be fairly summarized in the following terms: "all whom I have men-tioned failed to obtain happiness, for want of considering that mar-riage is the strictest tye of perpetual friendship; that there can be no friendship without confidence, and no confidence without integrity; and that he must expect to be wretched, who pays to beauty, riches, or politeness, that regard which only virtue and piety can claim" (*Rambler* 18, 3:103).

In fact, so many papers are devoted to those who marry for beauty, riches, or politeness that the Rambler feels obliged to include an essay that defends the institution of marriage: the problem resides, he explains, not in marriage as such but in the mortals who contract the bonds: "that they censure themselves for the indiscretion of their choice, is not a sufficient proof that they have chosen ill, since we see the same discontent at every other part of life which we cannot change" (*Rambler* 45, 3:244). But even after considering the unfortu-nate manner in which marriages are contracted—by parents who want heirs and do not consult their children or by adolescents in haste to leave home—the Rambler nevertheless concludes that in mar-riage, society has found "something in itself eminently agreeable to nature."

By comical means, the Idler goes one step further, demonstrating how a marriage can fail for lack of emotional and intellectual depth. Tim Warner describes his courtship of Miss Gentle in the most affable terms: "She did not in the days of courtship assume the privilege of imposing rigorous commands, or resenting slight offences. If I forgot any of her injunctions I was gently reminded; if I missed the minute of appointment I was easily forgiven." Surprisingly, after marriage Miss Gentle does not change in the least. She remains pliable, sweet, and calm; Tim Warner finds himself enmeshed in a life of civility, punctuality, and tact: "There are none whom she openly hates; for if once she suffers, or believes herself to suffer, any contempt or insult, she never dismisses it from her mind but takes all opportunities to tell how easily she can forgive. There are none whom she loves much better than others; for when any of her acquaintance decline in the opinion of the world she always finds it inconvenient to visit them; her affection continues unaltered but it is impossible to be intimate with the whole town" (*Idler* 100, 2:308).

Miss Gentle lives wholly on the surface. Her sole virtue is a cold propriety that finally is revealed to derive from a lack of passion and deep conviction. Thus Johnson, less than a year before writing *Rasselas,* introduces the element of passion into the marriage discussion, an issue that had not been of concern in the *Rambler* but one that will be important in our discussion of the marriage debate in *Rasselas.* Taken as a whole, the periodical essays on marriage contain all the ingredients of the marriage debate; the tale differs from the essays in the further development of the dialogic manner of presentation. After listening patiently to Nekayah's description of the difficulties of marriage—"in families, where there is no poverty, there is discord," "parents and children seldom act in concord," "few parents act in such a manner as . . . to enforce their maxims"—Rasselas wonders if his sister has been "unfortunate in her choice of acquaintances," for he finds it difficult to believe that "the most tender of all relations is thus impeded in its effects by natural necessity." The princess replies that while not necessary, "domestic discord" is seldom avoided. Despondent at his sister's report, Rasselas suddenly decides never to marry. Nekayah then further disconcerts her dispirited brother by asserting that "marriage has many pains, but celibacy has no pleasures."

Growing impatient, Rasselas accuses his sister of "exaggeratory declamation," that is, of overgeneralizing. "Marriage," he declares, echoing *Rambler* number 190, "is evidently the dictate of nature." Dourly, the princess replies, "I know not whether marriage be more than one of the innumerable modes of human misery" (*R* 28.73). The prince then triumphantly reminds Nekayah that she has just described celibacy as a less happy state than marriage: "both conditions may be bad, but they cannot both be worst. Thus it happens when wrong opinions are entertained, that they mutually destroy each other, and leave the mind open to truth." In response to her brother's warmth, the princess defends herself in terms that have a larger application than she intends. Since this particular part of the conversation contains the key to distinguishing the discussion of marriage in the periodical essays from that in *Rasselas,* it must be cited in full:

> "I did not expect," answered the princess, "to hear that imputed to falsehood which is the consequence only of frailty. To the mind, as to the eye, it is difficult to compare with exactness objects vast in their extent, and various in their parts.

Where we see or conceive the whole at once we readily note the discriminations and decide the preference: but of two systems, of which neither can be surveyed by any human being in its full compass of magnitude and multiplicity of complication, where is the wonder, that judging of the whole by the parts, I am alternately affected by one and the other as either presses on my memory or fancy? We differ from ourselves just as we differ from each other, when we see only part of the question, as in the multifarious relations of politicks and morality; but when we perceive the whole at once, as in numerical computations, all agree in one judgment, and none ever varies his opinion." [*R* 28.74]

The length of this speech distances the reader from the immediate occasion in order to suggest a broader application than the present conversation. At one remove from the conversation, the reader can see that the issues the prince and princess have been discussing—greatness versus domestic pleasure, celibacy versus marriage—are systems or, at the very least, parts of a vast system that no one can survey in its full compass. Furthermore, with reference to the whole, public and private gratification are seldom mutually exclusive concerns; most of us derive some of our pleasure from both realms. The debate about these matters thus becomes not merely a difference of opinion but also an example of two young people "alternately affected by one or the other" position, as "either possibility presses on [their] memory or fancy." And because the prince and his sister have become totally absorbed in their debate about the "parts" of life, Imlac interrupts to remind them of the larger "whole." "It seems to me," the sage points out, "that while you are making the choice of life, you neglect to live" (*R* 30.79). Imlac means that the decision about whether or not to marry cannot sensibly be arrived at in the abstract; it requires experience, living among married and single people.

But we cannot therefore dismiss the marriage debate as a mere youthful quarrel. The dispute itself represents an important element of marriage: passionately held differences of opinion must be included within the relationship, within the family. And here we see a further development of Johnson's consideration of the place of our profoundest emotions and beliefs in marriage that began with the *Idler* essay illustrating what results when deep beliefs and emotions are excluded from a marriage.

What we have at the end of the marriage debate in *Rasselas* is a marriage of perspectives, a brother and sister who must agree to differ while journeying together in search of a choice of life. Johnson skillfully creates a family situation that is not a literal marriage to emphasize that the relationship being established centers less upon the persons involved and more on their different perspectives. It is for this reason that the characters in *Rasselas* are more developed than the voices of the periodical essays but are not fully developed, like the "living and breathing" personalities of a Dickens or Thackeray novel. We are to accept the marriage of viewpoints of Rasselas and Nekayah without becoming concerned with whom they marry or whether they choose celibacy. The inappropriateness of such questions explains why the two sequels to *Rasselas* have passed into oblivion. Each continuation has pursued personal questions, providing the characters with spouses or with explicit religious convictions. But Johnson is interested not in the specific choice of life or of eternity for his characters but in the process of making a choice insofar as it helps one understand an important element of the human world as well as the formal basis of *Rasselas*. Characters who sound like voices from the *Rambler, Adventurer,* and *Idler* are placed in a literary context, a journey narrative, which is shown to be comprised of a family of perspectives, an intellectual marriage. The result is a dialectic of perspectives, not an organic form, a relationship of viewpoints to be applied in a learning situation.

The pyramid incident applies this marriage of perspectives to a learning situation, and the consideration of the astronomer will lead to a discussion of the principle of this process. Most modern critics agree that the pyramid episode (chapters 30-39) differs from what precedes it because of the new prominence given to action.[5] As a result of Pekuah's abduction the other main characters become involved in the search for and eventual rescue of the princess' favorite. From this point on in the narrative, the central characters both observe and participate in events. This new combination is reinforced in the last section, devoted to the astronomer, in which the travelers become so concerned about the scientist that they eventually include him in their group. An important indication of this change is to be found in the pyramid and astronomer episodes. Although topics from the essays, such as the effects of idleness and of the prevalence of the imagination, are present in the longer narrative, the central actions of these episodes are unique in Johnson's writings up to this point. *Rasselas* develops more fully ideas present in the periodicals, but it moves beyond the shorter works to take on an action and life of its own.

The two main issues from the periodicals that have a direct bearing on the pyramid section are idleness and sorrow. In *Rasselas*, at this advanced point in the narrative, these traditional Johnsonian ideas are not only modified and further developed but also, for the first time, subjected to irony. The sight of the pyramid evokes Imlac's speech on idleness, a subject that is perhaps more frequently considered than any other in the periodical essays. *Rambler* number 103 (March 1751) explains that idleness derives from curiosity, a key Johnsonian term. In its negative connotation, curiosity refers to a general and vague anxiety; as a positive term, it means an interest in an inquiry into the passing world. The latter "thirst of the soul" is as pure a delight in knowledge as can be found. The former, the focal point of this essay, entangles one in "trivial employments and minute studies. . . . The necessity of doing something, and the fear of undertaking much, sinks the historican to a genealogist, the philosopher to a journalist of the weather, and the mathematician to a constructer of dials" (*Rambler* 103, 4:187). But far more serious than the harm done to the self by this aimless curiosity or idleness is that done to others, and here the Rambler provides an example. Having begun life as a promising student of human actions, Nugaculus strays from his original purpose and becomes a "master of secret history," able to recount "the intrigues, private marriages, competitions, and stratagems of half a century." Although not ill-natured, Nugaculus obtains his knowledge by inadvertent acts of treachery, draining servants of their trust, flattering children into discoveries, and perpetually spying upon his neighbors. Having begun in a state of innocent and laudable curiosity, Nugaculus has wasted his intelligence and become a person marked by "vicious" idleness.

It is quite clear that Imlac sees the pyramid as a symbol of idleness. But it is important to hear the rhetoric of Imlac's diatribe, especially in view of what happens while he is speaking the following words:

> I consider this mighty structure as a monument of the insufficiency of human enjoyments. A king, whose power is unlimited, and whose treasures surmount all real and imaginary wants, is compelled to solace, by the erection of a pyramid, the satiety of dominion and tastelessness of pleasures, and to amuse the tediousness of declining life, by seeing thousands labouring without end, and one stone, for no purpose, laid upon another. Whoever thou art, that, not content with a moderate condition, imaginest happiness in royal magnificence, and dreamest that command or riches can feed the appetite of novelty with perpetual gratifications, survey the pyramids, and confess thy folly! [R 32.85]

Imlac's language suggests another enthusiastic fit, a suspicion confirmed by the final exclamation mark. While Imlac, safely inside the pyramid, lectures on the vacuity of life, outside, Pekuah is being kidnapped. The irony is, to be sure, of a delicate Johnsonian sort. Imlac is correct; most of our lives are punctuated by periods of vacancy. But, to paraphrase his own previous words to the travelers, in expatiating on the vacuity of life he neglects the fullness of life outside. Once again, Johnson has provided a double perspective, inside and outside the pyramids. But here, because the characters are participants rather than observers, their perspective becomes a contributing factor. Imlac's speech on the vacuity of life provides the Arabs sufficient time to abduct Pekuah, and Pekuah's superstitious fear of pyramids is the reason she remains outside alone, vulnerable to the kidnappers. For the first time in the tale, the characters find that their attitudes and mental postures have an effect upon what happens to them. Even Nekayah, who is relatively passive during this event, comes to realize that had she been less indulgent toward her servant and insisted on her going inside with the others, Pekuah would not have been abducted.

Johnson is here extending to the mental realm a notion first seen in a physical context in the incident involving the attempt at flight. There no one would have anticipated that the wings designed for flight in the air might sustain the inventor in the water. Similarly, no one could have divined that Pekuah's superstition, Nekayah's indulgence, and Imlac's oration would contribute to the abduction. Nevertheless, after the event, the reasons and causes for it are quite apparent. Because such events, however unexpected, are finally not mysterious but rather explicable in terms of body and mind, they will here be referred to as examples of human contingency. These examples emphasize that this notion applies not merely to physical acts but also to mental behavior, that is, to the manner in which our ideas, beliefs, hopes, and expectations contribute to what happens to us.

This specifically human contingent factor is reinforced in the pyramid incident when even the most intelligent Johnsonian assumptions become a part of and are manipulated by events. In Pekuah's history, for example, the Arab abductor is not a swarthy villain, but polite and well-behaved. Instead of ravishing his virgin captive, he treats her respectfully, teaches her astronomy, and enjoys her company. The world into which she is captured, that of an oriental outlaw with a harem and desert retreats, is not at all sinister and only slightly exotic. For the most part, it is boring. Moreover, having set a ransom for the captive, to whom he grows progressively more attached, the Arab is neither obsessed with his attraction for Pekuah nor anxious for the ransom money. Rather, he feels unable to refuse the treasure that he is unwilling to fetch.

While no one could be expected to have anticipated these results of Pekuah's abduction, nothing that happens is beyond explanation,

explanation that makes use of traditional Johnsonian principles. Such principles here become part of a surprising event. For instance, Pekuah points out that upon arriving at the Arab's castle on the Nile, she looked down at the river expecting "to see mermaids and tritons, which, as Imlac has told me, the European travelers have stationed in the Nile, but no such beings ever appeared, and the Arab, when I enquired after them, laughed at my credulity" (*R* 39.102). This laugh is not a sneer, for Imlac has drawn his inferences from reading the best sources, not unlike a studious Johnsonian familiar with the principles of the *Rambler, Idler,* and *Adventurer.* Moreover, the information Imlac has given to Pekuah is seldom a source of embarrassment to her; recognizing that Pekuah is much more intelligent than the ladies of his seraglio, the Arab converses with her about astronomy. Pekuah's education from Imlac enables her to learn from the Arab. But what she learns from captivity is another surprise. After her rescue, Pekuah is willing to enter into places of burial not, as we might have hoped, because she has ceased to credit her superstitious fears but because she is afraid of being abducted again.

The manner in which traditional Johnsonian dicta are manipulated, without being wholly undercut, by events at the pyramid can be seen in the section devoted to Nekayah's sorrow over the loss of Pekuah. Here again, it is important to recognize how Johnson applies irony to positions presented quite soberly in the periodicals. In August of 1750, the Rambler provided a detailed consideration of sorrow. The essay begins by distinguishing the sorrow of bereavement from all other passions in that the latter are directed toward some object or tangible goal that can lessen the pang or satisfy the desire. Sorrow for the loss of another, on the other hand, is an incessant wish that something were otherwise without the least prospect of achieving that end. For this reason, the Rambler asserts that sorrow, although at first laudable, must be temporary, for "we have no right to sacrifice, to the vain longings of affection, that time which providence allows us for the task of our station" (*Rambler* 47, 3:255). If, however, a "habitual sadness" seizes upon the soul, the following remedy is recommended by the essayist. Maintaining at first a general attitude "of neutrality and indifference," thereby eliminating any bonds of affection that when broken cause grief, the bereaved may reenter ordinary life, where he will experience the safest antidote for all sorrow, that of "employment."

Rambler number 47 avoids at once callousness and sentimentality, recognizing that although a natural expression of love, sorrow, if prolonged, can prove debilitating. Employment is the ultimate remedy, because anyone capable of feeling grief will soon experience a gradual return of concern for the living. But even the most astute reader of this essay could not anticipate the progress of Nekayah's sorrow. Soon after the abduction of her favorite, the princess despairs of finding Pekuah and decides to enter a covent. Imlac advises against taking religious vows: "do not entangle your mind by irrevocable determinations." Nekayah agrees to wait one year before retreating, and, fortunately, within a few months Pekuah returns. Although it is true that we have here an example of the function of encouraging the mourner not to turn away from life, the procedure of this chapter is singular. Heeding advice against irrevocable decisions, the princess replaces her intended religious vow with another one, her promise to wait a year. Because of her obedience to this vow the retreat is never carried out, since Pekuah returns before the year has elapsed. The following chapter continues in a similar vein, transforming our anticipations and those of Nekayah. Its subject is simply and succinctly summarized in the title, "Pekuah is still remembered. The progress of sorrow." The details, however, are more complex, not to say uncanny.

Gradually, the princess begins to forget her favorite servant, but she is occasionally reminded of Pekuah and thus of her own forgetfulness: "she rejoiced without her own consent at the suspension of her sorrows, and sometimes caught herself with indignation in the act of turning away her mind from the remembrance of her, whom she yet resolved never to forget" (R 36.94). Instead of the expected relief from "employment," the princess now grieves both for her favorite and for her own forgetfulness; Pekuah is remembered fitfully but more intensely by way of forgetfulness. Thus an examination of the period of Nekayah's waiting and mourning points to the uncommonness of the ordinary and is inverse preparation for Pekuah's narrative concerning the boredom of the occult.

The pyramid incident demonstrates how man's ideas and beliefs, his hopes and expectations, become threads in the tapestry of events. The mental baggage that the travelers have brought with them from the happy valley—from the naive hopes of Rasselas to the sophisticated reflections of Imlac—contribute to what happens to them on their journey. This principle of human contingency further complicates the choice-of-life quest because of the manner in which the prince's questions and Imlac's assumptions, their approaches to the events and subjects, become entwined with the conclusions concerning the choices of life, the learning resulting from the travels. The nature of the ability to comprehend the results of intermingling the travelers' assumptions with what and whom they visit is the subject of the astronomer incident.

This last section of *Rasselas* is devoted to a lengthy consideration of solitude and retirement, rounding out the narrative by returning to issues raised earlier in the happy valley section. But unlike that of the happy valley or even of the hermit, the isolation here is neither physical nor imposed upon one by others. And the way the astronomer is introduced to us establishes continuity with the previous episode by providing a further instance of human contingency. Once Imlac has told the others about this learned man, the travelers want to meet him but anticipate great difficulty in gaining access to such a solitary intellectual. After considerable discussion, Pekuah suggests introducing herself by way of an "honest pretence," her wish to continue the astronomical studies that were begun with the Arab. "'I am afraid,' said Imlac, 'that he will be soon weary of your company: men advanced far in knowledge do not love to repeat the elements of their art, and I am not certain, that even of the elements, as he will deliver them connected with inferences, and mingled with reflections, you are a very capable auditress'" (*R* 46.120-21). But Imlac's condescending preconception proves to be unfounded: Pekuah "told her tale with ease and elegance, and her conversation took possession of [the astronomer's] heart" (*R* 46.121).

In fact, all the travelers are surprised by his response to them. Having expected that access to the astronomer would be difficult, they discover that in fact he craves company: "They came again and again, and were every time more welcome than before. The sage endeavoured to amuse them, that they might prolong their visits" (*R* 46.121). Although entry to the observatory is considerably easier than any of the travelers had anticipated, the fact that they devote time and consideration to a means of entry is related to the kind of reception they receive. Having lived without company for some time, the astronomer is pleased to meet the travelers because they are polite, thoughtful, honest, and intelligent—the characteristics manifested by the "honest pretence." We see the principle of human contingency in operation; the travelers' mental attitudes contribute to the outcome of the event but not in ways that they could have anticipated.

The astronomer, however, unlike the others visited by the prince in his pursuit of a choice of life, from the outset employs the principle of human contingency, thus making the matter more explicit than before. When first revealing his "preternatural commission" to Imlac, the "man of learning" recognizes that his power can never be proven or scientifically demonstrated: "I know too well the laws of demonstration to think that my conviction ought to influence another, who cannot, like me, be conscious of its force. I, therefore, shall not attempt to gain credit by disputation. It is sufficient that I feel this power, that I have long possessed, and every day exerted it." Instead of proof, the sage recounts the circumstances surrounding his discovery of his miraculous power. "One day as I was looking on the fields withering with heat, I felt in my mind a sudden wish that I could send rain on the southern mountains, and raise the Nile to an inundation. In the hurry of my imagination I commanded rain to fall, and, by comparing the time of my command, with that of the inundation, I found that the clouds had listened to my lips" (R 42.111).

The pathos and humor of this confession are manifested in the ironical example of the astronomer's use of the concept of human contingency. Instead of asserting his power by decree or making false empirical claims, the astronomer reconstructs the moment when, to his astonishment, the weather was directed by his inner dictates. In order to relate his assumptions about the weather to the actual rainfall, the astronomer resorts to narrative; that the principle of human contingency is communicated by way of the technique of storytelling will be of moment later on in the analysis. Here my interest is in the response to the story. As a result of the above cited account, Imlac becomes involved in the action of *Rasselas* as he never has before, for he finds that he has been chosen as the heir apparent to the "preternatural" monarchy. "The care of appointing a successor," explains the astronomer, "has long disturbed me; the night and the day have been spent in comparisons of all the characters which have come to my knowledge, and I have yet found none so worthy as thyself" (R 42.112). Suddenly, Imlac has become deeply involved in a matter that only a moment previously he beheld as an observer. Now named prince of this imaginary kingdom, Imlac must feel as the astronomer did when the rain clouds listened to his lips. For it is Imlac's patient, responsible, and concerned attitude toward the astronomer that has qualified him as his successor—a further instance of a mental posture producing surprising but understandable results. The second ingredient in understanding an instance of human contingency is empathy, Imlac's putting himself in the situation of the astronomer.

Imlac's concern for the demented man of learning also causes the other travelers to become implicated in "the dangerous prevalence of the imagination". In recounting the history of the astronomer to the prince and princess, Imlac explains that the scientist's "integrity and benevolence are equal to his learning," a judgment borne out by the astronomer's behavior. After revealing to Imlac his preternatural commission and the manner in which he discovered his power, the astronomer earnestly warns his chosen successor not to tamper with the seasons or the weather. Having diligently studied the various possible positions of the earth and sun and having formed innumerable schemes to change their situation, the astronomer has "found it impossible to make a disposition by which the world may be advantaged; what one region gains, another loses by an imaginable alteration." In conclusion, he pleads: "Do not, therefore, in thy administration of the year, indulge thy pride by innovation; do not please thyself by thinking that thou canst make thyself renowned to all future ages, with disordering the seasons. The memory of mischief is no desirable fame. Much less will it become thee to let kindness or interest prevail. Never rob other countries of rain to pour it on thine own. For us the Nile is sufficient" (*R* 43.112-13).

Instead of gloating over his power, the astronomer thinks only about protecting his subjects from an arbitrary or unscrupulous monarch. In spite of his delusion, the scientist remains a man of integrity and benevolence, and for this reason Imlac rebukes the ladies for laughing at what he calls this "heaviest of human afflictions." Few people, Imlac continues, can equal the astronomer's knowledge and virtue, but "all may suffer his calamity." After this reminder, Rasselas, Nekayah, and Pekuah each confess to their own temporary but recurrent forms of the dangerous prevalence of the imagination. Their harmless "visionary schemes," or daydreams, are to be distinguished from those of the astronomer in that they are momentary and do not prevail. The travelers come to realize by way of the history of the astronomer that their assumption that the monarch of the seasons must be a megalomaniac is unfounded and that the hopes and wishes that led to his delusion are not different in kind from their own. Clearly, presentation of the astronomer's problem involves manipulation of the listeners' and readers' expectations. The precise nature of this literary technique begins to emerge when we compare this section of *Rasselas* to an appropriate periodical essay.

Rambler number 89 (January 1751) begins by citing a philosopher on the limitations of philosophy: "Locke, whom there is no reason to suspect of being a favourer of idleness or libertinism, has advanced, that whoever hopes to employ any part of his time with efficacy and vigour, must allow some of it to pass in trifles" (*Rambler* 89, 4:105). For this reason those who study the most are not necessarily the most learned; many who appear to be diligently at work in their study are, in fact, giving themselves up "to the luxury of fancy." Indeed, nothing is more dangerous to the thinker than "to have learned the art of regaling his mind with those airy gratifications." Unlike any other vice or folly, the prevalence of the imagination can remain totally secret, a private gratification never subject to correction because never known. Of course, those who dream instead of laboring will eventually produce little or nothing of consequence, but often by that time it is too late, the habit having become ingrained and much of life having been dissipated.

The cure for this unfortunate mental vice is complex. Close application to "some new study" requires solitude, the very milieu where imagination can prevail. But change of the topic of study, accompanied by "active employment or public pleasure," may help dispel the "airy gratifications." Once the balance has been turned against this "formidable and obstinate disease of the intellect," constant employment must be maintained so that idleness can be avoided at all costs. Moreover, the Rambler continues, since some part of every man's time must be spent on trivial tasks, it is far better to do so in company than alone, for "he that amuses himself among well chosen companions, can scarcely fail to receive, from the most careless and obstreperous merriment which virtue can allow, some useful hints." Social amusement, the essay concludes, produces happiness of a sort not available to the solitary man.

This *Rambler* essay certainly helps clarify the issues in the astronomer episode. Ensconced in his observatory, the scientist sees few people, too few to be reminded of how much he misses company. He creates an imaginary sky kingdom over which he presides, dispensing justice benevolently to the people below. Since this entire scheme functions chiefly to compensate him for the lack of society, the astronomer, even at his most demented stage, never loses his deep concern for people, a fact made evident in his advice to Imlac not to favor one nation over another. Understandably, the presence of people begins the return to sanity. Once Imlac and his charges interrupt the scientist's solitude, he starts to feel his belief in the preternatural commission weaken. "The sage confessed to Imlac, that since he had mingled in the gay tumults of life, and divided his hours by a succession of amusements, he found the conviction of his authority over the skies fade gradually from his mind" (*R* 46.123). Being in the company of others helps loosen the grip of the airy gratification, a procedure that follows the stages outlined in *Rambler* number 89. But at this point problems arise in *Rasselas* not anticipated in the periodical essay.

First, in response to the prince's question about a choice of life, the solitary scientist explains that his own career was a mistake: "'Of the various conditions which the world spreads before you, which you shall prefer,' said the sage, 'I am not able to instruct you. I can only tell you that I have chosen wrong . . . I have purchased knowledge at the expense of all the common comforts of life: I have missed the endearing elegance of female friendship, and the happy commerce of domestick tenderness'" (*R* 46.122-23). As we know, the astronomer acts in accord with these words, giving up his observatory to travel with the characters in the story. I shall describe the significance of this additional element in the progress of the diseased imagination first in psychological and then in narratological terms.

His first doubts about his powers are accompanied by depression: "When I have been for a few days lost in pleasing dissipation, I am always tempted to think that my enquiries have ended in errour, and that I have suffered much, and suffered it in vain" (*R* 46.123). Imlac, encouraged to see light dawning, presses forward, receiving the solitary man into "familiar friendship." Now the astronomer's intermittent doubts about his sky monarchy are interrupted by moments when he doubts his own doubt: "I am like a man habitually afraid of spectres, who is set at ease by a lamp, and wonders at the dread which harrassed him in the dark, yet, if his lamp be extinguished, feels again the terrours which he knows that when it is light he shall feel no more" (*R* 46.124). But even as the light predominates over the dark periods, the unfortunate man's cure is complicated by guilt. How "dreadful is my crime," he explains to Imlac, "if I neglect the great responsibility of the weather and seasons entrusted into me, betraying the peoples of my dominion." Imlac now addresses the problem directly, explaining to his learned friend that at this stage guilt is the only impediment to sanity. The astronomer replies that he often had similar thoughts on the matter but that his reason had been overpowered by his obsession, rendering him unable to trust in his own reflections.

Return to sanity is thus the result of more than filling the vacuity of life with pleasurable society or diverting the mind when imagination might otherwise have prevailed. Such distraction was necessary for the first stage, the introduction of doubts about the dominion. But then Imlac had to cultivate the friendship in order to be heeded and trusted when he encouraged the astronomer to discover the psychological barrier preventing total comprehension and alleviation of his problem.

To understand why the astronomer incident is what Walter Raleigh called a "skillful climax," we must distinguish it carefully from *Rambler* number 89. For example, Ernest Lee Tuveson, in *The Imagination as a Means of Grace,* generalized about the eighteenth century in a way applicable to the *Rambler* essay but not to *Rasselas.* The central thesis of Tuveson's book concerns the evolution of ideas. "Great cultural changes" are seen as the outcome of the gradual separation of imagination from other faculties of the mind, especially reason, until, in the late eighteenth century, imagination became a "means of grace" and was finally secularized in the nineteenth and twentieth centuries into the purely aesthetic. Tuveson therefore begins with Locke, who "had made necessary a new kind of thinking and creating for the artist, the critic, and theorist."[6] Tuveson's summary of Locke is in all essential respects applicable to *Rambler* number 89. Indeed, Tuveson's description of a Lockean case study is reminiscent of how Johnson applies such notions to the astronomer: "Locke cites the case of a man who, as a child, heard from a foolish maid stories which connect 'ideas of goblins and spirits' with darkness and who, as a result, shall never be able to separate them again so long as he lives, but darkness shall ever afterwards bring with it those frightful ideas, and they shall be so joined, that he can no more bear the one than the other!"

Readers of *Rasselas* are immediately reminded of that moment when the astronomer characterizes himself as one "habitually afraid of spectres, who is set at ease by a lamp." But according to Tuveson, Locke did not further investigate this issue nor suggest how "the associations, inspected under the white light of understanding, might lose their despotic power." "To take this step toward psychoanalysis," we are informed, "required almost two centuries."[7] But the preceding analysis has demonstrated that the astronomer is cured by precisely the procedure Tuveson places at two centuries' distance. Assisted by Imlac, the solitary scientist fishes "the associations out of the recess beyond the immediate awareness" by explaining the condition that led to his belief that the clouds listened to his lips. Examining the matter under the white light of understanding, the astronomer, again with the guidance of Imlac, comes to realize that only his unwarranted guilt prevents him from shedding his illusory mantle.

Of course, Tuveson is characterizing major trends of thought, and *Rasselas* may constitute an anomaly of little interest to the historian of ideas. But the point is important to criticism, because here literary interpretation has a direct link to human understanding. To clarify this link, we need to focus upon narrative technique, the manner in which the incident is unfolded for the reader, as opposed to the chronological order of events. We first hear of the "man of learning" after the prince has decided that he loves learning and intends to devote himself to "literary solitude." Imlac feels that before the prince makes a final decision he should hear about the astronomer. At the outset, the reader is alerted to the fact that the ensuing tale will exemplify the dangers of solitary knowledge. That knowledge is the subject of the tale is further reinforced when we are informed that Imlac, a poet, was introduced to the scientist as a "man of knowledge worthy of his notice." This story, like all stories, begins by promising a specific end, a conclusion that will resolve the question it raises. Moreover, Imlac remarks somewhat immodestly that the scientist "smiled at the narration of my travels," thus suggesting that we attend to both his tale and his manner of telling it.

Imlac begins by explaining that he was admitted as a regular visitor because his "history" gave pleasure to the astronomer; as a poet he recognizes that the first requirement of an author is to sustain the reader's interest by providing pleasure. From continual pleasure comes relaxation; the astronomer expresses himself freely, revealing his integrity, benevolence, and profound intelligence. At this point, the question raised by this tale becomes so apparent that Rasselas can no longer wait: "Surely," the prince exclaims, "this man is happy." Thus the listener's and, by implication, the reader's expectations are included in the story, a point reinforced when Imlac tells of the moment when he was selected as the heir apparent to the sky kingdom, when he too ceased to be an observer and became a participant.

The next stage is marked by an obvious change in narrative technique. Now the astronomer tells his own tale, providing us with a story within a story (Imlac's discourse) that is itself within a story (*Rasselas*). The scientist's design, however, is not to evoke pleasure and excite interest but to promote understanding. Unable to prove his claim of monarchy over the weather and seasons, he decides to reenact the moment when he first discovered his extraordinary power. Implanting the astronomer's direct address within but at two removes from his own tale, Johnson isolates this section concerned with human understanding, a topic reinforced when the astronomer cautions Imlac against tampering with the weather or seasons because the result will cause more harm than good to the people of his realm. Imlac is able to reiterate and apply this notion when, as a rebuke to Nekayah and Pekuah, who interrupt the tale with laughter, he points out that all humans are subject to the dangerous prevalence of the imagination.

This remark provokes another set of short narratives, the confessions of the young travelers concerning their daydreams; the listeners are thus further drawn into the astronomer's tale, sharing not merely in his initial psychological drives but also in the imaginary projection of desires. Now, suddenly, the entire episode is interrupted by the entrance of the old man, which occasions a separate chapter to be discussed in more detail shortly. Here it should be noted that the old man signals a change in kind of narrator; the speaker is not Imlac, the astronomer, or any character in the text, but the omniscient narrator who began *Rasselas* by addressing himself to "ye who listen with credulity to the whispers of fancy." Johnson's reason for taking the narrative away from Imlac and the astronomer at this point is that they must now become part of the action.

After the comfortless words of the old man, the astronomer's tale is resumed, but now we turn to the manner in which the astronomer regains his sanity. Imlac is the prime agent because he is equipped to use poetic and narrative techniques for purposes of human understanding. After the astronomer has begun to enjoy the company of the travelers, Rasselas asks his opinion about the choice of life, and the "man of learning" explains that he can offer little in the way of helpful advice because he has made the mistake of choosing study without experience. Imlac is delighted by this first glimmering of sanity and his delight is highlighted by the controlling or authorial narrator: "Imlac was delighted to find that the sage's understanding was breaking through its mists, and resolved to detain him from the planets till he should forget his task of ruling them, and reason should recover its original influence" (*R* 46.123).

The narrator of *Rasselas* interrupts Imlac to reemphasize delight because the literary procedure involves the evocation and manipulation of our deepest desires. Having discovered that the astronomer can be distracted from the planets by social amusements, Imlac arranges for him to be immersed in the "gay tumults of life." After engaging in the social world of the travelers for some time, the astronomer reappropriates the narrative and confesses to Imlac that his conviction about his authority "over the skies" begins to fade but that he fears that such doubt will lead to the neglect of his monarchical responsibility. Having moved the astronomer from solitude to society, having altered the context of his desires, Imlac now suggests another point of view appropriate to the new situation: perhaps the astronomer's guilt is delusive and prevents the recognition that he is no different from other human beings, having no "supernatural favors or afflictions." Once the astronomer is able to accept this more modest alternative, Imlac completes the artistic process by providing a means of closure that links the two points of view. Admitting that Imlac's doubts confirm his own, the astronomer ends by hoping that he will now be relieved of this immense responsibility and will live in peace. Imlac replies that "your learning and virtue may justly give you hopes," reminding us that knowledge and decency were the motivating forces behind both the sane and the insane view.

We have seen that the same structural elements of the astronomer episode given prominence by the psychological or "character" analysis are also featured by a narratological approach that analyzes the changes of and differences between speakers. Both explain the astronomer's disease and cure by way of human understanding. What we have discovered is that the psychological process pursued by the listeners *in* the tale is homologous with the narrative process followed by the reader *of* the tale. Literary interpretation journeys with the travelers and arrives at the same end point but at a higher level. For while the pilgrims unravel the astronomer's problem, the critical reader is led to a vantage point that reveals that human understanding is achieved through the method of literary interpretation.

Now we can appreciate fully the function of chapter 45, "They discourse with an old man."[8] This interruption of the successful use of literary analysis, the cure of the astronomer, serves to make the young critics hear the old man tell them that the wisdom of old age does not provide happiness. The message is religious and traditional: literary understanding cannot provide the consolation of religion. The reason we need such a reminder is made clear in chapter 48, the last episode of *Rasselas,* the visit to the Egyptian catacombs. This final outing is, as the prince puts it, one "which I have done, because I would do something." Those elemental drives from the happy valley have again appeared, and it is important that they figure in a chapter involving religion, "Imlac discourses on the nature of the soul." Occasioned by the question of why the Egyptians sought to preserve the human corpse, the discourse concerns the materiality or immateriality of the soul. Instead of attempting to argue for one or the other position, Imlac makes clear that each is defensible in its own terms. We return to the double perspective that first emerged with the paradise-on-earth desire, at once material and immaterial. Johnson is emphasizing that this kind of ultimate desire is essential to the literary process; literature engages our interest because it promises an end, the satisfaction of such desires.

Of course, that promise is not fulfilled; instead, these desires are manipulated, never fully realized. But no one was more aware than Johnson of the dangers of the belief that literature fulfilled this need, of what he called the perils of romance, the imprisoning capacity of the happy valley. Having allowed his travelers to escape from prison-paradise, Johnson concludes with their being informed that the paradise-on-earth drives manipulated by literature for the purpose of literary understanding can only be satisfied by religious faith. And, to return to the religious controversy of chapter 1, that is why religion hovers in the background of *Rasselas*, a question raised for the purpose of remaining a question. Manipulating but not satisfying religious aspirations, literature is clearly distinguished from religion.

The astronomer incident clarifies the nature of the enabling principle of *Rasselas.* To understand why the man of learning's choice of a solitary observatory was wrong is also to understand why Rasselas must escape from the happy valley and travel with Imlac in search of a choice of life. It is not enough to fill one's vacant life with amusements; the prince could have done that in the happy valley. Nor is it enough to associate oneself with acquaintances who will distract one from moments of the dangerous prevalence of the imagination;

the prince could also have availed himself of such company in the happy valley. It is necessary to break out of a situation that provides for only one way of life, be it the happy valley or the observatory, because only by changing situations, by traveling in a metaphoric and literal sense, can we come to understand how our mental assumptions and postures relate to what we experience. Furthermore, friendships, like that which develops between Imlac and the astronomer, allow for the sharing of dangerous elements of the imagination and for laughter at one another's foolish public spectacles.

This culminating episode of *Rasselas* is a social situation involving interaction of all mental faculties, emotional and rational. It concludes with the cured astronomer joining the travelers, who have discovered by helping him that they share in his flights of fancy. We are thus reminded of "the whispers of fancy" mentioned in the first sentence. In spite of the dangers of these desires, exemplified most notably by the demented astronomer, *Rasselas* includes and manipulates these desires because suppression of them is shown to be dangerous. The hermit, for instance, advises the prince to abandon all attempts at positive pleasure; the best he hopes for is avoidance of evil. But, as we have seen, he seems doomed to alternate disappointedly between hermitage and city; he has relegated his deepest passions to the realm of the unconscious, where their effects on his actions will remain unexamined. The astronomer realizes that such would be his fate if he chose to remain alone in his observatory. The desire represented by Rasselas' quest for the choice of life can never be abandoned; for that reason even experienced and sophisticated men like Imlac and the astronomer travel with Rasselas. But it is as dangerous to indulge such desires as to attempt to evade them. The first option is represented by the complacent happy valley residents and the latter by the hermit and the insane astronomer.

What conclusion, then, are we to come to about *Rasselas*; what are we to make of the last chapter, enigmatically entitled "The conclusion, in which nothing is concluded"? The comma in this chapter title serves as a reminder that both a conclusion and that in which nothing is concluded are here present. Rasselas concludes not with the choice of life but with the process of making a choice of life. The only resolution is a negative one: isolation or permanent retreat is a mistake because it prevents the self-correction possible in the society of the world at large. Nothing is concluded in that the choice of life quest never ends because, for active and inquiring minds, it is bound up with life itself. At the end of their journey, the young travelers divert themselves by revealing to one another their "various schemes of happiness," while Imlac and the astronomer are content "to be driven along the stream of life." But "of these wishes that they had formed they well knew that none could be obtained." Rasselas, Pekuah, and Nekayah now understand what the astronomer and Imlac recognized earlier, that the choice-of-life quest functions not to arrive at a choice of life but to impel one along the stream of life, a life of civilized inquiry like that pursued by the astronomer and Imlac.

It should be emphasized that while Imlac and the astronomer do not form specific wishes as do the younger travelers, they are not immune to such desires. At their advanced stage of life, they are impelled along the stream of life by the desire for intelligent diversion, the sort of motive that first led Imlac to leave the happy valley. They cannot therefore be excluded from the category of those "who listen with credulity to the whispers of fancy," those readers addressed at the beginning of *Rasselas*. Indeed, the manner of reading *Rasselas* is directly related to the procedure of the choice-of-life quest; the understanding of *Rasselas* is intertwined with the understanding that Rasselas finally acquires at the end of the tale. The innovative element of *Rasselas* is what I shall call the principle of literary understanding, an interpretive procedure unfolded *in* the text and available to the critical reader interested in accounting for the originality of *Rasselas*. On this level, it can be said that *Rasselas* is the story of how happy valley desires impel one into the human world where one can journey toward understanding the function of the quest set off by those desires. The travelers in *Rasselas* move gradually toward the employment of an interpretive procedure that thereby becomes available to the reader as a principle.

That *Rasselas* concludes with a process is evident in the final phrase of the book, which informs us that the travelers decided "to return to Abyssinia." Now we are able to understand why it took two centuries for the meaning of the term "Abyssinia" to be fully understood. As we know from chapter 1,[9] Abyssinia is not synonymous with the happy valley; it is also to be distinguished from the other locations of the journey. *Rasselas* concludes by suggesting that the journey has ceased in that the pilgrims now realize that change of geographical location will not produce the choice of life. Although the young characters still fantasize about the choice of life, they have now ceased to take the quest literally, thus ending the journey in the narrative. But they return to Abyssinia, not the happy valley, because the secluded paradise limits the choice-of-life desires essential to the life of inquiry. Abyssinia has caused considerable problems for critics because it is contiguous with the literary realm of *Rasselas* but not contained within it. In my view, Abyssinia signals the contiguity of the literary and the extraliterary, for it is the location of the happy valley and of actual events recounted in history books. The literary process of *Rasselas* is thus shown not to be restricted to literature; it is a procedure used in life, especially in choice-of-life situations, where we frame or contextualize elements from the flux of experience in order to interpret them.

The notion that literature is a form of knowledge was commonplace in the eighteenth century. But because the familiar formulation, "to instruct by pleasing," as Johnson put it in the *Preface* to Shakespeare, is presented in moral terms, we assume that the goal is the inculcation of principles of virtue and decency. While the ethical dimension is nearly always present, it is not the sole justification for art as instruction. Johnson pointed out early in his career that the writer was not only to "reform Vice" but also to "instruct Ignorance" and "reclaim Error." In *Rambler* number 3, he explains that the task of an author is either "to teach what is not known, or to recommend known truths." The former task is considered particularly difficult because readers "must not only confess their ignorance, but, what is still less pleasing, must allow that he from whom they are to learn is more knowing than themselves."

It is often overlooked that Johnson and his contemporaries took for granted that literature, apart from its moral commitment, provided knowledge in the form of information about the world. But the specific issue that pertains to the relationship between knowledge and fiction is usually labeled the problem of believability or credibility, an issue that concerned Johnson throughout his career. In his first published work, he declared that "he who tells nothing exceeding the bounds of probability, has a right to demand that they should believe him who cannot contradict him," and near the end of his life he reiterated the point: "Nothing is good but what is consistent with truth or probability." In the *Life of Gray,* Johnson addresses this issue in the context of literature. Concerning *The Bard,* he declares that it "disgusts us with apparent and unconquerable falsehood" and then generalizes in the following terms: "To select a singular event, and swell it to a giant's bulk by fabulous appendages of spectres and predictions, has little difficulty, for he that forsakes the probable may always find the marvellous."[10]

The term repeated in all three of the above citations is "probability." Johnson was not by any means the first to use probability as a bridge between literature and knowledge. In *Tom Jones,* Fielding declares that "every good author will confine himself within the bounds of probability." In the Postscript to *Clarissa,* Richardson precludes the possibility of a sudden conversion of Lovelace on the grounds that such an action would have "neither *art* nor *nature,* nor even *probability.*" Fanny Burney declares, in the Preface to *Evelina,* that her story is to be distinguished from Romance, "where Reason is an outcast, and where the sublimity of the marvellous rejects all aid from sober Probability." And Richard Cumberland promises the reader of his narrative, entitled *Henry,* that he shall not be required to "swim . . . against the stream of probability." In a pioneering and important scholarly contribution, Douglas Lane Patey examines Augustan theories and practical applications of the concept of probability. Patey demonstrates conclusively that probability was a major philosophic and critical concern throughout the eighteenth century. Most pertinent to the present discussion, Patey shows that probability was a recurrent term used to explain believability and credibility in literature. Indeed, probability is seen by Patey as the key notion that enabled eighteenth-century philosophers and critics to establish a link between poetics and what critics of the period called life. Theorists in Johnson's day, Patey demonstrates, sought an explanation for the probability of fictive literature and, in the second half of the century, focused on character because the notion of personality offered a mimetic counterpart for fictive creations.

While profiting greatly from Patey's study, I pursue a different method of inquiry.[11] Unlike Patey, who begins with theory and ends with practice, I begin with practice, drawing theoretical inferences from interpretations of literary texts. Specifically, the preceding analysis of *Rasselas* demonstrates that a relationship between literature and knowledge is achieved by way not of character but of literary structure. Yet neither Johnson nor his contemporaries discussed the matter in these terms: formalistic aesthetic methods were not conceived of for over a century. My contention is that in his practice as a writer Johnson created literary works that manifested a resolution of this problem, the theoretical ramifications of which have still to be fully understood.

The next two chapters are devoted to explaining how an analysis of Johnson's writing process leads to this resolution. But at this point we can understand why twentieth-century critics have made *Rasselas* a *locus criticus* and yet have been so troubled by it. Educated within one or another aspect of formalism or postformalism, modern critics locate significant structural elements in *Rasselas* that are seen to operate in opposition to the mimetic assertions in the text, the truth and instruction that it promises. This Janus-faced quality of Johnson's aesthetic—literature that proceeds by way of a method that also has extraliterary application—causes modern critics grave difficulties.

The precise nature of this problem can be clarified by considering briefly three essays that appeared in 1975, when *Rasselas* criticism manifested the move from formalism to postformalism. The former position is represented by a commentator who attempted to document a religious reading of *Rasselas* by recourse to a neglected section of the work. The evidence provided for "theodicy" is the incident in chapter 37 at the shrine of St. Anthony, where Pekuah is returned by the Arab abductor. The monks at St. Anthony represent, according to this critic, the "concrete choice of eternity—qualified like all else in the book."[12] But the conversation about the monks provides little evidence for this reading. In response to Rasselas' admiration for the monks, who do not complain about a life of "uniform hardship," Imlac points out that these men are less unhappy than the residents of the happy valley because the religious hermits live a life of purpose, preparing themselves "for endless liberty." Nekayah then asks Imlac if he believes "monastic rule is more holy" than any other way of life. After some hesitation, Imlac decides: "he that lives well in the world is better than he that lives well in a monastery" (*R* 47.126).

On the basis of this conversation, it is surely difficult to assert that Johnson recommends the choice of eternity as represented by the monks at St. Anthony. Rasselas refers to them merely in passing, and Imlac is willing to recommend a monastery only to those who are "not able to stem the temptations of public life." Moreover, although the episode involving the return of Pekuah takes place in chapter 37, the prince does not comment on the monks until chapter 47. Occurring so late in the narrative, Rasselas' words can hardly be said to provide preparation for a journey to theodicy that supposedly began ten chapters previously. But this attempt to base one's reading on evidence within the text is understandable in view of two archetypal approaches to *Rasselas* that also appeared in 1975. In chapter one I discussed a religious reading based on the notion that the choice of Prodicus and the tablet of Cebes were subverted. But another critic, employing the choice of Hercules, asserted that *Rasselas* was to be viewed in secular terms.[13]

This critical dilemma stems from an assumption shared by these and most critics of our time, succinctly stated by one of them as follows: "that all literature is referential to literature."[14] My own reading of *Rasselas* questions this assumption: the principle of the literary process is seen to have extraliterary application. I believe that form does not inhere in a text or in the archetypes evoked by the text; structure is uncovered by critics who select and emphasize aspects of a text as part of the act of interpretation. The attempt to locate a formal configuration in a text or the whole of literature only succeeds in reifying the process of interpretation. It is of course not coincidental that this problem arises at the end of *Rasselas,* a story that ends by pointing to the principle basic to the process of interpretation.

In the ensuing chapters, I shall follow the process of trial and error by which Johnson arrived at his Janus-faced aesthetic by analyzing his other literary works in chronological order. But it should be emphasized that, while following in the path of Johnson's struggles to perfect his method, my own approach is not synonymous with his. As mimesis, the method employed by Johnson and other eighteenth-century critics, was unable to resolve the difference between Hawkins and Boswell, so modern formalist and postformalist theories are unsuccessful at reconciling present-day differences. My own literary method entails a combination of elements from twentieth- and eighteenth-century approaches in the belief that literary analysis can have extraliterary application when we recognize that both are informed by the act of interpretation. But, taking my hint from *Rasselas*, I believe that the nature of this process will be more clearly understood if presented in its unfolding by way of a journey through the literature of Samuel Johnson.

PART II

A Literary-Critical Journey

5

Trial and Error
Irene and *London*

IN *RASSELAS,* Johnson successfully applies a dialectic of literary perspectives outside of the literary to the realm of action, to the proper conduct of the choice-of-life quest. When *Rasselas* first appeared, Johnson was nearly fifty years old, in the middle of his writing career. I want now, in this chapter and the next to turn back to his early career to analyze how he designed a linguistic form that pointed beyond the bounds of words. Proper conduct, in a moral and religious sense, is the subject of *The Vanity of Human Wishes,* which appeared a decade before *Rasselas;* the next chapter will demonstrate that in this great poem Johnson first created a literary structure that pertained to the world of action. The present chapter is concerned with two earlier works that prepared the way for the poetic and narrative achievements that followed. My aim here is to demonstrate that the literary technique first manifested in *The Vanity of Human Wishes* and then raised to the level of principle in *Rasselas* developed from the problems that arose in two early works, *Irene* and *London*. In this way it will become clear that *Rasselas* is the key to my approach to Johnson's writings because it marks the first point at which he presented his technique as a method. As we have seen, Johnson formulates himself in educational terms; in converting Rasselas' educational principle into a literary-critical method, I move beyond Johnson and, as will be suggested in the conclusion, arrive at a position that has application to eighteenth-century literature in general.

In 1736 Johnson began *Irene*, his only play, which was completed and revised in 1748 for its first stage appearance a year later. *London,* Johnson's earliest substantial poem, was first published in 1738. Both works are generally regarded as less successful than *The Vanity of Human Wishes* and *Rasselas*. This chapter is not an attempt to revise such an evaluation. Rather, it will demonstrate that the difficulties in *Irene* and *London* result primarily from the attempt to devise a technique for linking the literary with the extraliterary. *Irene* and *London* fail to achieve a balance between these two elements, the play being enclosed in the literary and the poem confined to the extraliterary. Examination of Johnson's early struggle with creative technique will clarify the nature of his achievement in *The Vanity of Human Wishes* (1749), *Rasselas* (1759), and *A Journey to the Western Islands of Scotland* (1775).

Exemplifying opposite kinds of imbalance, *Irene* and *London* will be shown to complement one another. The drama concludes by turning inward, accomplishing formal closure by transcending its own reference; the satire, on the other hand, presents a concrete reference but neglects consideration of its own radical of presentation.[1] Because my view of these two earliest of Johnson's literary endeavors does not alter the prevalent judgment of them, I shall restrict my analysis to selections from each work. My argument is that during this early period of his career Johnson discovered by way of trial and error that the successful expression of his views in literature required a balance between the mimetic and the formal elements, a balance he first achieved in *The Vanity of Human Wishes*.

Detailed scholarship on *Irene* began with David Nichol Smith's essay of 1929, which, in modified form, served as the introduction to the play in the 1941 Clarendon Press edition of *The Poems of Samuel Johnson*, a book so widely consulted that it was revised and reissued in 1974.[2] The nearly two centuries between the first staging of *Irene* and this scholarly landmark have provided less than one hundred pages of commentary.[3] Not surprisingly, Nichol Smith's judgment is still generally accepted: "The mere number of performances is thus in itself no proof that *Irene* had not succeeded on the stage. A more important indication is that neither Garrick nor any other actor thought of reviving it during Johnson's lifetime. Nor, it would appear, has it ever been acted since, though when it was included in Bell's *British Theatre* it was adorned with a frontispiece representing Miss Wallis as Aspasia—a part which she is not known to have played."

Using the terms Johnson applied to Addison's *Cato*, Nichol Smith suggested that the failure of *Irene* resides in its use of "dialogue too declamatory, of unaffecting elegance, and chill philosophy."[4] In 1944, further pursuing the problem of style in *Irene*, Bertrand Bronson concluded that the language fails because it is divorced from the reality of everyday speech.[5] In 1970, Donald Greene modified this position by suggesting that the diction is not flawed but does put off a twentieth-century reader: "the blank verse of *Irene* remains a barrier between the modern reader and what Johnson was trying to do in the play, which was well worth doing."[6] Greene's suggestion that eighteenth-century dramatic conventions impeded understanding of the significance of *Irene* led to two kinds of defense of the play. Shifting attention away from the didactic language and toward the organic structure, Marshall Waingrow in 1965 reminded us that the "heroine of *Irene* is Irene," the purveyor of the tragic theme.[7] Building upon Roy Wolper's historical research, which demonstrated that Johnson understood and appreciated the theater of his day, Philip Clayton, in 1974, asserted that, when properly understood in terms of its period and genre, that of "neo-classic tragedy," *Irene* is "curiously successful."[8] Nevertheless, in the most recent comprehensive study of the play, James Gray, after considering the various close readings of the structure of *Irene* and the research on the history of its genre, concluded in terms reminiscent of Nichol Smith's judgment of over fifty years ago: "It would be comforting after this extensive examination to record a verdict of 'great tragedy manqué' of 'great failure,' but we can only say with Johnson himself that we thought it had been better. The moralist gets in the way of the dramatist."[9]

Twentieth-century scholarship on *Irene* has demonstrated that Johnson understood the drama of his day and has clarified the nature of the stylistic and generic conventions available to him, but the defense of the drama has been unsuccessful. I shall analyze not the linguistic and dramatic conventions but the action or plot, because it highlights the connection between the literary and the extraliterary.

In fact, the plot of *Irene* has been neglected. Although, as recent scholars have rightly pointed out, eighteenth-century conventions of tragedy need to be kept in mind, we should also remember that the source for the Irene story is a historical text that Johnson admired because it subordinated literary technique to the aims of history. In *Rambler* number 122, Johnson laments the lack of good historians in his age; only one work receives his highest praise, Richard Knolles' *The Generall Historie of the Turkes*, the source of *Irene*. "This great historian" is applauded for narrative ability described in the following terms: "A wonderful multiplicity of events is so artfully arranged, and so distinctly explained, that each facilitates the knowledge of the next. Whenever a new personage is introduced, the reader is prepared by his character for his actions; when a nation is first attacked, or city besieged, he is made acquainted with its history, or situation. . . . Collateral events are so artfully woven into the contexture of his principal story, that they cannot be disjoined, without leaving it lacerated and broken" (*Rambler* 122, 4:290).

Johnson admires the way in which Knolles weaves every element of a historical event—people, places, and situation—into a narrative of action. Understandably, Knolles provides the plot of his drama. It is surprising, however, that Johnson selected this particular portion of the *Historie.* At the Turkish invasion of Constantinople in 1453, Irene, a Greek beauty, is captured and eventually becomes the mistress of Mohamet II. Because the Moslem leader neglects his duties and gives all of his attention to the Greek captive, the courtiers become restive. Hearing of this anxiety, Mohamet calls an assembly, explains that their misgivings are unfounded, and demonstrates his point, according to Knolles, in the following way: "And having so said, presently with one of his hands catching the faire Greeke by the haire of the head, and drawing his falchion with the other, at one blow struck off her head, to the great terror of all" (*Poems* 268). Why did Johnson choose this brutal, melodramatic incident as the source of his tragedy about religion? This episode vividly conveys the dilemma of an individual caught in the clutches of historical forces, and Johnson, in my view, was interested in how religious faith would operate in this situation. How could Christianity show Irene an alternative to the fate she suffers in Knolles, an alternative viable for Irene in her historical context? For this reason, Johnson created a new character, Aspasia, who shares Irene's dilemma but survives because she selects the possibility refused by Irene.

Johnson's interest in presenting the apostasy decision in a historical context distinguishes his drama from previous Irene plays: Gilbert Swinhoe's version of 1658, Roger L'Estrange's rendition of 1664, and Charles Goring's *Irene* of 1708. A contemporary drama that shares the same historical situation as *Irene* is Aaron Hill's *Zara.* These two dramas are not usually compared, probably because Hill's title suggests that his drama is patterned after the original French drama, Voltaire's *Zaïre,* a tragedy about religious intolerance, not apostasy. Hill, however, does introduce the question of apostasy; his heroine faces with Johnson's Irene a similar kind of choice in the same historical context. *Zara* was first performed at Drury Lane in 1737. Hill employed stylistic and dramatic conventions available to Johnson in what is essentially the Irene story. But while *Irene* has never been revived during the past two centuries, *Zara* was popular and reappeared on stage in 1742, 1767, 1776, 1796, and 1797.[10] *Zara* thus provides us with a specific example of a successful mid-eighteenth-century drama. Moreover, it is similar in so many respects to *Irene* that we cannot help but wonder if Johnson was influenced by Hill during the period 1738-1749, when *Zara* was part of the repertoire at Drury Lane and *Irene* was being prepared for the stage. *Zara* is, in my opinion, more successful than *Irene* because its heroine combines the characteristics of Irene and Aspasia. Johnson resorted to a double protagonist, a device that had been conventional since the Restoration, because he wished to go beyond the personal consequences of the tragedy to explore its historical dimension.[11]

The religious dilemma of Voltaire's *Zaïre* is different from that of *Zara* and *Irene*. Parted in infancy from her Christian parents and raised in the East, Voltaire's Zaïre has a natural respect for Mohammedanism: her ability to understand the Moslem religion while sympathizing with the Christian faith of her family makes her exemplary of religious tolerance. The tragedy is that her ability to love both man and God cannot prevail against the bigotry of Christians and Moslems: Voltaire shows how sectarianism defeats the soul of religion. Cutting a number of lines on religious tolerance, Hill alters the central issue from the theological problem to the political dilemma of the lovers; he thereby moves the play in the customary direction of the time, toward love and honor, a theme made quite explicit in the last four lines of act 1, which are the creation of the translator:

> Monarchs, by Forms of pompous Misery, press'd,
> In proud, unsocial Solitude unbless'd,
> Would but for Love's soft Influence, curse their Throne,
> And, among crowded Millions, live *alone*.[12]

Moreover, by shifting the emphasis from Voltaire's antisectarianism to the dilemma of love in a situation of political and religious crisis, Hill unites the two elements separated in *Irene*. Irene does not love Mohamet; her motivation for marrying him, to protect herself and her fellow Christians, is clearly political. Johnson transfers the love interest of the plot to Aspasia and Demetrius. Zara, on the other hand, being in love with a Mohammedan, faces both the political dilemma of Irene and the romantic difficulties confronted by Aspasia.

The crisis in Voltaire's *Zaïre* occurs when the heroine discovers among recent prisoners of war her father and brother, who prevail upon her to swear to become a Christian.[13] But having been raised in the East, Zaire knows little about Christianity and does not fully understand the implications of her promise. Hill's Zara, on the other hand, promises not to be an apostate (III.1), a term not in the French play, which suggests that Zara, like Irene, understands the significance of her religious commitment. Thus Zara's promise to her Christian father and her vow of fidelity to the Moslem place her in a situation combining the plights of Aspasia and Irene. Clearly, Hill introduces the apostasy question because it enables him to present his tragedy in terms familiar to the audience of his day—the conflict between love and honor. For this reason, the characters of the translation are motivated not only by love and religious commitment, as in Voltaire, but also by passion for their honor. The most striking of the British alterations to the original drama concerns one of the most famous moments in *Zaïre*. When the heroine is driven to the point of refusing the proposal of marriage offered by her beloved Moslem, her manner of refusal rekindles his love for her. In the translation, the Mohammedan is merely insulted, and for this reason Hill omits one of Voltaire's most famous lines, "Zaïre, vous m'aimez" (IV.2.1161). Most of the characters in Johnson's *Irene* resemble Hill's disloyal Mohammedans, for the action of *Irene* centers on the courtiers conspiring against their Moslem leader.

Typical of such characters is Abdalla, a creation of Johnson's who is crucial to understanding the dénouement of *Irene*. Here we can clearly see the difference between *Zara* and *Irene* by adopting the perspective of the stage directors of these two plays, who had to present the final act so that the death of the protagonists was acceptable to the audience. Hill, here faithful to Voltaire's version, requires that the audience understand how the Moslem, distressed by the postponement of the wedding and unaware that any of the Christian prisoners are relations of Zara, mistakes the hushed words between brother and sister for those of lovers. Johnson, on the other hand, has set a formidable task for the director, his old friend David Garrick. For the resolution of the problem faced by Irene and Aspasia requires making plain to the audience that each is subject to the same factors, since the point is that two women have selected opposite alternatives in what is essentially the same situation. (Possibly Garrick's presentation of the death of Irene on stage, a spectacle so badly received on the first night that it was never again repeated, served to contrast the fate of the apostate with that of the faithful Christian.) The difficulty is to establish a link between the political-religious context (Irene's story) and the religious-love context (Aspasia's story), since those characters having access to one of the heroines are for that very reason kept at a distance from the other.

Abdalla is the one exception. A member of Mohamet's court, he can influence Irene's fate; in love with Aspasia and involved with Demetrius in a conspiracy against Mohamet, he has direct contact with both sides. Clearly, Abdalla can only move freely between the two contexts by way of hypocrisy and treachery, by being willing to turn on his emperor or betray his coconspirators. This Machiavellianism must be defeated and punished; furthermore, such an evil agent must never be seen to overpower the forces of Christian virtue, if the argument against apostasy is to be sustained. In order to alter the controlling agency of the dénouement from villainy to virtue, Johnson introduces contingent and providential circumstances, making the final act extremely intricate, more complex than that of either Voltaire or Hill.

After the death of Zaïre and the revelation that she was the sister, not the lover, of the Christian prisoner, Voltaire's Moslem frees all the

Christians and then kills himself. In *Zaïre* the spirit and magnanimity of the Moslem, in *Zara* his love and honor, ensnare him in the same absolutism and political intrigue that destroyed his beloved. Johnson, on the other hand, resorts to the following intricacies. Foiled in his attempt to poison Aspasia's beloved, Abdalla turns his soldiers against his coconspirator and his Christian allies. Aspasia tries to convince Irene to flee with them, but the apostate believes that the rebellion is crushed and sends her servant to inform on the Christian lovers. Meanwhile, one of the conspirators confesses that the Moslem leader was to have been killed in Irene's bedroom; assuming the apostate's complicity in the conspiracy, the Sultan sends two servants to execute her. These men hesitate until urged on by Abdalla, who withholds the evidence that Irene is innocent, because she knows that he participated in the conspiracy. After Irene is strangled, the executioners explain that they only proceeded against Irene because of Abdalla's encouragement, and the villain is tortured, then executed.

We can perhaps thread our way through this Johnsonian maze by following the path of Abdalla. Once his attempt to poison his Christian rival Demetrius fails, he changes sides, hoping the Moslems will kill the Christian and leave Aspasia for him. To silence Irene, the only person who could expose him to the Sultan, Abdalla fabricates an order from the palace for her execution. Then and only then do Hasan and Caraza kill Irene. At this juncture, however, an attentive audience may well be puzzled. Why do Hasan and Caraza murder their emperor's mistress on the word of Abdalla, a man they know to be a traitor, having themselves informed against him in the previous act (IV.8.8-13)? Surely they should be suspicious of an order from one whom they have recently seen engaged in a treasonable conversation. Johnson, it would seem, has become entangled in the intricacies of his own drama. But the difficulty is instructive. The plot would in no essential respect be changed by cutting the five lines in act 4 exposing Abdalla, who will, in any case, be unmasked at the end of the play. Johnson's problem is that if Abdalla's disloyalty to the Sultan remains unrevealed until the end of the drama, the villain will control the major events of the last act and will be ruined only at the very end of the play. Instead of knowing that Abdalla was doomed from the beginning of the dénouement, the audience would see that evil, in the form of Abdalla, temporarily controlled the situation, a state of affairs that would bolster Irene's argument for the political expediency of apostasy. That evil can at times be a controlling force is not a notion offensive to Johnson's Christianity or unacceptable to eighteenth-century audiences of tragedy, but such potent evil makes it difficult to decide whether Irene or Aspasia made the wiser choice.

If malevolence can at a crucial historical moment control a political situation, apostasy may be justifiable, indeed necessary, as a means to restore to control the forces of virtue and justice.

Of course, most readers and spectators cannot be expected to notice this slight inconsistency. It does, however, highlight an aspect of *Irene* usually neglected: the question of apostasy is meant to be seen in its historical context, as a practical possibility for Irene in the Constantinople of 1453. This point is made at two crucial stages of the drama. In act 2, Mahomet courts Irene with promises of political power, eliciting a response indicating that she is tempted by this possibility:

> MAHOMET: O seize the Power to bless—Irene's Nod
> Shall break the Fetters of the groaning Christian:
> *Greece*, in her lovely Patroness secure,
> Shall mourn no more her plunder'd Palaces.
>
> IRENE: Forbear—O do not urge me to my Ruin!   [II.7.75-79]

Mahomet is clearly suggesting that Irene's conversion could alter the historical position of the Greek Christians. In the next act, Irene uses this same argument in her debate with Aspasia. When advised to think less about the materials of this world and more about the next, Irene asks where Aspasia was when the Turks besieged their city, occasioning the response that a woman's place is not at the battle front. Irene then makes the following eloquent plea for woman as a force in history:

> O! did IRENE shine the queen of *Turkey*,
> No more should *Greece* lament those Prayers rejected.
> Again should golden Splendour grace her Cities,
> Again her prostrate Palaces should rise,
> Again her Temples sound with holy Musick:
> No more should Danger fright, or Want distress
> The smiling Widows, and protected Orphans.   [III.8.51-57]

Unfortunately, we cannot know whether these fine words are a rationalization or a sincere belief. Irene's actions never make clear whether her decision in favor of apostasy is made merely on her own behalf or also as a means of aiding the Greek Christian community. *Irene* creates a context calling for a combination of Aspasia and Irene, steadfast loyalty to virtue and a capacity for concerted action, someone more like Zara than either of Johnson's heroines. Separated from one another, neither Aspasia nor Irene can resolve the dilemma of *Irene*. Zara, on the other hand, never has the historical possibility offered to Irene, for there is no suggestion that Zara could save her own life by choosing apostasy. Hill, like Voltaire, is interested in history for background purposes, as a means of explaining how an exceptional individual is trapped by forces beyond her control. Johnson's problem, in my view, stems from his foregrounding of history in order to pose a new question: what could a steadfast Christian, an Irene who refused apostasy, have done to help the Greek Christians? Aspasia is meant to embody the answer to this question. But at the final crisis she flees from Constantinople, leaving her fellow Christians behind. The apostate remains in Turkey and dies. Although the protagonists' separate fates are clearly demarcated, the drama ends in uncertainty. Could Aspasia have survived in Constantinople, and would her continued presence there have aided the captive Christians? If Irene had decided to leave, would that decision have been motivated by her Christian faith or by the wish to survive? These questions arise because Johnson has created a drama that illustrates how the decisions of key individuals affect the course of human history. The nature of such decisions cannot, however, be resolved by a conclusion concerned solely with those individuals. The larger historical issues must be faced.

To put it another way, in concluding *Irene*, Johnson failed to recognize the nature of his own achievement. The plot of the Irene story has been transformed into the action of history; closure of the tragedy is therefore not sufficient. Johnson's own response to *Irene* near the end of his life is made more comprehensible in these terms. As is well known, upon hearing the drama being read, Johnson left the room, remarking, "I thought it had been better." Another episode related to Johnson's later attitude concerns a man named Pot. Wishing to ingratiate himself with Johnson, Pot is reported to have referred to *Irene* as "the finest tragedy of modern times." Johnson's reply is often cited: "If Pot says so, Pot lies!"[14] Both of these responses suggest a mature author's awareness that in not completing its task, this play does not do justice to itself.

Recent scholars have demonstrated that *Irene* is an organic form, a "neo-classic tragedy." Johnson, however, was dissatisfied with the drama because he sought to create not traditional tragedy but historical tragedy, a fact that becomes apparent in the action of the play. Modern critics neglect this aspect of the tragedy, the action as a mirror of history, because it is a manifestation of mimeticism, an approach to literature that has been largely discarded in our time. I believe that Johnson's work will only be fully appreciated when we are able to account for both the formal and the mimetic elements. But, as has become clear with *Irene,* Johnson's creative struggle suggests how we can set about constructing such a critical method.

If the problem in *Irene* can be described as formal closure achieved by excluding a key element of the historical referent, *London* goes too far in the other direction, sacrificing form to mimesis. Modern critical commentary on *London* consists of attempts to demonstrate ways in which the satire is unsuccessful at achieving organic unity. Comparing the tone of *London* to that of Juvenal's original, Mary Lascelles finds that Johnson's poem "causes none of the vibrations of irony" present in the Latin work. Her comparison between the country estates described near the end of each poem reinforces this distinction: "Johnson turns *hortulus* into a country estate, and Juvenal's sour acceptance of a countryman's life into a little pastoral." This "piece of idealization" presented in a stately manner is intended, according to Lascelles, "to convey a sense of deep contentment" with country life. "In such a mood, [Johnson] might perhaps miss the irony in Juvenal's tale of country pleasures, yet find the denunciation of Rome (to which they had been a merely conventional foil) heartily congenial." Lascelles concludes that "Johnson's *London* has not the brilliance of its original, because it lacks the lightning flash of its irony."[15]

In reply to Lascelles, Howard Weinbrot extends the historical argument first presented in *The Formal Strain: Studies in Augustan Imitation and Satire*, in which he demonstrated that "the assumption that Johnson read Juvenal as we do leads to inappropriate methodology and mistaken literary criticism." In particular, Weinbrot attacks the assumption of Lascelles and a number of other critics that the modern ironic reading of Juvenal's poem was generally known and accepted in Johnson's day. Four kinds of historical evidence are adduced to demonstrate that in the eighteenth century Juvenal's narrator was not seen in ironical terms. Weinbrot does not, however, defend *London* as a successful poem. On the contrary, he argues that the poem is marked by two major flaws: an inconsistent speaker and a lack of structural unity. "Thales is marred by contradiction, suggestions of insincerity, self-pity, self-righteousness, and arrogance. . . . The satiric focus of the poem is also blurred: *London* consists of two alternating and only occasionally interlocking parts, rather than one satiric whole."[16] The problem for Weinbrot is that the country estate presented as an ideal does not adequately resolve the social and political problems of the city. Lascelles and Weinbrot both fault *London* for employing a unifying principle insufficiently comprehensive; the former focuses on the omission of the speaker's tone and the latter on what he describes. Essentially, the debate concerns whether the unifying principle in *London* is London or Thales.

In 1972, D.V. Boyd tried to resolve the critical difference by rising above it. He declared that both Thales and London are encompassed by a "structural level" but that Johnson strives toward a yet higher level, a fact indicated by the metaphorical texture of *London:* "In the chasm between the two infinities, he perceives the London scene as a given and inexplicable fact, a moral landscape in which the inherent miseries of the human condition and the willful perversities of man are inextricably mixed, and one in which satiric discrimination soon becomes an impossible task."[17] The failure of the poem for Boyd resides not in the portrait of London or the character of Thales but in the inability to complete the ascent above such issues: "Ultimately, we are left on our own to decide whether the nation's downfall has been brought about 'by folly or by fate.' " Boyd concludes that the "real context of the poem is therefore less ethical than ontological," for the "alternatives posed are not good and evil but being and nothingness," a problem only fully recognized and resolved at the end of *The Vanity of Human Wishes*. The level of the principle of organic unity is raised from the secular to the religious. But there is no evidence in *London* that Johnson intended to provide a conclusion like that of *The Vanity of Human Wishes*. My own interpretation of *London* does not entail a unifying principle on any level, historical or religious. Rather, I believe that *London* seeks to establish a relationship between a London poet and his poem in order to portray the London of a struggling eighteenth-century poet. The satire, in my view, can only be fully understood if it is seen as employing a formal structure for referential purposes.

Since *London*, like *Irene*, is another of Johnson's early attempts to employ literary form for extraliterary purposes, its innovative quality becomes apparent through comparison to Juvenal's original, John Oldham's imitation, and John Dryden's translation. All four poems begin with a narrator whose sole task is to introduce us to the speaker of the remainder of the satire. The introduction is very important in shaping the reader's attitude toward the speaker of all but the first thirty-four lines of *London* and all but the first twenty lines of *Satura III*.

Juvenal's introduction is divided into two parts. Explaining first that he is saddened by his old friend Umbricius' decision to leave Rome and take up residence in the country, the narrator nevertheless shares Umbricius' dissatisfaction with the city, pointing out that he has himself contemplated a country retreat because of the physical and intellectual degradation of Rome. Then, in the course of accompanying his friend out of the city, the narrator describes some changes that have occurred:

hic, ubi nocturnae Numa constituebat amicae,
nunc sacri fontis nemus et delubra locantur

Iudaeis, quorum cophinus faenumque supellex
(omnis enim populo mercedem pendere iussa est
arbor et eiectis mendicat silva Camenis).
in vallem Egeriae descendimus et speluncas
dissimiles veris. quanto praesentius esset
numen aquis, viridi si margine clauderet undas
herba, nec ingenuum violarent marmora tofum.   [*JIS* 12-20]

This description illustrates the previous comment on the intellectual and physical decline of Rome. At the site where Numa, an ancient King of Rome, recited love poetry, the poor are being exploited by the slightly less poor who collect rent for small plots of ground on which beggars sleep. Moreover, the valley of Egeria now contains more marble than grass; monetary considerations have won out over the country-lover's concern for one of the few pieces of natural landscape remaining in the city.

Oldham—and we should keep in mind that Oldham's version is an imitation, while Dryden's is a translation—changes place names to London, Fleet Street, and Mile-end and calls his speaker Timon, a man who looks back upon London "with just rage." Dryden expands Juvenal's twenty-line introduction to thirty-six lines, adding details about the dilapidated condition of Rome and the decay of its monuments and characterizing the counterpart of Umbricius as "my sullen discontented Friend." Oldham and Dryden accentuate an element only implicit in the Juvenal, that although the narrator sympathizes with his friend, he differs from him in temperament, not being so disillusioned as to move away from the city. Johnson's introduction, however, leads the reader to question the narrator's sympathy with the decision to leave the city:

For who would leave, unbrib'd, *Hibernia's* Land,
Or change the Rocks of *Scotland* for the *Strand*?
There none are swept by sudden Fate away,
But all whom Hunger spares, with Age decay: [*London* 9-12]

The rhyme of "*Strand*" and "Land" suggests that in either city or country people are stranded or isolated from one another; the rhyme of "away" and "decay" implies that any change of place, to or from the country, alters only the form of one's fate, a slow, tedious death in the country or a fast, violent urban end. The distance in Johnson's satire between the narrator and his friend is most pronounced, however, in the following couplet: "While THALES waits the Wherry that contains / Of dissipated Wealth the small Remains" (*London* 19-20). "Dissipated" is a very pejorative term, defined in Johnson's *Dictionary* as "to spend a fortune," and illustrated by the citation of this very line from *London*. Juvenal has no equivalent for the idea of dissipation; "tota domus" is translated by Dryden as "all his Goods" (*DTS* 18) and is omitted by Oldham. Perhaps the dissipaters are the merchants and landlords who exploit Thales, but in view of the previous couplets it seems more likely that the dissipater is Thales himself. After the Valley of Egeria passage, which in *London* becomes a jingoistic and nostalgic catalog of "Britannia's Glories" during the reign of Queen Elizabeth, Johnson concludes his introduction with an image of Thales' posture:

> A transient Calm the happy Scenes bestow,
> And for a Moment lull the Sense of Woe.
> At length awaking, with contemptuous Frown,
> Indignant THALES eyes the neighb'ring Town.   [*London* 31-34]

Johnson's interest in point of view is quite apparent here. Juvenal's narrator hands the poem over to Umbricius without comment: "Hic tunc Umbricius," which Oldham renders in a full line, "Thus, with just Rage, the good old Timon spake" (*OTS* p. 55). Dryden presents a couplet, placing in parentheses his own addition: "Then thus *Umbricius* (With an Angry Frown, / And looking back on this degen'rate Town)" (*DTS* 37-38). Johnson, influenced by Dryden, expands upon the backward look, having Thales turn from the glorious past in order to "eye" the degenerate present. The speaker of *London* awakens from his preoccupation with the past and is placed not, as in Dryden, on the edge of the city looking backward, but outside it altogether, in Greenwich, looking toward "the neighbr'ing Town." What we previously described as fully achieved in *Rasselas*, the dialectic of points of view, is here being attempted, twenty years earlier, in the form of the narrator in London and Thales looking back at the city. However, the nature of the relationship between these viewpoints is not made clear in the poem. How and in what respect does the view of the narrator who remains within relate to Thales' view from without? The picture of the dissipation of "the neighbr'ing Town" is vivid and clear, but we are left in doubt as to how or even if the speaker is implicated in his own urban landscape.

One passage in *London*, however, is devoted to the relationship between Thales and London:

> But hark! th'affrighted Crowd's tumultuous Cries
> Roll thro' the Streets, and thunder to the Skies;
> Rais'd from some pleasing Dream of Wealth and Pow'r,
> Some pompous Palace, or some blissful Bow'r,
> Aghast you start, and scarce with aking Sight
> Sustain th' approaching Fire's tremendous Light:

Swift from pursuing Horrors take your Way,
And leave your little ALL to Flames a Prey;
Then thro' the World a wretched Vagrant roam,
For where can starving Merit find a Home?
In vain your mournful Narrative disclose,
While all neglect, and most insult your Woes.   [*London* 182-93]

The last couplet is particularly suggestive of the dilemma of Thales, who is clearly a destitute poet without hope of being heeded or helped. Juvenal, however, makes no reference to the "Narrative": "ultimus autem / aerumnae est cumulus, quod nudum et frusta rogantem / nemo cibo, nemo hospitio tectoque iuvabit" (*JTS* 209-11). Oldham concludes with a reference to the fact that in case of fire the garret-dweller's only consolation is that his abode will be the last to be burned: "For if the Mischief from the Cellar came, / Be sure the Garret is the last takes Flame" (*OTS* p. 66). In Dryden, the destitute "Codrus" finds in Rome no one to feed him or "take him home."

Johnson, more ambitious than his predecessors, connects Thales to his narration, the speaker in *London* to London, as is indicated by the rhyme of "disclose" and "Woes." Paradoxically, this passage in *London* is a striking description of a city fire but does not successfully complete the relationship between the speaker and his story. The power and originality derive from the image uniting the fire and the crowd: the "Roll" of the latter in the street and of the former through the house combine to pursue the unfortunate poet huddled in his garret. Finally, he loses both his possessions and any hope of finding a friend or concerned listener. The crowd responds to his tale as the fire did to his possessions. The reader of *London*, however, has access to the speaker's tale of wretchedness because of the narrator, the initial presenter of the poem, who has distinguished himself from the speaker's life of dissipation. This marked distinction between the narrator and the speaker leads us to wonder if Thales is unable to manage because he dissipates his income, burning his own possessions. Or do the vividness of the London fire image and others like it confirm the accuracy of Thales' view? Enclosing the narrator's poem within a lively and vivid referential picture of the satirist's dilemma in London, Johnson has lost control of the poem, for the speaker's literary achievement, the poem in process, modifies and complicates the portrait. The result is a series of brilliant insights into eighteenth-century urban literary life but also leaves unanswered questions about the conclusions to be drawn from these perceptions.

The difficulties of *London* become most apparent near the conclusion. A brief examination of two town scenes, one successful and the other unsuccessful, may help illustrate the manner in which the questions about the speaker finally become intrusive. Consider the following example.

> Has Heaven reserv'd, in Pity to the Poor,
> No pathless Waste, or undiscover'd Shore?
> No secret Island in the boundless Main?
> No peaceful Desart yet unclaim'd by SPAIN?
> Quick let us rise, the happy Seats explore,
> And bear Oppression's Insolence no more.
> This mournful Truth is ev'ry where confest,
> SLOW RISES WORTH, BY POVERTY DEPREST:
> But here more slow, where all are Slaves to Gold,
> Where Looks are Merchandise, and Smiles are sold,
> Where won by Bribes, by Flatteries implor'd,
> The Groom retails the Favours of his Lord.   [*London* 170-81]

The first six lines contrast sharply with the final quatrain. The three initial couplets voice a shrill patriotic complaint: the last two couplets are more dense. Mercantile corruption, in lines 178-79, moves from slaves and gold to looks and smiles, and, in the last couplet, bribes and flatteries become favors. The "Lord" at the end recalls the "slaves" of the beginning; the synechdochical progress shows people becoming looks or flatteries, man being reduced to his mercantile postures. Lord and slave alike are victims in a monetary world where humanity is merely another form of merchandise. This degradation explains the most important line of the verse paragraph: "SLOW RISES WORTH, BY POVERTY DEPREST." The patriotic couplets preceding this line function to show us a humane, whole speaker, a man of spirit, who is swallowed up in the commercial maw of London. The image of the city is very penetrating, but the last line, with the probably unintentional double entendre on "retails," raises a question as to whether Thales' tale is itself town merchandise.

Juvenal portrays what one translator has called "pretentious poverty," a social situation in which the free man can only be distinguished from the slave by the amount of money he gives his servants. Umbricius complains of being financially enslaved to the slaves; the alternative to this inverted hierarchy is retirement to the countryside, where slaves are not needed. Although the desire to be above the slaves is itself a symptom of urban life, the reader accepts as accurate the picture of the urbanite who in the countryside will cease to be a slave to slaves. Oldham has essentially the same idea as Juvenal; so too does Dryden, although his translation is more suggestive than the Restoration imitation:

> But here Attir'd beyond our Purse we go,

> For useless Ornament and flaunting Show:
> We take on trust, in Purple Robes to shine;
> And Poor, are yet Ambitious to be fine.   [*DTS* 296-99]

Dryden makes clear by the rhyme in the first couplet that those who "go" to the "show" are implicated in the "show"; the second couplet suggests that success or prosperity in the city requires that one "shine" even if the finery is only borrowed or rented. The only alternative to such false finery is to retreat to the countryside, where one need not shine. The speaker is as involved in this false show as anyone else in the city. Thales, however, begins his equivalent passage with a patriotic declaration not found in Juvenal, Oldham, or Dryden. We cannot therefore be certain whether Johnson's speaker has alienated himself from the city by way of his jingoistic idealism or is the victim of the corruption and cynicism of London.

The distinction between Thales and Umbricius becomes more distinct when they describe their ideal places of retreat in the countryside. Umbricius addresses his friend as if he were a wealthy Roman:

> Si potes avelli circensibus, optima Sorae
> aut Fabrateriae domus aut Frusinone paratur
> quanti nunc tenebras unum conducis in annum.
> hortulus hic puteusque brevis nec reste movendus
> in tenuis plantas facili diffunditur haustu.
> vive bidentis amans et culti vilicus horti,
> unde epulum possis centum dare Pythagoreis.   [*JTS* 223-29]

Again, Dryden's translation is accurate but inspired:

> But cou'd you be content to bid adieu
> To the dear Play-house, and the Players too,
> Sweet Country Seats are purchas'd ev'ry where,
> With Lands and Gardens, at less price, than here
> You hire a darksom Doghole by the year.
> A small convenience, decently prepar'd,
> A shallow Well, that rises in your yard,
> That spreads his easie Crystal Streams around;
> And waters all the pretty spot of Ground.
> There, lift the Fork; thy Garden cultivate;
> And give thy frugal Friends a *Pythagorean* Treat.
> "Tis somewhat to be Lord of some small Ground;
> In which a Lizard may, at least, turn round.   [*DTS* 363-75]

Juvenal suggests at once a healthy, sensible alternative to the city and a deserted bit of dusty ground more suited to lizards than men. His point, and here Dryden and Oldham follow him, is that man naturally craves society and therefore puts up with the problems of the city. Even when these become unbearable, he nonetheless addresses his desire for a quiet country life to another person, a city-dweller. Umbricius' inconsistency is typical, making plain why most people live in cities.

Thales' description of the country lacks this double edge.

> Could'st thou resign the Park and Play content,
> For the fair Banks of *Severn* or of *Trent*;
> There might'st thou find some elegant Retreat,
> Some hireling Senator's deserted Seat;
> And stretch thy Prospects o'er the smiling Land,
> For less than rent the Dungeons of the *Strand;*
> There prune thy Walks, support thy drooping Flow'rs,
> Direct thy Rivulets, and twine thy Bow'rs;
> And while thy Grounds a cheap Repast afford,
> Despise the Dainties of a venal Lord:
> There ev'ry Bush with Nature's Music rings,
> There ev'ry Breeze bears Health upon its Wings;
> On all thy Hours Security shall smile,
> And bless thine Evening Walk and Morning Toil.
> [*London* 210-23]

Juvenal has no equivalent for the pruned walks, twined bowers, and supported flowers. This "seat" seems more appropriate for a countrified dandy or displaced urbanite than a poor poet. Is the man who supports the drooping flowers likely to "Despise the Dainties of a venal Lord"? Has this dweller in the "smiling Land" resigned the "Park and Play," or has he transformed the countryside into a park? Again, Johnson has created a lively, satiric picture of a city-Lord's estate, but we remain in doubt about how it relates to Thales. Is he seriously presenting this "Seat" as his ideal or offering it as an ironic version of a "hireling Senator's" rural garden?

At the conclusion of *London*, therefore, we are confronted with a problem not found in Juvenal. The nature of Johnson's innovation becomes apparent when one compares the final couplets of the four versions of the satire.

> saturarum ego, ni pudet illas,
> auditor gelidos veniam caligatus in agros. [Juvenal]

> And, when you write again, may be of Use
> To furnish Satire for your daring Muse. [Oldham]

> Then, to assist your Satyrs, I will come
> And add new Venom, when you write of *Rome*. [Dryden]

In Virtue's Cause once more exert his Rage,
Thy Satire point, and animate thy Page. [Johnson]

Juvenal's speaker listens to the satire; Oldham's and Dryden's contribute "Venom" to the satire. Thales, however, seems to be in the satire itself, his presence animating the page.[18] Is he not only the provider of material for the poem but also a butt of the satire? As we shall see, when Swedish Charles, in *The Vanity of Human Wishes*, is said to "point a moral," the moral, although his own sentiment, turns upon the King.

The end of *London*, however, raises a new question that it does not resolve. The romanticized image of the country estate directs the irony at the projection of an urbanite exiled to the country. But this satire destabilizes the poem, for the suggestion is that Thales' tale (all but thirty-four lines of *London*) is one of the satirical targets of *London*. At this point, it is well to remind ourselves that no less a satirist than Alexander Pope remarked upon reading *London* that its author would soon be "déterré." No such compliment was lavished on *Irene*. The failure of *London* is a result of the penetration of its satire in implicating Thales, a self-exiled London poet, in his own poem. For this reason, the reader of Johnson's poem feels that a profound picture of literary London has been rendered, one that, in some respects, goes beyond Juvenal's Rome. Pope was moved by this picture, and of course he was correct in judging that its author would soon be known. The achievement of *London* resides in its referential aspect, the extra-literary realm indicated by the poem. For whether one believes that *London* presents Thales' "paysage intérieur" or an urban landscape, an aspect of London has been manifested.

The difficulty is that we have no means in *London* of distinguishing interior from exterior landscape. As previous critics have pointed out, the matter is further complicated by the historical and political situation of 1738. The Licensing Act, mentioned in the poem, which muzzled the theater is but one of many factors affecting the writer during these last years of Walpole's regime, making it impossible to decide who is responsible for Thales' dissipation.[19] To remedy this difficulty, Johnson had to devise a means of inscribing and accounting for the speaker's radical of presentation. In *Rasselas*, as we have seen, he employed the technique of the tale within a tale, which was raised to the level of principle when the tale within a tale was itself inscribed in another interpolated tale. But even in *Rasselas* this principle is manifested in practice, since the theory behind such a technique cannot be explained in the terms available to the eighteenth-century critic. Johnson discovered the utility of this technique in *The Vanity of Human Wishes*, where he was able for the first time to combine the formal properties of *Irene* with the mimetic capacity of *London*. Halfway between *London* (1738) and *Rasselas* (1759), *The Vanity of Human Wishes* (1749) combines the satire of the former with the religious impetus of the latter to demonstrate that the vain choice of life is bound up with the form or manner in which it is presented.

6

Form and Reference
The Vanity of Human Wishes

IN CHAPTER 1 we saw that throughout the nineteenth century and until the middle of the present century *Rasselas* was considered to be a prose version of *The Vanity of Human Wishes*. But recent criticism and scholarship have established that these works are related to separate generic traditions and evince different formal characteristics. In 1969 Howard Weinbrot provided an introduction to the genre of *The Vanity*,[1] that of the imitation, a popular form in the eighteenth century, and in 1975 R.G. Peterson explained how Johnson employed this literary tradition: "Johnson, for all his knowledge of Latin and Greek . . . approached the Classics . . . with an attempt to extract what would be useful or morally elevating for himself and others. With disguise and pretense, with the grotesque and the extravagant, antiquity had intoxicated the mind of Europe and led it into dreams. In Greek and Latin Samuel Johnson found tools he could use superbly, but he did not use them for escape in any dream, rather in that celestial wisdom which 'calms the mind, / And makes the happiness she does not find.' "[2]

As a result of this scholarship, the religious conclusion of *The Vanity of Human Wishes* is now generally believed to be the organizing principle of the poem. In 1975 William Kupersmith demonstrated that Johnson employed a rhetorical structure related to but different from that of Juvenal;[3] in the same year Paul McGlynn located a stylistic microcosm in *The Vanity* that was seen to serve not merely the exigencies of the heroic couplet but also those of Johnson's "broad philosophic structure."[4] In 1976 Lawrence Lipking took this position to its logical conclusion by comparing "The Vision of Theodore" with *The Vanity* to show that they represent two forms of a similar Johnsonian religious idea.[5]

In my view, the study of religion in *The Vanity* has overemphasized the conclusion at the expense of the body of the poem. Of course, the title and the very first couplet make abundantly clear that terrestrial concerns will finally be replaced by celestial consolation. But my interest is in the manner in which Johnson connects the concerns of this world with those of the hereafter, because this procedure creates a context for the axis of perspectives. Furthermore, focusing upon the body of *The Vanity of Human Wishes* reveals the chief source of its originality and greatness. Specifically, in *The Vanity of Human Wishes* Johnson implicates his own perspective *on* vanity *in* the vanity, thereby resolving the problems he faced in *Irene* and *London*. In more theoretical terms, I shall demonstrate that the poem develops a double perspective, a dialectic of its formal and referential aspects, that shows the reader how each human vanity points to a less vain alternative and leads to the celestial consolation at the end of the poem. Discrimination among vanities reveals in *The Vanity* the literary function of religion; in *Rasselas* it becomes a principle of human understanding.

Eighteenth-century imitators adapted an original text to their own day by changing the names of places, people, and any other aspect of the earlier work that was considered dated or inappropriate. The original work was, however, constantly to be kept in mind, if only to emphasize the disparity between past and present. For this reason, in his first imitation, *London*, Johnson included at the foot of each page the passage from Juvenal's *Third Satire* that was being imitated, and in the first edition of *The Vanity of Human Wishes* he indicated by way of footnotes on each page which line numbers of Juvenal's *Tenth Satire* were equivalent to his own. Since the changing of certain key Juvenalian passages is an essential part of Johnson's imitation, I shall compare selections from *The Vanity of Human Wishes* to appropriate sections of *Satura X* to demonstrate how the eighteenth-century poem develops a different moral attitude and more hopeful themes than the Roman satire. A Restoration version of *Satura X*, the translation by John Dryden, published in 1693, will also be referred to because Johnson was often influenced by Dryden. But the imitation goes beyond the art of translation. While employing certain of Dryden's linguistic changes, Johnson locates his satire firmly in England and diverges most radically from Dryden in that he does not preserve Juvenal's conclusion.

In fact, Johnson's originality begins to emerge at the outset. The opening section of *The Vanity of Human Wishes* differs markedly from that of Juvenal in both attitude and tone.[6] *Satura X* begins by reminding us that throughout the world few people listen to reason.

Most men are driven by their desires and fears even though they see around them people who have been or are being ruined by similar irrational impulses. Great orators are continually displaced by the eloquent animosity of the opposition, and the wealthy man's position is coveted in spite of its precariousness. Juvenal implies that this thoughtless behavior is seen for what it is by the satirist and by us while reading him, but that when once again involved in our daily routine, we forget the absurdity and futility of such desires. These first lines make no mention of an observer[7] or of the perspective from which the world is seen. Dryden begins with the phrase "Look round" (*DSX* 1), introducing a spectator whose range of vision is wide but not above that of the rest of mankind. Johnson personifies observation: "Let Observation with extensive View / Survey Mankind from *China* to *Peru*" (*VHW* 1-2). This famous opening couplet was much criticized in the nineteenth century for being redundant.[8] Commentators argued that an "extensive view" is already implicit in the personification of observation and that the phrase "from *China* to *Peru*" is merely a geographical variation on the word "Mankind." Johnson expands into a couplet this single line by Dryden: "Look round the Habitable World" (*DSX* 1). "Look" becomes the first line of *The Vanity*, and "round the Habitable World" is lengthened to "Survey Mankind from *China* to *Peru*."

Johnson's expansion serves to recommend more than the momentary "Look" urged by Dryden: his reader must examine searchingly and (in line 2) raise himself above in order to include within his range both the Far East (China) and the Far West (Peru). In his *Dictionary*, Johnson defines "survey" as: "To overlook; to have under view; to view as from a higher place," and the manuscript version of *The Vanity of Human Wishes* contains the word "o'erlook" in place of the later emendation "survey."[9] While Juvenal invites his audience to pause from its daily toil and take note of its human folly, and Dryden begins to separate the viewer from the viewed, Johnson completes the process, establishing a separate vantage point above vanity, one which, as will soon become clear, serves to expose vanity in a special way while not itself remaining immune to vanity. That Johnson's first couplet is not redundant can be demonstrated by noting what this new point of view discloses. Combining elements of Dryden and Juvenal, Johnson displays an original scene:

> Then say how Hope and Fear, Desire and Hate,
> O'erspread with Snares the Clouded Maze of Fate,
> Where wav'ring Man, betray'd by vent'rous Pride,
> To tread the dreary Paths without a guide,

As treach'rous Phantoms in the Mist delude,
Shuns fancied Ills, or chases airy Good. [*VHW* 5-10]

Engulfed by numerous abstract and personified nouns ("Hope,"
"Fear," "Desire," "Hate," and others), a man struggles in a "Maze,"
seemingly entrapped by the words surrounding him. There is, after
all, nothing more substantial here than such "Phantoms" as "fancied
Ills" and "airy Good." Yet there is some substance, for mists, although
not delusions, do delude. The words "clouded" and "Mist" are derived
from Juvenal's image of the cloud of error: "pauci dinoscere pos-
sunt / vera bona atque illis multum diversa, remota / erroris nebula"
(*JSX* 2-4). Omitting any reference to external phenomena, Dryden
asserts that man's fate results from his own passions: "how void of
Reason are our Hopes and Fears!" (*DSX* 3). Although portraying men
as incapable of true discernment, Juvenal implies that they are
blinded not merely by inner passions but also by the external "erroris
nebula." Johnson's "clouded Maze," beset by the snares of our own
hopes and fears, combines Dryden's notion of man's responsibility for
his fate with the external element stressed by Juvenal. This combination of the Classical and Restoration positions suggests that human
vanity has an inner and an outer aspect: a double perspective will be
required of the reader to perceive both. Johnson's passage is less
submissive and resigned to man's errors than the corresponding lines
in Juvenal and less emphatic than Dryden's concerning the divorce
between reason and emotion.

But one important element of Juvenal's and Dryden's opening
lines is omitted by Johnson. Juvenal's "cenacula," Dryden's "Garret"
has no parallel in *The Vanity of Human Wishes* "Rarus venit in
cenacula miles" (*JSX* 18) is translated as "The Mob, Commission'd by
the Government, / Are seldom to an Empty Garret, sent" (*DSX*
27-28). For Dryden and Juvenal, man's folly is chiefly found in the
world at large, in the scramble for money and prestige. The poor
inhabitant of the garret is left in peace because he owns nothing
worth stealing. Omitting any mention of the garret, Johnson implies
that retirement and seclusion offer no relief; nor is the impoverished
man free, as he was in the earlier poems, to study from afar the bustle
of life. By implication, the observer with extensive view—the occu-
pant of the garret in Dryden and Juvenal—has, in *The Vanity of
Human Wishes*, lost his privileged position. Johnson has set for himself a more ambitious task than that of his predecessors, for the poet's
own perspective, the poetic process itself, is to be implicated in the
poem, as becomes most clear in my ensuing analysis of the "young
enthusiast" passage. For this reason, Johnson's labyrinth of fate com-

bines the errors of judgment seen in *Satura X* with the blindness of passion portrayed in *Satire X*.

> How rarely Reason guides the stubborn Choice,
> Rules the bold Hand, or prompts the suppliant Voice,
> How Nations sink, by darling Schemes oppress'd
> When Vengeance listens to the Fool's Request.   [*VHW* 11-14]

This quatrain moves from microcosm to macrocosm: the subject of the first couplet is the individual, that of the second is nations. Rulers are as unreasonable as their subjects, fool or suppliant. The irrational is as apparent in the actions of the one as in the schemes of the other.

Juvenal and Dryden concentrate on the desire for wealth, which both feel is the most pervasive and most ruinous of all evils; Johnson examines the nature of several passions.

> Fate wings with eve'ry Wish th' afflictive Dart,
> Each Gift of Nature, and each Grace of Art,
> With fatal Heat impetuous Courage glows,
> With fatal Sweetness Elocution flows,
> Impeachment stops the Speaker's pow'rful Breath,
> And restless Fire precipitates on Death.   [*VHW* 15-20]

"Th' afflictive Dart," a phrase found in neither Dryden nor Juvenal, is reminiscent of Milton's "fatal dart" (*Paradise Lost* 2.786). The fatal arrow, at once internal and external, turns our own wishes, gifts, and graces upon us; to use a metaphor Johnson borrowed from Waller, the eagle is "shot with an arrow feathered from his own wing." Impeachment puts a stop to powerful breath by means of powerful breath, and heated courage expires in the fiery duel or battle. Vanity is inherent in any human wish, not simply in those uninformed or hastily formed. The "Knowing" and the "Bold" in *The Vanity of Human Wishes* "Fall in the gen'ral Massacre of Gold" (*VHW* 21-22); neither intelligence nor valor is immune to this most pervasive of follies. In his introduction, Johnson eliminates reason and moderation, the worldly alternatives to vanity suggested by his predecessors. Observation informed by reason has its function in *The Vanity of Human Wishes*; lines 21-28 expose the self-defeating obsession with gold so prevalent that it is "scarce observed." But in the following passages, Johnson reveals how informed observation is also subject to vanity. This added dimension explains why the "needy Traveller" passage is twice the length of that in Juvenal, who portrays his "viator" in the following manner:

> pauca licet portes argenti vascula puri
> nocte iter ingressus, gladium contumque timebis

et motae ad lunam trepidabis harundinis umbram:
cantabit vacuus coram latrone viator.   [*JSX* 19-22]

In the moonlight, the sheen of the silver plate is indistinguishable
from the glimmer of the sword, and the figure of the trembling
traveler blends in with the tall wavering reed. Indeed, the juxtaposition of the bandit's weapons and the victim's fear ("gladium con-
tumque timebis") brings together the sword, cudgel, and shivering
man, respectively, shimmering, shaking, and quaking. Both the pos-
sessor and the pursuer of silver are apprehensive in the dim light that
veils the distinction between sword and silver, offensive and defensive
agents. But unlike the man who carries even a few possessions, the
pauper ("vacuus viator") faces the outlaw at close quarters ("coram")
so that the latter can see that there is nothing to be gained. At the end
of the passage, literally and lexically, the outlaw and the penniless
traveller meet ("latrone viator"). Relaxedly, the latter sings; the former, although holding the sword, is silent and tense. In a world
marked by constant strife over possessions, only the pauper is secure.

Devoting a couplet to the "Beggar," Dryden implies that his
fearlessness enables him to reach his destination without being way-
laid: "The Beggar Sings, ev'n when he sees the place / Beset with
Thieves, and never mends his Pace" (*DSX* 33-34). Johnson's "Traveller" is at first carefree, like Dryden's beggar, and then becomes
anxious, like the Juvenalian wayfarer bearing his few valuables. The
shift from one of these conditions to the other is established by way of
the second couplet in the following quotation, a couplet without an
equivalent in *Satura X* or *Satire X*.

The Needy Traveller, serene and gay,
Walks the wild Heath, and sings his Toil away.
Does Envy seize thee? crush th' upbraiding Joy,
Encrease his Riches and his Peace destroy,
Now Fears in dire Vicissitude invade,
The rustling Brake alarms, and quiv'ring Shade,
Nor Light nor Darkness bring his Pain Relief,
One shews the Plunder, and one hides the Thief.   [*VHW* 37-44]

Here Johnson has introduced a new vanity, for "thee" envies not the
state of the bearer of the "Paltry Plate" (*DSX* 30) but that of the
beggar. The singing pauper who alone enjoys security in Juvenal and
Dryden is an object of envy in Johnson. Indigence has here become a
coveted possession.[10] To inquire why need excites envy is to confront
again the issue I have already discussed at length. For my present
purpose, it need only be recalled that envy for Johnson is "the hope of

alleviating the sense of our disparity by lessening others, although we gain nothing to ourselves."

A comparison between the first portions of these three satires indicates that Johnson has created a clear perspective for the surveyor of vanity in order to investigate how that observer is related to the vanity he perceives. In involving himself in the vanity of his poem, the narrator of *The Vanity* distinguishes himself from his equivalent in *London* and, by implication, commits himself to demonstrating how his own literary process is a kind of vanity. At the same time, the obverse is also implied. The pervasiveness of all terrestrial vanity is pursued to arrive at celestial consolation; the end of *The Vanity of Human Wishes* includes its own literary process among the vanities.

At this point, we should recognize that by way of envy Johnson has introduced a new kind of vanity, one which, because it can be located in agent and/or object, implicates not only the poet but also his reader. The observing reader may be envied for his detachment or may feel envious of the carefree beggar. An axis of viewpoints on the level of reading now emerges, reminiscent of that noted in the marriage debate of *Rasselas*. The difference between the two works is that in *Rasselas* the points of view concern knowledge; in *The Vanity of Human Wishes*, the issue, a moral one, is whether you covet the carefree posture of the pauper or the repose of the observer of the pauper. But now that it is clear that the observer *qua* observer can be involved in what he observes, why should he attempt to view vanity from the perspective of "Observation with extensive view"? To answer this question, Johnson calls upon Democritus, the classical satirist, to survey the vanity of the present:

> Once more *Democritus,* arise on Earth,
> With chearful Wisdom and instructive Mirth,
> See motley Life in Modern Trappings dress'd
> And feed with varied Fools th' eternal Jest: [*VHW* 49-52]

Democritus plays a more complex role in the imitation than he does in the original or in the translation. In the two earlier versions, the satirical philosopher is a figure from the past who finds in modern society new causes for laughter. But in the imitation, as a figure from classical antiquity viewing the present, Democritus not only laughs at modern follies but also is symbolic of imitation itself, the juxtaposition of the past and the present. Johnson's title indicates that Democritus' classical perspective will have a moral and Christian function, one that will move beyond the ironies of Juvenal's *Satura X*. What will the ancient philosopher do in eighteenth-century England that

will guide us beyond classical satire? How will he employ his characteristic "eternal Jest?"

> How wouldst thou [Democritus] shake at Britain's modish Tribe,
> Dart the quick Taunt, and edge the piercing Gibe?
> Attentive Truth and Nature to descry,
> And pierce each Scene with Philosophic Eye.   [VHW 61-64]

This "Philosophic Eye" represents the position taken by the poem
toward the various vanities; the stance of the imitation itself is among
the British vanities.[11]

The most vivid of the first vanities shown to Democritus is,
significantly, an image within an image, that of the response of the
people to the frequent changes of the portraits of great men hung in
the "Palladium."

> For now no more we trace in ev'ry Line
> Heroic Worth, Benevolence Divine:
> The Form distorted justifies the Fall,
> And Detestation rids th' indignant Wall.   [VHW 87-90]

The vanity described here concerns a superficial view of vanity, a
perception that involves form devoid of content, the portrait rather
than the inner man. That one has fallen from favor is here deemed
sufficient evidence of vanity, an evaluation as vain, spiritless, and
lacking in benevolent concern for worth as is the location of the
portrait, the wall. Johnson thus confronts Democritus with a problem
not presented to him by Juvenal. How are we to awaken "Britain" to
the fact that in justifying anyone's fall (of fortune) in terms of "Form"
alone—in seeing the defeat of any man as exemplary of his vanity—
"she" prevents herself from "Sign[ing] her Foes Doom, or guard[ing]
her Fav'rites zeal"? In response, the passage concludes with a savage
picture of British elections, which should represent the opportunity
for men to discriminate between inner "human Worth" and outward
vanity.

> Our supple Tribes repress their Patriot Throats,
> And ask no Questions but the Price of Votes;
> With Weekly Libels and Septennial Ale,
> Their Wish is full to riot and to rail.   [VHW 95-98]

A privilege almost unique to the British at the time, the vote, is
abused, preparing the reader for the alternative—what might be
called the poetic election process, the search for less vain alternatives.

Having arrived at this new British vanity and the implicit promise of
a remedy for it, Johnson displays Wolsey for Democritus' scorn. This

first lengthy section of *The Vanity of Human Wishes* devoted to an individual is the equivalent of the Sejanus section in *Satura X*. The emperor Tiberius having retired to Capri, Sejanus, left in charge of Rome, plots to displace his superior and is eventually sentenced to death. Juvenal calls attention to two facets of this ambitious man's fall: the destruction of his personal monument and the fickleness of his followers.

> iam strident ignes, iam follibus atque caminis
> ardet adoratum populo caput et crepat ingens
> Seianus, deinde ex facie toto orbe secunda
> fiunt urceoli pelves sartago matellae.   [*JSX* 61-64]

The dismemberment and destruction of the statue have both historical and symbolic significance. Torn to pieces by his executioners, Sejanus was also totally consumed by the desire for material self-aggrandizement. His career is therefore fittingly compared to the fall of the massive, top-heavy statue, for he did little but amass a fortune. His subjects merely followed his example in treating his brass monument as a source of wealth and scrambling for fragments of metal. Sejanus was as soulless as his own metallic image. But the conversation after his fall is extremely animated:

> "quae labra, quis illi
> vultus erat! numquam, si quid mihi credis, amavi
> hunc hominem. sed quo cecidit sub crimine? quisnam
> delator? quibus indicibus, quo teste probavit?"
> "nil horum; verbosa et grandis epistula venit
> a Capreis." "bene habet, nil plus interrogo."   [*JSV* 67-72]

Bowing to Caesar, the crowd claims to have disapproved of his appointed minister and is therefore as disloyal to Sejanus as he himself was to Tiberius. Yet they survive and he perishes. The infidelity tolerated and even expected of the "rabble" is intolerable in a leader.

But Sejanus contributes to his own downfall by drawing attention to his egotism, by ordering the construction of his ostentatious monument. Like a massive statue, Sejanus' ambition towers above that of the emperor's other subjects and is therefore sufficiently conspicuous to be seen by Tiberius in Capri. A fitting monument to pretentious ambition, it tumbles from excessive weight and height.

Developing this metaphor, Dryden declares that the Roman "Rais'd a Top-Heavy Tow'r, of monstrous height, / Which Mould'ring, crush'd him underneath the Weight" (*DSX* 170-71). First mentioned in the translation, the deteriorating foundation of the monument represents the corruption of Sejanus' constituency, the "people," who are fickle, as in Juvenal, and "degenerate and base," actively participating in overthrowing the "first Minister of State." Dryden's addition, the power of the mob, reflects his concern about the political instability of the Restoration.

Although Johnson alters the subject of this section from Sejanus to Wolsey, he retains both Juvenal's toppling tower and Dryden's corrupt foundation. Cardinal Wolsey is a historical figure who would have been known to most readers of Johnson's day from Shakespeare's *Henry VIII*.[12] In the play, he is portrayed as a shrewd man of inordinate ambition who falls when the king discovers that the prelate kept more for himself than he gave to the state. After his disgrace, Wolsey retired to Cawood—referred to in the poem as "the Refuge of Monastic Rest" (*VHW* 118) because, although not technically a monastery, it was the residence of the Archbishop of York—where he engaged in a conspiracy against the King and was arrested. Wolsey's final speech in Shakespeare's play was doubtless familiar to Johnson: "Had I but serv'd my God with half the zeal / I serv'd my King, he would not in mine age / Have left me naked to mine enemies" (III.2.455-58).

Shakespeare balances the king's perfidy and the cardinal's lack of faith. For Johnson, however, the latter predominates. Wolsey's final reproach concerns only the king (*VHW* 120). Unlike the drama, the poem does not mention God, a conspicuous omission from the last words of a churchman. Sejanus, a secular figure marked by ambition and blind greed, is replaced by an intelligent but proud prelate. If Sejanus in *Satura X* is the man made brass, then Wolsey is the statue become flesh:

> In full-blown Dignity, see *Wolsey* stand,
> Law in his Voice, and Fortune in his Hand:
> To him the Church, the Realm, their Pow'rs consign,
> Thro' him the Rays of regal Bounty shine,   [*VHW* 99-102]

At the height of his career, this man held powers unequalled by an English subject before or since. "Alter Rex," as he was called, the butcher's son from Ipswich became Lord High Chancellor as well as papal legate and was reputed to be the richest man in all Christendom.

Johnson describes Wolsey's disgrace in terms similar to those of Dryden. The king and his followers act in concert but for no apparent reason: "At length his Sov'reign frowns—the Train of State / Mark the keen Glance, and watch the Sign to hate" (*VHW* 109-10). The courtiers resemble Dryden's "Mob," not needing a reason to hate the first minister of state. Like the Roman Sejanus, the English prelate is overtly ambitious; like the Restoration Sejanus, he is surrounded by degenerate followers. But unlike Tiberius' favorite, Wolsey is a clever and adroit diplomat. Another question therefore arises:

> For why did *Wolsey* near the Steeps of Fate,
> On weak Foundations raise th' enormous Weight?
> Why but to sink beneath Misfortune's Blow,
> With louder Ruin to the Gulphs below?   [*VHW* 125-28]

The phrase "near the Steeps of Fate" has puzzled some editors who believe it to be inferior to an earlier version, "near the Steps of Fate."[13] It seems to me that Johnson changed the phrase because the first version implied predestination, while the revision suggests doom not in the classical sense but in the everyday meaning of the word. Wolsey is doomed not because he climbs the preordained steps of fate but because anyone who approaches too near is likely to fall because of the steepness. To demystify the descent—it is a predictable political occurrence, not an act of the gods—raises another question. Why does Wolsey not see the obvious peril? After all, any prelate who gains political power is subject to reversal, a fact that only underlines the transitory nature of temporal power.

Here we come to understand why Johnson considers Wolsey *after* his fall from political favor, thereby introducing an entirely new issue:

> With Age, with Cares, with Maladies oppress'd,
> He seeks the Refuge of Monastic Rest.
> Grief aids Disease, remember'd Folly stings,
> And his last Sighs reproach the Faith of Kings.   [*VHW* 117-20]

Sejanus is never shown reacting to his disgrace, but the important moment for a Christian is that of adversity. Wolsey ends his life with none of the piety one would expect in a man of his calling. He does not even attempt to adopt the appearance of holiness. Furthermore, Wolsey compounds his political errors by plotting with Charles V and François I against Henry VIII.[14]

Mary Lascelles finds Juvenal's portrait of Sejanus to be more successful than its counterpart in *The Vanity of Human Wishes*:

> Juvenal's approach to the fall of Sejanus is tactically unsurpassable. He makes eavesdroppers of us: we listen sometimes to the nobles, sometimes to the populace, sometimes to the poet himself; we overhear fragments of whispered or muttered talk, scraps of eye witness reports—rumors, hints, allusions, in the voices of those concerned in the final crash. This it is (the voices suggest) to be an emperor's favourite; yet who would have the resolution to refuse, or strength to abide by

the consequences of refusal? . . . Johnson's tale . . . proceeds
as simple narration, in the single voice of the poet, and the
tone of that voice is grave, compassionate, devoid of irony.[15]

This statement does not do justice to Johnson's portrait. Juvenal
(and it should be noted that Dryden follows him) is describing the
brutal destruction of a tyrant by the masses. The various voices of the
crowd, all speaking against the defeated leader, represent collective
tyranny. Wolsey, a man protected by the church, is less vulnerable to
popular despotism. The "single voice" that Lascelles finds devoid of
irony is, in fact, the vehicle of Johnson's irony. The narrator adopts the
tone of a preacher because Wolsey's entire career can be appropriately
"heard" as part of a sermon on the distinction between temporal and
spiritual power. Yet the poet, not the cardinal, delivers the homily: it
is Wolsey's neglect of religious principles that makes his end so bitter
and his career fit material for satire. The Church can withstand the
perfidy of the sovereign and the loss of such of its ornaments as he
considers himself to be.

The vocabulary of this section of *The Vanity of Human Wishes* is
an important indication of how the observer's philosophic eye (and
ear) points the way toward an alternative to Wolsey's bitter end. Ian
Jack attends to the "rhetorical skill" here, characterizing the language as abstract, aiming at "the grandeur of generality. What could
be simpler? *The* + generalized adjective + generic noun."[16] This
formulation, however, is itself too simple. The rhetoric in this part of
the poem is not general but "sublime." The language is specific but
elevated—for example, "Steeps," "Gulphs," "Heights," "Tow'r," "regal
Palace." Marjorie Nicolson and Samuel Monk have endeavored to
explain the eighteenth-century conception of the sublime in different
ways, but the double perspective evoked by Johnson requires both
concepts of the sublime. Nicolson, in *Mountain Gloom and Mountain
Glory*, seeks to show that the "rhetorical sublime" formulated by
Longinus had less and less influence in Augustan England and was
finally displaced by the "natural sublime," a response to certain
kinds of rural landscapes.[17] Monk, on the other hand, believes that
during this same period the rhetorical sublime gradually blended
and interacted with the natural sublime.[18]

In fact, Johnson uses these two types of sublime vocabulary in a
more complex way than is defined by either Monk or Nicolson. The
rhetorical sublime is employed in the description of Wolsey's station,
the "Dignity" of his "awful State," the "golden Canopy," the "glitt'ring
Plate," and his "liv'ried Army." The natural sublime appears in the
fall from the "Steeps" to the "Gulphs" below. The two are neither
blended nor separated but related dialectically. Wolsey's fall from his

lofty station arouses in the reader both respect for the position and amazement at the completeness of his defeat. Inured to the excesses of power, to the accoutrements presented in the rhetorical sublime, the Cardinal had to be reminded of the sublimity of his responsibility by way of a natural experience, a fall from power to the abyss below. Johnson employs the two forms of the sublime to establish a dialectic of viewpoints, the one permitting us to look up at "full blown" Wolsey and the other enabling us to look down at the Cardinal in the "Gulphs below."

But at this point Johnson adds a section to the Wolsey episode that has no equivalent in his predecessors' poems and is directly connected to the reader's point of view toward Wolsey:

> Speak thou, whose Thoughts at humble Peace repine,
> Shall *Wolsey's* Wealth, with *Wolsey's* End be thine?
> Or liv'st thou now, with safer Pride content,
> The wisest Justice on the Banks of *Trent*?   [*VHW* 121-24]

Wolsey is not condemned for his proud ambition: that vanity is to be found in abundance in the provinces, on the "Banks of Trent," and few achieve power without it. But a Cardinal at court in London must expect that his eminence will be brief and realize that "the Doom of Man [will not be] revers'd for thee." Wolsey's reproach of the king contains a tacit awareness of this truth, but in his case it leads to bitterness and political machination rather than renewed faith. Johnson uses the viewpoint of the justice on the banks of the Trent to reveal Wolsey's axis of perspectives in history, to show that the Cardinal's response to his own vanity is what produces his final degradation. Johnson broadens the scope of the satire, including within the framework of vanity the process of responding to vanity that unfolds in the episode.

For this reason, the next section concerns the "young Enthusiast," whose vanity involves essentially the point of view adopted by an intelligent reader of the Wolsey passage. Juvenal begins his equivalent section with a schoolboy, not a university entrant, thereby emphasizing the small and dependent state of the student. The change from a schoolboy to a university student enables Johnson to introduce a perspective on his own perspective. The Oxford entrant discovers his goals above him: "O'er *Bodley's* Dome his future Labours spread, / And *Bacon's* Mansion trembles o'er his Head" (*VHW* 139-40).

The ascent is difficult and arduous, fraught with the temptations of "Kindness," "Praise," "Novelty," and "Beauty." Even if he remains unmoved by this dazzling array of distractions and achieves the level of Bodley's Dome, he will find the following below him:

Deign on the passing World to turn thine Eyes,
And pause awhile from Letters to be wise;
There mark what Ills the Scholar's Life assail,
Toil, Envy, Want, the Patron, and the Jail.   [*VHW* 157-60]

In addition to these material "Ills," the scholar must also accept obscurity. Recognition for his work will occur, if ever, after his death, and the tribute to his "buried Merit" will probably not be appreciation of his contribution but a "tardy Bust."

Johnson's other well-known version of this notion is in the prologue to *Comus* occasioned by the performance of the masque in 1751 for the purpose of raising money for Milton's last surviving relative. Here Johnson points out that although the poet finally has been recognized after his death, his indigent granddaughter is neglected:

While Crowds aloft the laureat Bust behold,
Or trace his Form on circulating Gold,
Unknown, unheeded, long his Offspring lay,
And Want hung threat'ning o'er her slow Decay.
[*Poems* 137-38.23-26]

The bust and the image on the coin are of little use to the poet's needy family. After the enthusiast in *The Vanity* has cultivated his ray of reason and is thereby enabled to "pour on misty Doubt resistless Day" (*VHW* 146), he will see sad spectacles like that of Milton's granddaughter, which represent the neglect of literary merit. Upon rereading this section, Johnson burst into tears[19], a response understandable in that the vanity being described is that of the poet/narrator. Cognizance of vanity may point the way toward less vain alternatives but can provide no escape from the vanity of all human endeavor. The phrase "nor think the Doom of Man revers'd for Thee" has become part of an inner dialogue.

The final and most devastating vanity of learning resides in its highest achievement, however rare. Should the young enthusiast master his subject and communicate it to others in his lifetime, he may then be victimized for spreading the truth, like Laud, whose "fatal Learning" led him "to the Block" (*VHW* 172). In the terms of the perspective advanced by the poem itself, the young enthusiast's training enables him to discover what would have been a less vain "choice of life" for Wolsey, but Wolsey would probably have responded to the enthusiast's knowledge not as disinterested learning but as a threat to his power. The vanity Johnson finally arrives at involves the function of the axis of perspectives in the ever-changing world of human contingency, where the scholar's insight is, from one point of view, truth, and, from another, a menace to established political figures.

Thus, the question becomes how the enlightened perspective upon vanity can prevail, can have any effect on the "passing world," if it is cultivated by those like the university student who have no political power. This issue is central in the most famous passage of *The Vanity of Human Wishes*, that devoted to Charles XII, King of Sweden. Charles replaces Hannibal in the original because of a similarity in their military careers. During the Second Punic War, Hannibal three times achieved the seemingly impossible: he crossed the Pyrenees, scaled the Alps, and defeated the numerically superior Romans at the battle of Cannae. Finally, the wheel of fortune turned. The Romans gradually crushed the Carthaginian army, and Hannibal fled to Bithynia, where he was pursued and finally resorted to suicide. Swedish Charles, before reaching the age of tweny, miraculously defeated Denmark, Poland, and Russia. He was finally overpowered by Peter the Great at the battle of Pultowa but escaped to Turkey. Undaunted after six years of exile, he returned home to gather some troops for an invasion of Norway, where he was killed by a stray bullet from either his own camp or that of the enemy.

In spite of Hannibal's military victories, Juvenal presents him as a ridiculous figure: "O qualis facies et quali digna tabella, / cum Gaetula ducem portaret belua luscum!" (*JSX* 157-58). Perched upon an elephant, one of the many unfortunate beasts he has driven from Africa, first to Spain, then over the Pyrenees and the Alps into Italy, the half-blind, monomaniacal leader pits himself against the vast forces of nature. "additur imperiis Hispania, Pyrenaeum / transilit; opposuit natura Alpemque nivemque: / diducit scopulos et montem rumpit aceto" (*JSX* 151-53). Juvenal further diminishes Hannibal's exploits by physically weighing them: "expende Hannibalem; quot libras in duce summo / invenies?" (*JSX* 147-48). Placing Hannibal in the scale of posterity is apt, since he strove throughout his life against containment, bursting the boundaries of Africa, Spain, and Italy. Having given himself entirely to overcoming physical limitations, he is epitomized by his weight in the scales of history.

Moreover, his career is symbolized by the poison ring that ended it. Hannibal searched constantly for the unsurpassable, and his enemies had only to wait for him to find it. Juvenal makes the obsessive desire to break down barriers worthy of our scorn because it invariably leads to the achievement of its goal, finding that which it cannot overcome.

Beginning with the image of "Great *Hannibal* . . . whom *Affrick* was not able to contain" (*DSX* 234, 236), Dryden develops the spectacle of a man attempting to conquer the world itself.

> *Spain* first he won, the *Pyreneans* past,
> And steepy *Alps*, the Mounds that Nature cast:
> And with Corroding Juices, as he went,
> A passage through the living Rocks he rent.   [*DSX* 242-45]

Having burst through the Alps, "like a Torrent, rowling from on high, / He pours his head-long Rage on Italy" (*DTS* 246-47). The torrent image transforms the man into a force of nature and leads to a change of tone. Dryden turns from the geography of Hannibal's feats to the man himself, a paltry figure, one "A Sign-Post Dawber wou'd disdain to paint" (*DTS* 254). Hannibal's fame resides not in his conquest of foreign peoples but in his defiance of nature. Crossing the highest and most perilous mountains in Europe, Hannibal led his forces into devastating defeat.

Dryden's Hannibal treats people as if they were mere physical obstacles: in neglecting humanity he has, in the deepest sense, ceased himself to be human. Johnson, again influenced by Dryden, pursues the human side of the warrior. Swedish Charles' distinguishing mark as a military leader was his great personal dignity. His career was well known in the eighteenth century; Voltaire's biography, the *Histoire de Charles XII*, available in English by 1731, was widely circulated in *Read's Weekly Journal* and was probably known to Johnson.[20] Voltaire portrays Charles' fall as the consequence not of any fault but of excessive virtue.[21]

Johnson's description of Charles is greatly admired; in fact, a number of commentators feel that it is "tragic."[22] The texture of the language is certainly rich and merits detailed analysis. The final couplet, for instance, is justly celebrated: "He left the Name, at which the World grew pale. / To point a Moral, or adorn a Tale" (*VHW* 221-22). This coda contains two seemingly contradictory notions. On the one hand, the story of Charles is exhilarating; the reader grows pale in awe and respect for the "Name" or reputation of this king even as the "World," during his lifetime, was frightened and amazed by his deeds. On the other hand, all that now remains of this dynamic, powerful warrior is his name in a didactic story, a "Tale" that can be but a "pale" imitation of the vigorous historical activity it depicts. In fact, all Charles' victories were nullified even before his death: at the end of his life, he had less territory than his father had originally bequeathed to him. In a very literal sense, the warrior's great feats are to be found only in history books or moral tales like that contained in *The Vanity of Human Wishes*.

These two perspectives function contrapuntally. In less than a decade, a young king created a military reputation for himself that has seldom been surpassed. In the same amount of time, he lost territory almost equal to that of Eastern Europe, leaving his beloved Sweden, which twenty years previously had been one of the most powerful forces in the western world, a defeated and weakened nation. To understand this unique king we may begin, as does Johnson, by asking "On what Foundation stands the Warrior's Pride?" (*VHW* 191).

Charles' personality is the key to his entire career:

A Frame of Adamant, a Soul of Fire,
No Dangers fright him, and no Labours tire;
O'er Love, o'er Fear, extends his wide Domain,
Unconquer'd Lord of Pleasure and of Pain;   [*VHW* 193-96]

The above quatrain skillfully interweaves the image of the "Lord" with his "Domain." The frequent use of personification in this portion of *The Vanity* serves to emphasize the sheer power of personality: "War sounds the Trump," "Peace courts his Hand" in vain, and "blushing Glory" hides "*Pultowa's* Day." Entire nations "on his Eye suspended wait," because Charles leads simply by means of his adamantine frame and fiery soul, that is, his singular personality. In calling upon nothing external to himself, he suggests to his followers that every man can mold himself into a warrior, and he paralyzes his enemies, witnesses to his use of the resources at any individual's disposal. Yet this quatrain also contains the shadow of defeat, for Charles has conquered himself. In refusing to feel pleasure or pain, he grows insensitive also to signs of impending defeat or approaching death. "Not Want and Cold his Course delay" (*VHW* 209), even when more provisions and warmer weather would have turned the balance in his favor.

Charles is not, like Hannibal, simply an overly ambitious general. As a human being, he is superior to the Carthaginian because, instead of losing his humanity, Charles uses it as his greatest weapon in battle. This king of Sweden, the epitome of military ambition, transcends every form of militarism. Hannibel loved conflict and can be characterized solely in terms of his obsession. Charles XII passes by the opportunity for the usual military spoils as if they were the baubles of children. Although the term "Pride" is used in reference to the Swede and has application to him, Swedish Charles was famous for his piety. To those familiar with this legendary individual, Johnson's phrase "no Joys to him pacific Scepters yield" (*VHW* 197) applies to both the physical and the emotional rewards of war. Charles attained the goal of every conceivable form of military ambition but never even paused to gather the spoils. Moreover, he was a virtuous man, especially when compared to the half-mad, half-blind Hannibal.

Yet he who appears to have every accomplishment attainable by mortals dies in a petty and dubious fashion: "His Fall was destin'd to a barren Strand / A petty Fortress, and a dubious Hand" (*VHW* 219-20). While Voltaire painstakingly seeks to prove that the king died gallantly,[23] Johnson concludes with disapproval. *The Vanity of Human Wishes* characterizes Charles' final battle as unworthy of him. His end occurs not in heroic combat but in a skirmish for a minor fortress. For Johnson, Charles' fault, a vanity far beyond that of military ambition, resides in not realizing that his personal dignity was more important than any military victory and could endure in spite of defeat. Such a perspective on himself might have enabled the Swedish leader to avoid the last battle; his name could then have pointed to a less vain tale. In insisting on leading an unnecessary expedition after he has achieved his fame, Charles misunderstands the nature of his own greatness, which rests not in continual victory but in the manner in which he inspires his troops. Charles is blind to the other perspective on himself, the view of him adopted by the reader of *The Vanity*. The less vain alternative for Charles is to retire after Pultowa to the secular equivalent of what Wolsey had at Cawood, the opportunity for a dignified instead of petty and dubious end.

But few have such opportunities, and even those few seldom pursue the possibility viewed from such an enlightened perspective. Johnson recognized that most of those in positions of power acted like Xerxes, whose final retreat is described in lines said by Boswell to be Johnson's favorites and that serve as a coda to this section of *The Vanity of Human Wishes.*

> Th' insulted Sea with humbler Thoughts he gains,
> A single Skiff to speed his Flight remains;
> Th' incumber'd Oar scarce leaves the dreaded Coast
> Through purple Billows and a floating Host.   [*VHW* 237-40]

Xerxes can only be brought to an awareness of the myriads of individuals who have died as a result of his ambition when their corpses impede his retreat. This image vividly depicts how people in positions of power come to witness their effect upon the ordinary man only when it is too late.

The question that then arises is, what alternative to "vanitas vanitatum" is offered to the ordinary man, one who has not the sway of Xerxes, Wolsey, or Charles and is therefore more likely to be included among the floating host? Johnson answers this question in the next section of the poem (255-343), which prepares us for the religious conclusion. The key notion here is the manner in which human energy and desire are seen to burst naturally out of all mortal forms. Old age is the first subject because it involves the physical juxtaposition of man and the realm of spirit, thereby evoking two opposite attitudes toward death. Old age can take two forms, acceptance or resistance. The latter is portrayed as a prolonged disease gradually closing all sources of pleasure: "Time hovers o'er, impatient to destroy, / And shuts up all the Passages of Joy" (*VHW* 259-60). But despite his maladies, the old man's "unextinguish'd Av'rice still remains," even to the point of his being pained by monetary losses after he is physically unable to use his money. Finally, gazing with "suspicious eyes" upon his "Coffers," and counting his money with "cripled Hands," he dies. Avarice has become another physical manifestation of this painful, protracted death because the desperate holding on to life symbolizes the essence of avarice; embracing a body in pain is like doting upon gold for its own sake. Unlike the equivalent section in Juvenal (see 346-66) where inner anguish is only a contributing factor, Johnson suggests that a major source of torment is the insistence on dwelling in the dying body, the refusal to yield the self to the spirit. The poem offers itself, specifically in its Christian conclusion, as an alternative to the anguish of resistance.

But that alternative is, as ever in Johnson, a process, entailing an arduous ascent, since even the few who experience healthy old age are not immune to vanity. The healthy octogenarian sees relatives sicken or has the misfortune to outlive his own child. Even if he is able and fortunate enough to continue working at an occupation he enjoys, new techniques and fashions will render him obsolete. Of those who remain sound in body and mind, only a few are permitted by "Nature" to die in peace. Others end by undermining the bravery and wisdom of their life: "From *Marlb'rough's* Eyes the Streams of Dotage flow, / And *Swift* expires a Driv'ler and a Show" (*VHW* 317-18). For Johnson, it is appropriate that Swift and Marlborough, two famous men who in different ways strove too hard for public recognition, ended by being on public view, like inmates of Bedlam. Their over-commitment to public life was accentuated in their manner of dying. The less vain alternative implicit in *The Vanity of Human Wishes* is made explicit in "On the Death of Dr. Robert Levet." This tribute to the former lodger in Johnson's house who devoted his life to tending to the medical needs of the poor begins by demonstrating how Levet lived among the ill and died, in a sort of "mine."

> Condemn'd to hope's delusive mine,
>   As on we toil from day to day,

By sudden blasts, or slow decline,
    Our social comforts drop away.   [*Poems* 233.1-4]

Devoted to a life in a mine of disease, Levet is released quickly from his own body because he so totally dedicated himself to alleviating the bodily pains of others:

Then with no throbbing fiery pain,
    No cold gradations of decay,
Death broke at once the vital chain,
    And free'd his soul the nearest way.   [*Poems* 235.33-36]

A life spent watching the poor and the obscure die has prepared Levet for acceptance of the private and isolated quality of death. He thereby achieves the final quiet dignity denied to Swift and Marlborough.[24]

In *The Vanity*, the foibles of old age, from avarice to the obstinate clinging to life, are forms of misdirected energy; the religious coda commences with the following question:

Where then shall Hope and Fear their Objects find?
Must dull Suspence corrupt the stagnant Mind?
Must helpless Man, in Ignorance sedate,
Roll darkling down the Torrent of his fate?   [*VHW* 343-46]

The negative terms of corruption and stagnancy apply to that which is "down"; the proper direction for helpless man must be upward. While Juvenal and Dryden merely point from below to the inscrutable gods above, Johnson makes us climb up step by step, introducing for the first time an endeavor not vain: "nor deem Religion vain" (*VHW* 350). Since mortal goals are never achieved, the secular task is to choose the least vain form of behavior. The religious task is more mysterious: "Still raise for Good the supplicating Voice, / But leave to Heav'n the Measure and the Choice" (*VHW* 351-52). The supplicator may only be able to grope, but even this fumbling and uncertain activity goes beyond the Juvenalian passive resignation and is an initial form of salvation:

Safe in his Pow'r, whose Eyes discern afar
The secret Ambush of a specious Pray'r.
Implore His Aid, in his Decisions rest,
Secure whate'er he gives, he gives the best.   [*VHW* 353-56]

The specious prayer is a terrestrial petition beyond which we have been guided earlier in the poem. The petitioner knows that he must crave celestial peace, not worldly delight.

This lesson Johnson rendered some years later in a fairy tale entitled "The Fountains." Floretta rescues a goldfinch from a hovering hawk, but when her mother suggests that it be kept in a cage, the young girl releases the creature into the air. As a reward for such benevolence, the bird reveals its true identity as Lady Lillinet, chief of the fairies, and offers her rescuer the use of two fountains. The sweet water of one fulfills any wish, which can be cancelled or modified by the bitter water of the other. Floretta asks for beauty, "a spirit to do her own way," wealth, and wit. After experiencing the negative consequences of each of these attributes, she returns to the second fountain to modify each of her wishes except wit: "Being now a wit for life, she surveyed the various conditions of mankind with such superiority of sentiment, that she found few distinctions to be envied or desired, and therefore did not very soon make another visit to the fountain" (*Works* 2:511).

Later, however, desiring length of life, the young girl returns to the fountain, but upon discovering that longevity does not include perpetual health, she returns to drink of the bitter fountain water that will nullify her last wish: "she drank the bitter water. They walked back to the favourite bush pensive and silent; 'and now,' said she, 'accept my thanks for the last benefit that Floretta can receive.' Lady Lillinet dropped a tear, impressed upon her lips the final kiss, and resigned her, as she resigned herself, to the course of nature" (*Works* 2:511). Thus the tale ends with Floretta being released into her own natural element, as it began with the protagonist freeing the bird into the air; Floretta has understood the gift of death and, in the terms of *The Vanity of Human Wishes*, is prepared now to cease looking down below and begin her ascent toward faith.

This difficult upward movement is begun in *The Vanity* when we are lifted above the "Ambush" of false prayers. Cognizance of this high perspective gradually develops into a "Sense of Sacred Presence":

> Yet when the Sense of sacred Presence fires,
> And strong Devotion to the Skies aspires,
> Pour forth thy Fervours for a healthful Mind,
> Obedient Passions, and a Will resign'd;   [*VHW* 357-60]

This fervent search begins to resemble worship. Instead of seeking full comprehension, the poet concentrates on his inspiration, however unclear, in the realization that his instinctive fervor is healthier than his mental doubt. He strives to make the "strong Devotion" dominate, longing

> For Love, which scarce collective Man can fill;
> For Patience, sov'reign o'er transmuted Ill;

For Faith, that panting for a happier Seat,
Counts Death kind Nature's Signal of Retreat.   [*VHW* 361-64]

The paradox of these lines is that at the moment one prays for the love, patience, and faith of God, one manifests each of these virtues—in loving God, who has in Himself that which "scarce collective Man can fill"; in the patience of the prayer, which is itself temporarily "sov'reign o'er transmuted Ill"; and in the feeling of faith, which allows one to view death as a kind of signal of "Retreat." The final profundity of this passage is that as a momentary process it applies to man, and as a continuous state, to God. Now understanding that the supplication for a proper prayer can itself become the best prayer, the mind is temporarily calmed with the belief that the gaining of this blessing promises further blessings in heaven.

We can now understand why in *The Vanity of Human Wishes* Johnson first uses the process of literary understanding that he raises to the level of principle ten years later in *Rasselas*. Johnson's religious faith drove him to pursue a process that commenced with the insight that the viewing of vanity is itself a form of human vanity. This response to vanity contextualized it, permitting another viewpoint that posited a less vain alternative. The final part of the poem then reflects upon this process in religious terms, concluding that the drive to achieve a perspective on "Observation with extensive View" is the manifestation of the Spirit, man's impetus toward religious consolation. Johnson first realized this literary understanding in his great Christian poem because his own deep faith pressed him to discover less vain alternatives. For that reason the force of religion remains in the background of all of his literary works, a basso continuo reminding us that this driving force of literary understanding can never be fully satisfied within the realm of literature.

Johnson's first successful manifestation of the process of literary understanding occurs in a religious context because the force that enables man to assess his own assessment of his vanity is also the moment of the "sacred presence." In 1749 Johnson achieved what he had been struggling toward in *Irene* and *London*. Ten years later, in *Rasselas*, he presented the principle of this achievement. But the question first put forth in *Irene* remained unanswered. What effect does the comprehension of less vain alternatives have upon history? The task of answering that question was assigned to his last literary work, *A Journey to the Western Islands of Scotland* (1774).

7

Historical Understanding
A *Journey to the Western Islands of Scotland*

AFTER THE publication of *Rasselas* in 1759, Johnson wrote only one more lengthy literary work. Most of his efforts during the 1760s and 1770s were devoted to literary-critical projects. In fact, during this period he produced his longest and most important critical works, the edition of Shakespeare (1765) and the *Lives of the Poets* (1779-1781). The title alone of the latter, *Prefaces Biographical and Critical to the Works of the English Poets,* makes plain an interest in the relationship between literature and history. Halfway between these two great monuments, Johnson published *A Journey to the Western Islands of Scotland,* which was based on his own historical experiences as a traveler. The *Journey* marks an important moment in Johnson's life and a new development in his literary career. On only two other occasions did he leave England, and only the account of the trip to Scotland was prepared by Johnson himself for publication. With Boswell's encouragement, Johnson grew interested in and became a part of Scottish history, leaving home for longer than ever before to experience a rural environment radically different from his beloved London.

The *Journey* represents a new departure for Johnson in a historical and a literary sense: his only travel diary intended for publication, it is the record of a voyage different in kind from the few others in his life. This chapter will explore the relationship between these two elements to explain how Johnson applied his literary procedure to history. Having perfected the technique of crossing the literary boundary by focusing in *Rasselas* on an individual concern, the choice of life, Johnson then broadened his range by placing the journey motif in a cultural and historical context.

If *Rasselas* has almost always been commented on, the *Journey* has only recently been considered worthy of critical scrutiny. The reason for its relative neglect, I believe, relates to assumptions about its genre; as a journal, it is usually categorized with personal papers and letters, works not considered appropriate for literary analysis. But in 1960 Jeffrey Hart discovered that the *Journey* contained literary themes, an assertion that set off increased critical interest in the work.[1] Shortly thereafter, the assumption that the narrator throughout maintained the posture of the unassailably English "Dr. Johnson" was called into question. In 1969, Francis Hart pointed out that the narrator's attitude changed during his travels,[2] and in 1970 Richard Schwartz noted the emphasis in the *Journey* on the process rather than the product of Johnson's thinking.[3] More recently, Thomas Curley argued that for Johnson the trip was a form of education,[4] while André Perraux pointed out that the narrative reveals some unusual aspects of Johnson's personality: "Pourtant le récit de Johnson laisse entrevoir des aspects moins évidents de sa personnalité. Non seulement il lui est arrivé d'apprécier ce paysage écossais, mais c'est ce paysage qui lui a fourni en quelque sorte le point de départ de son inspiration."[5]

I agree with those who believe that Johnson changed during the course of his travels. My purpose in this chapter is to demonstrate how Johnson creates a literary context for his own various viewpoints, thereby applying the concept of literary understanding articulated in *Rasselas* to the history of the Western Islands of Scotland.

First, some clarification of the generic question will prove helpful. Johnson provides some assistance in this respect. He mentions two earlier accounts of travels in the Western Islands, that of Martin Martin, published in the early eighteenth century, and that of Thomas Pennant, part of which appeared just prior to Johnson's account (see *JTH*, 168). Since the travelers comment succinctly but respectfully on Iona, we may be able to distinguish the kind of work Johnson produced by comparing briefly the different versions of this sample section.

Martin's *A Description of the Western Islands of Scotland* (1703) was probably read by Johnson when he was still young, browsing in his father's bookshop. Martin paints a fascinating picture of the Highlands, one that would have aroused even the most sober young man who had never been north of the Border. A quaint yet important ecclesiastical island, Iona contains tombstones of the kings of Ireland, Scotland, and Norway, which are described in detail, as are the primitive beliefs of the inhabitants. For example, the people assert, according to Martin, that "Columbus," the founder of Christianity in Iona, was so opposed to women that he would have no cows on the island. This same eccentric prelate is said to have laid a curse upon his people: no family was to have more than four members. When that number was exceeded, the islanders "say one of the five was sure to die; and this they affirm . . . to this day."[6]

A native of the Highlands, Martin published his *Description* before the Battle of Culloden in 1746. Born in Wales, Pennant, a zoologist, journeyed north in the late 1760s and early 1770s; the portion of his *Tour* of concern here appeared before Johnson's *Journey* was published. His tone is analytic, not eulogistic. The naturalist's eye is immediately apparent: the flora and fauna are explained in greater detail and with more detachment than by Martin. Although mentioned, the legends, such as those about Columbus, are subordinate to the physical beauty of the island. Moreover, the attitude of the narrator toward the decaying religious traditions of Iona is clearly disapproving.[7]

While indebted to Martin and Pennant, Johnson goes beyond his predecessors by assimilating elements of both into his description of Iona, the first paragraph of which so moved Boswell that he cited it in his own *Tour:*

> We were now treading that illustrious Island, which was once the luminary of the *Caledonian* regions, whence savage clans and roving barbarians derived the benefits of knowledge, and the blessings of religion. To abstract the mind from all local emotion would be impossible, if it were endeavoured, and would be foolish, if it were possible. Whatever withdraws us from the power of our senses; whatever makes the past, the distant, or the future predominate over the present, advances us in the dignity of thinking beings. Far from me and from my friends, be such frigid philosophy as may conduct us indifferent and unmoved over any ground which has been dignified by wisdom, bravery, or virtue. That man is little to be envied, whose patriotism would not gain force upon the plain of *Marathon,* or whose piety would not grow warmer among the ruins of *Iona!* [*JWI* 123-24]

The reverence for the religious heritage of Iona Johnson shares with Martin. But both before and after this famous passage Johnson comments on physical details—the roughness of the water, the rocky, inaccessible shore, the ruinous state of the church. These geographical facts show the influence of Pennant.[8]

By creating a dramatic scene, however, Johnson achieves a sublimity not found in the works of Martin or Pennant. No one but a "frigid philosopher" could fail to be impressed by the ruins of Iona and by Johnson's fervent description of the island. Neither Martin nor Pennant attempted to recreate the scene for a spectator. Boswell points out that upon arriving at this sacred place, Johnson was "no less affected by it than I was." In fact, Boswell shares with Johnson an interest in dramatic spectacle. But they produce different kinds of scenes because each strives for a different effect. Boswell explains that after landing at Iona he embraced his companion and awaited an opportunity to return to the cathedral in order to "indulge in solitude and devout meditation." "While contemplating the venerable ruins, I reflected with much satisfaction, that the solemn scenes of piety never lose their sanctity and influence . . . . I hoped, that, ever after having been in this holy place, I should maintain an exemplary conduct" (*JTH* 336-37).

Johnson's *Journey* contains no equivalent passage. The younger traveler leaves his companion and goes to the ruined church for a private confessional moment. As ever in Boswell's *Tour,* individuals predominate over the landscape. Johnson, on the other hand, maintains a balance between the world within and that without. The difference here is rather subtle. The *Tour* is a form of autobiography that borders on biography; the *Journey* takes autobiography to the brink of history.

This distinction becomes more apparent when the two travelers use the same story. After mentioning the ruins only briefly, Boswell focuses on Johnson and a man named M'Ginnis who was erroneously reported to have refused to send some rum to his landlord and was rebuked by his superior in the following terms: " 'Refuse to send rum to me, you rascal! Don't you know that, if I order you to go and cut a man's throat, you are to do it?— 'Yes, an't please your honor! and my own too and hang myself too!' " Boswell is pleased "to find such attachment to a Chief," for M'Ginnis "had no connection with the island, and had not been there for fourteen years" (*JTH* 337-38). The ruins of the church evoke pious feelings in Boswell, a Lowlander without direct Highland ancestors, as the ancient tradition of honoring the chief is revered by M'Ginnis, a man whose forebears were not of the clan. Boswell develops an analogy between the biographical tale of M'Ginnis and his own biographical and autobiographical narrative.

The Englishman, on the other hand, calls attention to inanimate objects as well as to the people, using this same incident for another purpose. After pointing out that this island "which was once the metropolis of learning and piety" has only two inhabitants who can speak English and not one who can write or read, Johnson narrates the incident as an illustration of the primitiveness of these poor people: "one of [the tenants] being sharply reprehended by [the chief], for not sending him some rum, declared after his departure, in Mr. *Boswell's* presence, that he had no design of disappointing him, '*for,*' said he, '*I would cut my bones for him; and if he had sent his dog for it, he should have had it'* " (*JWI* 127). Here the primitive loyalty seems almost savage, and the chief is reminiscent of a heathen idol. Lacking religious education and guidance, the Highlander can only lavish his respectful fervor upon his chief. For Johnson, this man's loyalty is analogous to the fertile soil of Iona upon which once flourished a religious establishment now in ruins. The resources, profound spiritual needs, and rich terrain, are still there, but the great leaders are gone, and the institutions are in disrepair. In fact, Johnson concludes this section of his *Journey* by relating his own impressions to those of Boswell: "We now left those illustrious ruins, by which Mr. *Boswell* was much affected, nor would I willingly be thought to have looked upon them without some emotion. Perhaps, in the revolutions of the world, *Iona* may be sometime again the instructress of the Western Regions" (*JWI* 127).

The final sentence establishes a relationship between the way people like Johnson and Boswell respond to Iona and what in the future will happen to the island. By extension, Johnson is interested in how the records of their responses, *The Tour* and the *Journey,* will affect the Western Islands of Scotland, that is, how the literary process will be subsumed in the historical one. We have seen this generic strategy used before in *Rasselas,* where allusions to different but related genres or to contrary modes of the same genre are presented to guide the reader to the point of interest for Johnson, the border line between the literary and the extraliterary. Here Johnson signals that his account combines biography/autobiography with travel tale; aptly titled, the *Journey* is neither a journal, like Boswell's, nor a tour, like Martin's or Pennant's. But the visit to Iona occurs near the end of the travels; the manner in which Johnson distinguishes his account from those of his predecessors by mixing and interrelating their different generic techniques only gradually becomes apparent.

To understand the means by which Johnson found a generic mixture that suited his purpose, we must attend to the narrative unfolding of the travels. At this point, however, we can understand why the *Journey* has been misunderstood generically: combining autobiography and travel tale, journal and tour, Johnson places literature in history.[9] The principle embodied in *Rasselas* is used in the *Journey* to go one step beyond the story of the prince of Abyssinia. I shall demonstrate that the achievement of the *Journey* resides in the application of the literary technique employed in the account of the trip to the historical dilemma encountered in the Western Islands of Scotland.

Johnson begins his *Journey* by explaining that he is the Londoner who wanders north for no apparent reason—"I scarcely remember how the wish was originally excited"—and who amuses himself by considering how different a small island near Edinburgh would be if it were located close to London. We know from Boswell that this stance is exaggerated, a literary device whereby Johnson reveals a central truth about himself: "Dr. Johnson has said in his *Journey*, that he scarcely remembered how the wish to visit the Hebrides was excited: but he told me, in summer 1763, that his father put Martin's Account into his hands when he was very young, and that he was much pleased with it." (*JTH* 13). Wishing to emphasize that he has little knowledge of the Hebrides, Johnson omits any mention of his familiarity with Martin's travels.

Although reminiscent of Rasselas upon first leaving the happy valley, the narrator of the *Journey* differs from the young prince in being a man of the world with definite predilections and beliefs, which soon emerge. At St. Andrews, a town in decay because of the desecration of its church and the decline of its university, the narrator comments: "the kindness of the professors did not contribute to abate the uneasy remembrance of an university declining, a college alienated, and a church profaned and hastening to the ground" (*JWI* 5-6). As a high churchman and scholar, Johnson—and these characteristic attitudes make plain that the narrator is meant to be taken as Johnson—finds that no amount of hospitality can distract him from the mournful sight of ecclesiastical and academic neglect. In the equivalent section of Boswell's *Tour* (*JTH* 61), Johnson indicates his awareness of the thriving commerce in St. Andrews; he omits this conversation from his own account to stress that he begins with the posture traditionally expected of the typical Londoner.

Although the speaker here and throughout the *Journey* is clearly identified as Samuel Johnson, making manifest a strand of autobiography, I use the term "persona" because he is located in a literary text and subjected to the forces of that context. The narrator's comments on trees make the relationship between autobiographical journal and travel tale apparent. Johnson was, in fact, always interested in trees as representative of culture. One of his earliest poems, "On the Stream at Stowe Mill, Lichfield," contains remarks on the disappearance of trees remembered from his childhood: "Nunc veteres duris periêre securibus umbrae, / Longinquisque oculis nuda lavacra patent" (*Poems* 261.7-8).

This topic is introduced in the third section of the *Journey*, entitled "Aberbrothick": "From the bank of the Tweed to St. Andrews I had never seen a single tree, which I did not believe to have grown up far within the present century" (*JWI* 6). As there are over a dozen references to trees in the *Journey*, the reader soon recognizes that the persona's obsession develops into a literary motif. Some of the first

Scottish reviewers of the *Journey* mentioned older Hebridean trees present at the time that were not seen by the English visitor.[10] Johnson's assertion, however, applies not to all of the Hebrides, but only to that portion he observed during his travels. The use of the first person pronoun, itself a relative rarity in the canon, and the constant mention of place names, dates, and specific people, such as his companion Boswell and the Highlanders who provided them with hospitality, serve to locate every general observation in a concrete historical context. Johnson notes not the scarcity of trees in the Hebrides but the few old trees "I" saw on "my" itinerary of 1773. The biographical truth, when placed in a literary structure, takes on a new significance. Trees represent for Johnson not merely a personal quirk but a belief in posterity, both in planting the sapling and in nurturing and protecting the growing tree. "To drop a seed into the ground can cost nothing," but the willingness to do so presupposes "the least thought of future supply."

The lack of consideration for the future disturbs Johnson because to plant a tree in one age for the benefit of the next represents a physical manifestation of a belief in and commitment to the future of civilization. At Mull, Johnson explains that the need to cultivate trees, although particularly acute in the Highlands, is a relatively recent phenomenon because "all the woods, by which the wants of man have been supplied from the Deluge till now, were self-sown." The planting of trees takes on a double significance, literary and historical. The persona's attitude toward tree-planting, which changes and develops, is a literary means of rendering the effect of the Western Islands on Johnson. At the same time, the physical activity involved in placing a seed in the soil signals that Johnson's commitment is not merely to writing history or what is now called historical discourse but to active participation in history. *A Journey to the Western Islands of Scotland,* unlike *The Vanity of Human Wishes* and *Rasselas*, develops a means of locating the Johnsonian persona in history.[11] In this sense, what Johnson set out to do in his first literary work, *Irene,* is finally achieved in the *Journey.* But this movement into history is only achieved at the end of the journey, the culmination of an accretive progression that must be understood in its unfolding.

At the outset of the travels, the persona is a man of letters in his sixties who has never before crossed the Border. In his innocence about Scotland and his strong views on such matters as education and religion, the narrator of the *Journey* reveals himself to be a learned but inexperienced explorer. Johnson's initial stance is not simply that of a Londoner insensitive to the countryside. On the contrary, deeply committed to the importance of all aspects of culture, he insists that the beauties of pastoral life require attention and care; the monuments and natural beauties of the landscape can no more be neglected than can those of the city. At the same time, however, this sophisticated Englishman visiting the wilds of Scotland is not without humor about his own posture, thus preparing us for changes to come: "At our inn we did not find a reception such as we thought proportionate to the commercial opulence of the place; but Mr. Boswell desired me to observe that the innkeeper was an Englishman, and I defended him as well as I could" (*JWI* 8). The narrator recognizes that the humor of the episode turns upon him and emphasizes the point by explaining that he defended himself as well as he could. The journey is already exerting pressure on the English traveler.

Traveling now to the north, Johnson, although indignant about the desecration of two churches at Elgin, reflects upon his own country: "Let us not however make too much haste to despise our neighbours. Our own cathedrals are mouldering by unregarded dilapidation" (*JWI* 18). And at the next stop, near a plantation of oaks, Johnson makes his first favorable, although double-edged, comment on trees. What can be accomplished at Fores, a location in the far North, Johnson believes can certainly be more than equalled in the South. Nevertheless, the oak plantation is applauded as a Scottish accomplishment, a new level of awareness which is made more emphatic by Johnson's pointing to his own limitations. Having admired Fort George, he feels it necessary to add that "my suffrage is of little value, because this and Fort *Augustus* are the only garrisons that I ever saw" (*JWI* 19). This public revelation by the self of the limits of the self constitutes both a personal discovery and an attempt to suggest the general function of such a revelation: what the Highlands reveals to anyone depends on the nature of the perceiver, on what he has seen before and is capable of seeing now. In addition to causing a change of perspective, the historical journey demonstrates that in learning from history man also discovers his own limitations.

At the next stage of the *Journey*, which begins at Inverness, paradoxical oppositions are first developed. The elegance of the literature and "politer studies" is contrasted with the filth inside the houses and the coarseness of the food. Although poetry has been cultivated here since the sixteenth century, the sons of gentlemen still go barefoot, and the farmers had to be taught by Cromwell's soldiers how to raise kale: "I know not whether it be not peculiar to the Scots to have attained the liberal, without the manual arts, to have excelled in ornamental knowledge, and to have wanted not only the elegancies, but the conveniences of common life" (*JWI* 20).

The separation of liberal from manual arts requires on the part of the ordinary person, we are shown in the next village, considerable strength and ingenuity. For instance, a peasant woman with five children and an eighty-year-old husband must grow her own potatoes and barley in addition to trading her goats and chickens for other necessities. Nearby, however, is an inn well stocked with provisions. While Boswell entertains us with a tale of the "coquetry" of this woman when asked by Johnson where she slept, Johnson compares the industriousness of this cottager with the dissolute luxury at the inn. The publican at Anoch, in the next section of the *Journey*, seems to combine the best of both worlds. Well-spoken, civil, and competently educated, this "gentleman" farms the land, manages a comfortable hostelry, and has a charming and intelligent daughter. Unfortunately, he is emigrating to America because he is charged an excessive rent: "From him we first heard of the general dissatisfaction, which is now driving the Highlanders into the other hemisphere; and when I asked him whether they would stay at home, if they were well treated, he answered with indignation, that no man willingly left his native country" (*JWI* 29). The patriotic dignity of this unfortunate but upright man is very moving to the narrator, and it is surely because of such people that Johnson wrote his *Journey*. Indeed, this section of the *Journey* contains the story of how the idea of writing the book was first conceived: "I sat down on a bank, such as a writer of Romance might have delighted to feign. I had indeed no trees to whisper over my head, but a clear rivulet streamed at my feet. The day was calm, the air soft, and all was rudeness, silence, and solitude. Before me, and on either side, were high hills, which by hindering the eye from ranging, forced the mind to find entertainment for itself. Whether I spent the hour well I know not; for here I first conceived the thought of this narration" (*JWI* 31).

In placing the decision to write the *Journey* in the text, Johnson inscribes one literary process in another, but this moment initiates the attempt not to enclose the literary process but to open it to history. The passage itself warns the reader that his literary expectations will be employed but thwarted; the "bank" may have delighted a reader of romance, but a traveler in the Highlands would soon find that the realities of Scotland were not wholly suitable for that genre. Instead of whispering trees, he will be subjected to the rudeness, silence, and solitude of the high hills. Nevertheless, with a clear rivulet streaming at his feet, Johnson records the image derived from romance to demonstrate how careful attention to the physical particulars of the Western Islands of Scotland thwarts his literary expectations. Romance has been inscribed within geography.

By way of general introduction to the region, the reader is informed that the high, isolated mountains protect the people from invasion but also sustain the absoluteness of the laird's rough form of justice. The civilized Augustan's attitude towards these clan laws is predictable: "Those who had thus the dispensation of law, were by consequence themselves lawless. Their vassals had no shelter from outrages and oppressions; but were condemned to endure, without resistance, the caprices of wantonness, and the rage of cruelty" (*JWI* 36). The laird's law may be primitive and outmoded, but in the first episode after this introductory note on the Highlands, the English traveler experiences the benefits of the ancient forms of civility among the rocks. Climbing to Glenelg, Johnson's horse loses its footing, and the rider admits that "this was the only moment of my journey, in which I thought myself endangered" (*JWI* 38). Having finally reached their destination, the tired, hungry, and irritable travelers find no milk, bread, eggs, or wine. Suddenly, a servant of a gentleman appears with rum and sugar from his master. Highland hospitality is now not merely a quaint custom but a practical offer of assistance. Danger, hunger, and fatigue have resulted in a radical change of viewpoint toward Highland customs of hospitality.

Johnson next arrives at Skye, where the civilized world within and the rugged world without confront one another. The contrast between the storms and rocks outside and the peaceful interior is also described in Johnson's "Ode upon the Isle of Skye," in which the island is portrayed as being "Strepens procellis, rupibus obsita," but the home of "blanda certe pax" (*Poems* 193. 2, 6). The ode concludes by urging submission to God's power. The *Journey*, however, remains in the terrestrial realm, where brute physical forces threaten even the chief's castle. The weather is not cruel, "yet the dark months are here a time of great distress; because the summer can do little more than feed itself, and winter comes with its cold and its scarcity upon families very slenderly provided" (*JWI* 42). The untillable moors are treacherous to walkers because "the land could not be trusted": "In travelling this watery flat, I perceived that it had a visable declivity, and might without much expence or difficulty be drained. But difficulty and expence are relative terms, which have different meanings in different places" (*JWI* 54). The last sentence indicates an important development. The *Journey* never ceases to mention unrealized possibilities in the Hebrides; the lack of old trees is the most often repeated example. And upon first landing in Skye, Johnson calls our attention to an orchard as an indication "that the present nakedness of the Hebrides is not wholly the fault of nature." The scarcity of aged timber will continue to be remarked upon, but the "fault of Nature" and the "difficulty and expence" also become considerations at this midway point of the voyage.

Even at Raasay, a neighboring island where he is lavishly entertained, Johnson remains keenly aware of the physical surroundings.

While the "air of festivity" predominates—thirty-six people dance, dine, and are entertained with "Erse songs" (*JWI* 47-48)—the island itself is described as barren and craggy. The few cows sustained must seek pasturage on perilous slopes, often perishing from a fall down a precipice. In fact, *"Raasay* has little that can detain a traveller, except the Laird and his family" (*JWI* 53-54). The distinction between inside and outside is extreme: "Without is the rough ocean and the rocky land, the beating billows, and the howling storm: within is plenty and elegance, beauty and gaiety, the song and the dance" (*JWI* 54).

At this point, the observer's attitude toward the inner Highland world grows more nuanced. In the past, the craggy shore enabled the laird to pursue civilized pastimes, for his guests and his books were protected from enemy invaders. Now the drawing-room culture has developed to the point that the smoothing of the path to the house would hardly be noticed, since, in any case, the ladies in dancing slippers will be carried over it. For this reason, the farmer's lot has not changed. He drives a plow similar to that of his feudal ancestors, and his cattle graze on terrain essentially unimproved since the days of serfdom.

From this vantage point, it now appears that the chasm between the rich and the poor is a function of the separation of interior from exterior. Feudalism was ended abruptly in 1745. The claymore and the kilt were outlawed. The laird could no longer require loyalty, for he was unable to offer protection. Traces of the past are occasionally visible—a furtive tartan-wearer or a remnant of a clan feud—for the present is still arriving. Disarmed, the people feel unprotected and would, in fact, be defenseless against foreign invasion. The imperfect law of the laird has ceased, but by the time a dispute reaches the courts in the south, the disagreement is obsolete. Finally, the laird himself, deprived of his ancient power, seeks the modern surrogate, money. His tenants must pay more rent but no longer receive his feudal services, protection and rough justice.

These well-known historical facts are repeated by the traveling narrator to emphasize that they have taken on a new meaning for him during his experience of life in the Western Islands. By means of narrative process, the *Journey* renders historical understanding. Having begun with a distant and disapproving view of the dichotomy between inside and outside, between manual and polite arts, between the drawing rooms and the craggy landscape, Johnson has come to realize that the rocky terrain that once protected the elegant culture now insulates it from the dilemma of the farmer. Having arrived at a viewpoint opposed to his initial one, Johnson seeks a context that can accommodate both of his perspectives. On his way to Iona, Johnson is forced by bad weather to land at Col, where the inhabitants, unlike those of Skye and most of the other Western Islands, are content and do not wish to emigrate to America. This tiny island seems to have solved the problem of life in the Hebrides. In large part, the islanders' happiness is due to the young laird Col, a leader who combines a respect for tradition with modern ingenuity. Although the most advanced of the Western Islands, Col is less than ideal; its minister "has no publick edifice for the exericse of his ministry; and can officiate to no greater number than a room can contain" (*JWI* 100). Moreover, its prosperity is precarious. Such a small island, with its restriction on immigration, could be devastated by an epidemic or a hard winter. In fact, soon after the visitors leave Col, its young laird is drowned at sea, a death announced with a solemnity suggesting that the island is doomed by the loss of its leader.

Johnson reports the death in the same section that contains the description of the ruins of Iona. Col is a barren land made habitable by a leader; Iona has a fertile soil but lacks proper management. Religion on both islands is in decline: the churches are in ruins, and now, with the death of the laird, both seem destined for further hardship. Spiritual as well as material leadership is necessary if prosperity is to endure. Thus, neither Col nor Iona separately can be held up as the ideal island. But each points to the essential ingredients necessary for a renaissance of Highland culture, and each corresponds to the poles of Johnson's axis of perspectives. Iona provides evidence that the secular aspect of civilization needs religion to sustain it through the ages; Johnson's initial dismay at the unrepaired church roofs is thus reinforced. On the other hand, the late laird, a leader who recognized the nature of the physical limitations of Highland life, manifests another dimension of life in the Western Islands. If the Church or any other institution allows itself to become insulated from the lot of the man who plows the field, it will perish with the culture. Thus, the second viewpoint, the geographic insight that Johnson acquired by climbing the hills and living among the people, is also sustained. Clearly, the ideal would be a laird like Col residing on the island of Iona, a leader in touch with his people who resides in a place with the resources of a spiritual community that could be rebuilt. But Col is dead, and Iona seems doomed to further decay. Johnson could have resorted at this point to a posture familiar to us from the *Life* and delivered one of his many taunts directed at Boswell—i.e., the best road for a Scotsman is that which leads to England.[12]

But he does not. Instead, he makes plain his genuine concern about the future of the Western Isles: here the *Journey* makes a clear move beyond autobiography, beyond personal assertion, toward history. This displacement entails depiction of the narrator's own autobio-

graphical process. We come now to visit to Braidwood's academy for
the deaf and dumb. Full appreciation of its literary function entails
viewing it in relation to the progress of the narrator.

At the beginning of the *Journey*, the traveler from London was ap-
palled to find that the only unbroken relic of the past was the way of
life of the farmer, who used the implements of a serf upon land with no
more arable acreage than was available hundreds of years ago. He
also soon noticed that the decline of churches and universities meant
that the eighteenth-century Highlander toiled without the religious
and intellectual guidance available to the Medieval serf. But as he
made his way over the hills and rocks, the Englishman came to
understand how the Highland past had led to the dilemma of the
present. Seeing at select residences an inverse relationship between
the elegance inside and the harshness outside, he realized that civilization had been able to thrive in such an environment by employing
the barren rocks as protection. The problem is one of historical
development: the Highland culture has been in the past so continuously protected from the environment that it has now become insulated from its own source of sustenance and protection, separated
from the man who toils in the field. The laird festively entertains
Boswell and Johnson while his tenants emigrate to America. In the
past, the spiritual mediator between the people and their laird had
been the parish priest, but since the Reformation, ministers are few,
places of worship are in disrepair, and congregations are dispersed.
   Now not content merely to comment on the remnants of the past
in the Highlands, the narrator is deeply troubled about the region's
future. He concludes by describing the "wonderful" improvement
made by Mr. Braidwood of Edinburgh in teaching the deaf and dumb
to speak, read, write, and do "arthimetick": "whatever enlarges hope,
will exalt courage; after having seen the deaf taught arithmetick,
who would be afraid to cultivate the *Hebrides*?" (*JWI* 137).
   The comparison between cultivating the Hebrides and educating
the deaf signals a new level of understanding. Braidwood's accomplishment in eliciting articulate sound from the deaf and dumb is
perhaps no less wonderful than the transformation of a High Church
Londoner contemptuous of Scottish customs into a man who has come
to understand the dilemma of the Highlands and to sympathize so
much that he feels compelled to conclude by seeking for the basis of a
renaissance. Johnson finally offers himself as a historical specimen,
saying in effect: promoters of Highland culture need not despair if it
can inspire care and concern in people like myself. Now the full
significance of the final words of the *Journey* becomes clear: "Such
are the things which this journey has given me an opportunity of

seeing, and such are the reflections which that sight has raised. Having passed my time almost wholly in cities, I may have been surprised by modes of life and appearances of nature, that are familiar to men of wider survey and more varied conversation. Novelty and ignorance must always be reciprocal, and I cannot but be conscious that my thoughts on national matters, are the thoughts of one who has seen but little" (*JWI* 137).

This final paragraph is a startling statement from a man who had for at least a decade established himself as the most famous and respected literary figure of his day; one need not be imbued with the Victorian "image" of Dr. Johnson to be impressed by the modesty of these remarks. But their profundity resides in the fact that the narrator places himself in history, for he is saying that only future historians, from the vantage point provided by future events, will be able to judge the *Journey*. The assessment of posterity will concern whether or not the literary process of the *Journey,* the development and change in Samuel Johnson's attitude during his travels, constitutes an accurate and fruitful insight into the historical situation of the Western Islands of Scotland.

In the end, *A Journey to the Western Islands of Scotland* goes beyond the bounds of historical discourse, whether biography and autobiography or journal, and of literary discourse, whether travel tale or novel. Johnson inscribes both kinds of discourse, presentation of self and aesthetically structured travel tale, within history. In its conclusion, the *Journey* presents itself as a historical act, the implantation of a literary tree, that will, like the seedling, be subject to the natural and human forces of future events. The judgment of posterity alluded to concerns more than the literary merit and autobiographical justness of the *Journey:* the narrator believes that his book should be assessed as a historical act. Did Johnson's account of his tour of the Hebrides aid in the process of transforming the Western Islands into a modern civilization? The realization of that goal, affecting the future, rests upon an accurate and meaningfully structured rendering of the past. The *Journey* demonstrates that the author's process of coming to terms with the Hebrides furnishes an insight into the historical dilemma of the islands.

The *Journey* cannot be taken in solely mimetic terms as a fictionalized history of the Western Islands or merely as an autobiography. The interaction between the two is a literary representation of a historical process. With great artistic skill, Johnson concludes by seeing his narrative as a historical event. Such a move involves more than crossing over into another discourse; history itself, not historical discourse, looms at the end of the *Journey.* Indeed, *Rasselas* and the *Journey* can be differentiated in terms of their final arrival at different locations on the periphery of literature. The Abyssinian tale points to a principle of literary understanding that applies to our everyday world of private decisions, choices of life, and the narrative about Scotland concludes by applying that principle to the realm of public events, the question of the future of Scotland's Western Islands.

I believe that *A Journey to the Western Islands of Scotland* presents a problem for both historians and literary critics because it interweaves two disciplines, using literary understanding for historical purposes. For Johnson, literary understanding is by its nature Janus-faced, at once literary and extraliterary: the skillful writer must employ art to show us how and where to apply the literary process. Those familiar with Johnson as a moralist were probably not surprised to find that *Rasselas* was designed to have application to the reader's process of seeking a choice of life. But in the *Journey to the Western Islands of Scotland,* the literary process is applied to history, an assertion more radical than it seems since it rests on the assumption that history is different from historical discourse. My point is that at the end Johnson asks us to conceive of his *Journey* as a happening. The question that now arises is how the literary process is to be distinguished from the historical one; in more familiar terms, how literature is to be distinguished from events or occurrences in life. This problem Johnson confronts most profoundly in his last great work, *The Lives of the Poets*.

8

The Limitations of Perspectivism
The Lives of Rasselas and Pope

FROM THE beginning of his career, Johnson sought a means of presenting the relationship between the literary and the extraliterary. In *Irene,* the tragic dilemma was to be situated in the historical context of fifteenth-century Constantinople; in *London,* the problem of the urban poet was to be firmly placed in London. In *The Vanity of Human Wishes*, Johnson first found a means of creating a balanced relationship between these two opposing elements, a dialectic favoring neither of its poles. Johnson's profound religious faith led him to recognize that the observer of vanity qua observer can become involved in various forms of vanity; the poet-narrator who provides the literary structure of the satire becomes a part of the world he observes, the poetic referent. The Christian position of the *Vanity* differs from that of *Irene* in that it involves not a celestial transcendence above the terrestrial in the manner of Aspasia but an awareness of the self-implicating nature of the poetic process, the sorts of vanity presented by "Observation with extensive View." At the conclusion of the great poem, our understanding of the relationship between observer and observed provides a path to the "sacred Presence." But since this credo involves a transformation of, instead of a movement above, the human world, Johnson can now turn his attention to problems in the vain world where this process of implicating the observer has particular application, the choice of life and cultural history. In *Rasselas* and *A Journey to the Western Islands of Scotland,* religion, while evident in the catacombs or Iona episodes, remains for the most part in the background.

In the prince of Abyssinia's quest, however, we move a step beyond the observer's awareness of his implication in the vanities of the world; the solipsism of the astronomer or the vacillation between city and country of the hermit, both of whom evidence self-awareness, are avoided by means of the principle of literary understanding. Similarly, the *Journey*, after establishing a relationship between history and literature, concludes with literary understanding displaying itself as a historical event.

Rasselas and *A Journey to the Western Islands of Scotland* nonetheless conclude at different locations on the border between the literary and the extraliterary. The former ends with a principle of literary understanding, a paradoxical notion since it applies to the extraliterary. The latter ends with a narrative attempt to place itself beyond narrative. In these terms we can understand why one work has been the subject of two centuries of controversy and why the other has posed a problem for historians and literary critics. Both literary works insist in the end that the application and utility of their literary motifs consists in subverting their own literariness. *The Vanity of Human Wishes,* on the other hand, has been neither neglected nor subject to controversy, because it concludes with religious faith, and religion is generally accepted as a form of closure that undermines mortal endeavors for closure. But how can literary-critical methods be applied to *Rasselas* and *A Journey to the Western Islands of Scotland,* which conclude by moving beyond the confines of literature?

One of the first questions raised by the notion that the literary only fully achieves its goal by passing into the extraliterary is how we are then to distinguish between these two realms. Johnson's last major work attends to this issue. In *The Prefaces Biographical and Critical to the Works of the English Poets* (the original title of *The Lives of the Poets*) he confronts this problem by establishing a relationship and a distinction between poetry in a biographical context and poetry as the object of literary criticism. Nowhere is this problem more central than in the *Life of Pope* because Johnson demonstrates that Pope's life, more than that of any other poet in the two volumes, was entwined with his poetry. My concluding chapter will compare the function of literary understanding in *Rasselas* and in the *Life of Pope*. The analysis of the *Life of Pope* will be brief, for my object is to demonstrate that in the context of Pope's life Johnson maintained a dialectic of perspectives that he could not sustain in the analysis of Pope's poetry. In this way, we shall understand why the concept of literary understanding remained implicit in Johnson's own creative writing and was never manifested in his own literary criticism.

Since Johnson believed that Pope's life was pervaded by his poetry, it is not apparent how Johnson could defend contrary evaluations of the man and his work. The *Life of Pope,* like all the other *Lives,* is divided into two sections, a biographical discussion followed by a critical assessment. The first section establishes that Johnson saw each of

Pope's major works as connected to specific persons and as occasioned by personal problems. Beginning with the pastorals that affected the short-lived friendship with William Wycherley, Johnson goes on to the attack by John Dennis on the *Essay on Criticism*. *The Rape of the Lock* is discussed in relation to the Fermor family and is followed by the translation of *The Iliad*, which is related to the shabby treatment of Halifax, and the translation of *The Odyssey*, which led to the end of the friendship with Addison. Then we are told how *The Dunciad* occasioned the friendship with Swift and alienation of Theobald. Pope's *Letters* are seen as the cause of his animosity toward Curll, and the *Essay on Man* is described as having Bolingbroke as its apparent influence and Warburton as its defender. Finally, the second edition of *The Dunciad* is viewed as Pope's rendering of the quarrel with Cibber. The catalog makes obvious one salient fact. Although great poetry, Pope's formidable satire was considerably less successful at making or keeping friends than at creating enemies. In this sense, the great social satirist was a social failure.

Pope had few friends, according to Johnson, and even those few were not loyal. When the poet on his deathbed asked to see his "favourite," Martha Blount, she is reported to have said to the Earl of Marchmont: "What, is he not dead yet?" (*LP* 190). Of Marchmont and Bolingbroke, Pope's most trusted friends and the executors of his will, Johnson provides the following account: "He left the care of his papers to his executors, first to Lord Bolingbroke, and if he should not be living to the Earl of Marchmont, undoubtedly expecting them to be proud of the trust and eager to extend his fame. But let no man dream of influence beyond his life. After a decent time Dodsley the book-seller went to solicit preference as the publisher, and was told that the parcel had not been yet inspected; and whatever was the reason the world has been disappointed of what was 'reserved for the next age'" (*LP* 192.)

Lest we assume that Pope actually preferred to live without friends, Johnson cites the satirist's last words: "In the morning, after the priest had given him the last sacraments, he said, 'There is nothing that is meritorious but virtue and friendship, and indeed friendship itself is only a part of virtue' " (*LP* 192). Johnson believed that although Pope professed to value friendship above all else, he died with few good friends. The description of Pope's grotto serves as a metaphoric explanation for this paradox: "Here he planted the vines and quincunx which his verses mention, and being under the necessity of making a subterraneous passage to a garden on the other side of the road he adorned it with fossil bodies, and dignified it with the title of a grotto: a place of silence and retreat, from which he endeavoured to persuade his friends and himself that cares and passions could be excluded" (*LP* 134-35).

Although brief, this paragraph involves a reading process with a beginning, middle, and end, the significance of which derives from accretion. We are introduced to the garden by way of Pope's verses, suggestive of the way Pope himself appropriated elements from his own existence to embellish his poetry. But the garden requires something very unpoetic, an underground passage. The middle of Pope's garden was marred by an unavoidable and unsightly physical obstacle, a road so wide that the only practical means of passage was by way of a tunnel. Now, in the middle of the paragraph, like visitors within the grotto, we come upon Pope's artistry. He decorated the cave with sparkling fossils, so lovely and so skillfully arranged that they served as more than mere providers of light. Pope completes his creation by entitling it not "tunnel" or "underground passage" or even "cave" but "grotto," a term that referred to the lavish garden features fashionable at the time in Europe, particularly in Italy.[1] But the Mediterranean climate provided a justification for a grotto not available to Pope. A cool refuge from the hot sun is seldom needed by the British gardener. Pope therefore justified his grotto in intellectual terms as a retreat for himself and his friends from the cares of the world.

Here we come to the final stage, which for Johnson involves some doubt that the spectacular design of the grotto achieved Pope's goal. The "endeavour" failed in one respect because of its success in another. The elaborately decorated, somewhat incongruous garden retreat serves more to recall than to remove the frustrations of the world beyond the poet's control. Our final impression of the grotto thus comes to resemble that evoked by many amateur artifacts—and Pope claimed to be only an amateur gardener—that the deepest and most personal feelings are expressed in this "weekend" result of "relaxation."

The precise nature of the contradiction inherent in the grotto is made clear by Johnson: "Pope's excavation was requisite as an entrance to his garden, and, as some men try to be proud of their defects, he extracted *an ornament from an inconvenience,* and vanity produced a grotto where necessity enforced a passage" (*LP* 135; italics mine). At once an ornament and an inconvenience, the grotto simultaneously exemplifies skillful and deceitful artifice, both the definitions of "artifice" found in Johnson's *Dictionary:* 1) "art; trade; skill obtained by practice or science" 2) "trick; fraud; stratagem." Pope cleverly converted a dark cave into a luminous and beautiful retreat. The stratagem for Johnson, however, involves attempting to pass off as desirable in itself what was, in fact, occasioned by the inconvenient location of a public highway.

A proper understanding of Johnson's presentation of Pope's grotto calls for the dialectic of perspectives already found in the literary understanding procedure. In this instance, artifice as art and artifice as deceit correspond to the poem and the poet. The poet was embarrassed by the presence of a mundane public road on his property in Twickenham; he attempted, Johnson believes unuccessfully, to mask his discomfiture by making the inconvenience into an ornament. The poet, however, succeeded in crafting his underground passage into a beautiful grotto. Johnson's admiration for the positive element of the grotto is attested to in his translation into Latin of Pope's poem on the subject. Friends frequent the cave—Bolingbroke, Wyndham, and Marchmont—which inspires the poem that concludes by urging visitors to approach the grotto with respect: "Temnere opes pretium sceleris, patriamque tueri / Fortis, ades, solus tangas venerabile limen" (*Poems* 93.15-16).

Nonetheless, Johnson faults Pope for alternating between these two viewpoints and not seeing them in relationship to one another or recognizing that a skillful creation can be seen as deceitful artifice and vice versa. The clearest application of the axis of perspectives to Pope's life occurs in the discussion of the verses on Addison. Johnson begins by citing Pope's admission that this great poem was a key event in a personal quarrel: "The next day, while I was heated with what I had heard, I wrote a letter to Mr. Addison, to let him know that I was not unacquainted with this behaviour of his; that if I was to speak severely of him, in return for it, it should not be in such a dirty way, that I should rather tell him, himself, fairly of his faults, and allow his good qualities; and that it should be something in the following manner. I then adjoined [subjoined] the first sketch of what has been since called my satire on Addison. Mr. Addison used me very civilly ever after" (*LP* 133).

The initial motivation for the poem was self-defense, a frequent necessity for Pope. But the resulting satire was something more than an act of reprisal against Addison: "the verses on Addison, when they were sent to Atterbury were considered by him as the most excellent of Pope's performances; and the writer was advised, since he knew where his strength lay, not to suffer it to remain unemployed" (*LP* 134). The satire was recognized as being of interest in itself apart from the author's anger at Addision. These verses are one of many examples showing that Pope's satirical weapon was so highly wrought that it became of interest to those who neither knew nor cared about the satirist's vengeful motives.

Pope's ability to transform completely his personal social world of factionalism and rivalry into a public and artistic one of great poetry was his talent. And yet it was also his bane, for he wanted Addison as a friend. Johnson points out that Pope "paid court" to Addison by composing a prologue to *Cato,* by siding with Addison against Dennis, and by giving him high praise in the *Dialogue on Medals.* "In all this," Johnson concludes, "there was no hypocrisy; for he confessed that he found in Addison something more pleasing than in any other man" (*LP* 129). But Pope's attack on Addison took the form of a brilliant work of art that stood on its own merits as a work of art. Addison realized that to attempt a retort would be self-defeating. To deny the applicability of the poem to himself would entail suggesting to the public how he might be taken as the possible target of the satire. Addison had no choice but to maintain an outward appearance of civility and to leave the poem unanswered, but understandably the friendship ended. Since the poem was well received in its own right, most readers need never have known that its main target was Addison.

Thus Pope had a choice: he might have withheld from the general public his personal intent and availed himself of the possibility of patching up the quarrel, which Johnson would have us believe is what Pope wanted. Here we are reminded of Rasselas, driven away by the derisive laughter of his new friends, the young men of spirit and gaiety. Drawing the young prince away from these revellers who are unwilling to reflect upon their way of life, Imlac leads him on a journey toward a new perspective upon his quest. Pope lacks such direction. He wants Addison as a friend yet insists on announcing to the world that his satire is an attack· on Addison. Pope seems to believe that his poetic success will somehow bring Addison back into the fold, as if satire could secure friendship. For Johnson this belief constitutes a grave error, which he calls Pope's "vanity."

The verses on Addison are one of many examples of Pope's conversion of an inconvenience into an ornament. Two distinct viewpoints are again apparent. On the one hand, having converted a personal quarrel into great poetry, Pope has transcended petty factionalism. On the other hand, the satirist can be seen as merely protecting himself behind the mask of the poet, exploiting his obvious satirical talent in order to wound a friend. The procedure of literary understanding enables us to locate the difference between the literary and the extraliterary. Indeed, the center of the dialectic is precisely at that border line where, looking inward, Pope's social satire is the highest of poetic achievements and, looking outward, it is self-defeating to the sociable poet. Unfortunately, Pope's behavior reveals, according to Johnson, that the latter prevailed. The need for personal defense became more important than the wish to preserve the artistic integrity of his poetry. This fact removed his last line of defense, namely, that he cared more about art than about friends. On the contrary, the satirist revised his poetry, even to its detriment, to pursue a personal vendetta: "But Pope's irascibility prevailed, and he resolved to tell the whole English world that he was at war with Cibber; and to shew that he thought him no common adversary he prepared no common vengeance: he published a new edition of *The Dunciad,* in which he degraded Theobald from his painful pre-eminence, and enthroned Cibber in his stead. Unhappily the two heroes were of opposite characters, and Pope was unwilling to lose what he had already written; he has therefore depraved his poem by giving to Cibber the old books, the cold pedantry and sluggish pertinacity of Theobald" (*LP* 186).

The first edition of The *Dunciad,* containing Theobald as the king of the dunces, was an example of personal invective employed for a higher artistic purpose. Johnson believed, however, that the second version manifested a conflict between vengefulness and art: the brilliant couplets that had applied so aptly to Theobald were recognized as such by Pope and left in the text, but the substitution for Theobald of another chief dunce whose personality was radically different detracted from the appropriateness of the satire. *The Dunciad* as a poem was thereby "depraved," a fact indirectly admitted by Pope when he published a variorum edition that preserved the original— for Johnson, the best version of the poem. In addition to its aesthetic consequences, Pope's alteration was self-defeating on a more practical level. Johnson asserts that the poetic enthroning of Cibber was unnecessary; the man's clumsy attacks on Pope provided the best illustration of his stupidity. "Silence only could have made him despicable: the blow which did not appear to be felt would have been struck in vain" (*LP* 186). Instead of providing his enemy with negative publicity, Pope should have left Cibber's work to fall "stillborn from the press." Too irascible to be silent, Pope damaged his poem and gave Cibber public recognition he could not have achieved on his own. We should here recall that point in the marriage debate of *Rasselas* when the prince and princess lose their tempers until Nekayah remarks that in arguing about particulars we often lose sight of the whole. Johnson's point concerning *The Dunciad* is that Pope lost sight of the whole, for the overall purpose of the satire is surely better served by enthroning a king of dullness who best exemplifies the faults being satirized.

Considering how severely critical he was of Swift for abusive social satire, Johnson is remarkably tolerant of the original purpose of *The Dunciad:* "In this design there was petulance and malignity enough; but I cannot think it very criminal. An author places himself uncalled before the tribunal of criticism, and solicits fame at the hazard of disgrace. Dulness or deformity are not culpable in themselves, but may be very justly reproached when they pretend to the honour of wit or the influence of beauty" (*LP* 241).

Aside from the "grossness" of some of its images, *The Dunciad* is said to contain a number of excellent passages. Johnson found, however, two major faults. One, as we have seen, concerned the change of the king of the dunces. The other is different, although not unrelated to this difficulty. Johnson explains that he is not convinced that the design of the poem is "moral." Although not specified, the implication seems to be that with both editions of *The Dunciad* the reader would discover that the same satire had been pointed at two contrary kinds of personalities, Theobald and Cibber. Since the ostensible moral end of *The Dunciad* is to demonstrate the social and intellectual dangers of poor writing, that purpose could only be properly achieved by radically altering the satire and withdrawing the earlier version, precisely what Pope refused to do. Pope had, in Johnson's opinion, misused his own writing in the manner of the dunces and thus enthroned himself as the king of the dunces.

Here, it seems to me, most modern readers part company with Johnson. Few of us are concerned about whether or not the satire that applied to Theobald is valid for Cibber. Even the acute reader of *The Dunciad* who discovers that the two dunces manifest different kinds of stupidity will see Pope's dilemma in accommodating his poem to both men as indicative of the difficulties experienced by a genius surrounded by mediocrity. Johnson is unable to entertain this possibility because of the limitations of his literary-critical framework. A satire with reference to a man like Theobald cannot apply to one like Cibber without undermining its own moral because, for Johnson, the moral referent predominates over literary structure. In this respect Johnson is representative of the mimetic tradition. Moderns, on the other hand, have long recognized that the skillful poet can include mimetic elements in an artistic form that is essentially fictive. In particular, Pope's great achievement in *The Dunciad* is to have demonstrated that some dunces respond to satire of their work by producing opposite kinds of bad writing that are as susceptible to satire as the original. Johnson is unable to see that Pope has, in a sense, anticipated Johnson's point of view and accounted for it in the final version of *The Dunciad*. For the notes to the variorum *Dunciad* imply that Cibber crowns himself king of the dunces by believing that he cannot be a dunce because his writing is different from Theobald's.

Johnson's limitations become particularly prominent here because only in the final version of *The Dunciad* did Pope alter the target of his satire and establish the applicability of the same poem to two different kinds of people. To view such an attempt as a success would, for Johnson, be tantamount to admitting that poetry can convert evil into good. That, in my view, is precisely what Pope did accomplish. The desire to be revenged on both Cibber and Theobald at the same time leads Pope to show us how dunces see only superficial differences between one another and miss their underlying similarity. Pope's pride becomes a poetic means by which he exposes the pride of others. Even as a mere possibility, such a notion strikes at the basis of mimeticism, for it means that within the confines of poetry the referent may be transformed into its opposite, and fact can become fiction.

For this reason, Johnson is able to see a dialectic of viewpoints in Pope's life that he cannot consistently recognize within the confines of a work of art. His comments on *The Rape of the Lock* are in this respect exemplary. We are first informed of the circumstances of the creation of this "the most airy, the most ingenious, and the most delightful" of Pope's writings. The satirist was asked by Caryll, a political figure and a "wit" of the day, to write a poem reconciling a breach of friendship "occasioned by a frolick of gallantry, rather too familiar, in which Lord Petre cut off a lock of Mrs. Arabella Fermor's hair" (*LP* 101). On the basis of new evidence gathered while traveling in France, Johnson reassesses the "event" of the poem, a term referring to the fact that the satire was commissioned for the purpose of reconciling a quarrel between two families. The widely held belief that Pope's satire had restored the friendship between Lord Petre and the Fermors is questioned on the basis of personal experience: "at Paris, a few years ago, a niece of Mrs. Fermor, who presided in an English Convent, mentioned Pope's work with very little gratitude, rather as an insult than an honour: and she may be supposed to have inherited the opinion of her family" (*LP* 103). Ridiculing "the little unguarded follies of the sex" in *The Rape of the Lock,* Pope nonetheless offered the poem as a compliment to Mrs. Fermor, the chief exemplar of the follies of her sex.

At first, it would seem, Mrs. Fermor, not on her guard, "liked it well enough to shew it" (*LP* 102) and, we may surmise, was eventually led by more perceptive readers to understand that the poem was considerably less of a compliment to her than the poet's presentation had suggested. Johnson's point is that in giving the satire to Mrs. Fermor, the poet himself manifested the vanity depicted in the poem and made plain to the world that his purpose in the satire was to expose the folly of the participants, not to reconcile them to one another.

Again Johnson is implying that Pope belongs in his own poem.

Johnson points out that *The Rape of the Lock,* a very successful satire, was unsuccessful at reconciling the quarrel that occasioned the poem. But, to pursue the comparison with the *Dunciad,* Pope did not alter *The Rape of the Lock* to satirize those who expected the poem to heal the difference between the two families. Johnson sees great art manifesting the social folly of the artist. He is unable to conceive that Pope could have employed his "unsuccessful" presentation of the poem to exemplify how Belinda brings out the folly of others. (It seems to me that Pope includes the letter of presentation with the final published version of the poem for precisely this purpose.) In short, Johnson is keenly aware of how the referent of poetry can be subverted by the extraliterary or what he called life, but not of the possibility of the reverse process. Pope thus presents a particularly challenging problem for Johnson because the great satirist is seen as quintessentially the writer who employed almost every aspect of his life in his writing.

If Pope and his poetry are almost synonymous, how can his successful poetry be used as evidence of his failure as a man? Once again, a complex question is answered in the form of an image: "Not long after Pope was returning home from a visit in a friend's coach, which, in passing a bridge, was overturned into the water; the windows were closed, and being unable to force them open, he was in danger of immediate death, when the postilion snatched him out by breaking the glass, of which the fragments cut two of his fingers in such a manner that he lost their use" (*LP* 143).

Before analyzing this passage in detail, two preliminary matters need to be settled. First, Johnson's structuring of a historical event or series of facts into an image or anecdote is a technique not restricted to the *Life of Pope.* Similar episodes are found in most of *The Lives:* Milton being read to by his daughters, Cowley in retirement, Savage wandering the streets of London, Swift secretly visiting Stella, or Gray shunning his fellow residents at college are some that immediately come to mind. These key moments, it can be demonstrated, reveal a relationship between the literary and the extraliterary. Second, the above cited passage is unclear concerning one fact, whose fingers were cut, those of the poet or of the postilion. Most readers of the day would have known that Pope injured his fingers in this accident. For those unaware of this fact, Johnson might have found the ambiguity functional, suggesting that the poet struggling within and the servant rushing to his aid were both vulnerable to injury.

In either case, this image functions as a metaphor for Pope's inability to separate and distinguish his life from his poetry. The carriage conveying Pope home from a friend became a trap for the helpless poet, who was only saved from drowning when the postilion broke the window and dragged the passenger to safety. Pope's poetry, like the windowed coach, was or purported to be a vehicle of friendship, entailing, as it often did, dedications, direct addresses, or presentations to friends and acquaintances. However, the poet was continually thwarted in his efforts to make friends. In fact, the windowed coach image suggests that these conveyances of friendship revealed the vulnerability of the poet and subjected his friends to possible injury. Not surprisingly, Pope's poetic overtures were often interpreted by their addressees as dangerous and unwelcome gifts. For those who were attacked, on the other hand, the means of revenge was suggested by the vehicle of attack. And they, accordingly, struck at the vulnerable little poet displaying himself in his poem. Less dignified and more dangerous than Addison's silence, this response was nonetheless adopted by several critics.

The first major attack on Pope was perhaps the most devastating because it concerned the *Essay on Criticism,* the earliest of his writings, which as Johnson points out "displays such extent of comprehension, such nicety of distinction, such acquaintance with mankind, and such knowledge both of ancient and modern learning as are not often attained by the maturest age and longest experience" (*LP* 94). Although Addison praised the *Essay,* Dennis was enraged, finding himself attacked, as he claimed, in his person, not his writings by "a little affected hypocrite, who had nothing in his mouth at the same time but truth, candour, friendship, good-nature, humanity, and magnanimity" (*LP* 95). Dennis was angered by what he perceived as Pope's use of the *Essay* as a kind of facade for an unprovoked personal attack. For this reason, he responded in kind, gravitating quickly to the physical vulnerability made visible by the coach windows. The following lengthy quotation is one of many that Johnson presents to exemplify the nature of the opposition of Pope:

"Enquire between Sunninghill and Oakingham for a young, short, squab gentleman, the very bow of the God of Love, and tell me whether he be a proper author to make personal reflections—He may extol the antients, but he has reason to thank the gods that he was born a modern; for had he been born of Grecian parents, and his father consequently had by law had the absolute disposal of him, his life had been no longer than that of one of his poems, the life of half a day.—Let the person of a gentleman of his parts be never so contemptible, his inward man is ten times more ridiculous; it being impossible that his outward form, though it be that of a downright monkey, should differ so much from human shape,

as his unthinking immaterial part does from human understanding."   [*LP* 97-98]

Dennis sees Pope's poetry as an attempt to compensate for his
physical deformities. Others, less able but equally vitriolic, followed
Dennis by attacking Pope on the level of physical appearance, where
they were certain of wounding the poet. Johnson suggests that Pope's
problem stems in great measure from the fact that his physical
deformities were constantly on public display and were mocked by
those who could find no other means of self-defense. For this reason,
Johnson describes Pope's physical person in detail. The satirist was
from birth vulnerable and delicate. Unable to dress himself even as
an adult, he was so thin and subject to cold that he always wore a fur
doublet underneath his shirt. Upon awaking in the morning, Pope
could not raise himself up until his servant had laced him in a stiff
canvas corset and flannel waistcoat. His maid then helped him with
the three pairs of stockings necessary for leg support. When at last
dressed and made presentable, Pope was still subject to continual,
public physical indignity: "his weakness made it very difficult for him
to be clean."

While Johnson shows compassion for Pope's physical deformities,
he is critical of Pope's means of defending himself. In response to those
like Dennis who ignored the brilliant poetry and pointed to Pope's
person, Pope resorted to poetic exaggerations. Here Johnson believes
Pope made his second major error. As we have seen, Pope attempted to
subsume historical events involving friends and enemies in his
poetry but was, according to Johnson, subsumed by them. A similar
pattern emerges with regard to physical facts, even those concerning
his own body. For instance, Johnson describes with impatience Pope's
"ridiculous and romantick" complaints of the secret sale and seizure
of his papers. "He tells, in tragick strains, how 'the cabinets of the
Sick and the closets of the Dead have been broken open and ran-
sacked'; as if those violences were often committed for papers of uncertain and accidental value, which are rarely provoked by real treasures, as if the epigrams and essays were in danger where gold and
diamonds are safe. A cat hunted for his musk is, according to Pope's
account, but the emblem of a wit winded by booksellers" (*LP* 144-45).

Pope is swallowed up by the literary world, which at creative
moments he was able to manipulate so adroitly. Ironically, this poetic
hypochondria, like the more ordinary kind, brought on the disease.
Taking the hint from Pope's complaint, Curll later published some of
the poet's letters without his permission. But the final phase, when
the satirist tried to retreat from his physical dilemma by dwelling in
his poetry, coincided with and was presented by Pope in *The Dunciad.*

Here Johnson finally makes overt what he sees as Pope's vanity. If those who were satirized in *The Dunciad* had remained silent, the satire, Johnson informs us, "would have made its way very slowly in the world." "This, however, was not to be expected: every man is of importance to himself, and therefore, in his own opinion, to others, and, supposing the world already acquainted with all his pleasures and his pains, is perhaps the first to publish injuries or misfortunes which had never been known unless related by himself, and at which those that hear them will only laugh; for no man sympathises with the sorrows of vanity" (*LP* 147).

Unfortunately, instead of sitting back and enjoying the profits of this battle over his book, Pope reentered the fray and in *The Dunciad* displayed his vulnerable self, thus inviting further attack. Johnson accuses Pope of poetic pride. Nevertheless, Pope is regarded as a great poet; before the nature of the poet's vanity is analyzed, the following assessment of his poetry must be kept in mind: "After all this it is surely superfluous to answer the question that has once been asked, Whether Pope was a poet? otherwise than by asking in return, If Pope be not a poet, where is poetry to be found? . . . Let us look round upon the present time, and back upon the past; let us enquire to whom the voice of mankind has decreed the wreath of poetry; let their productions be examined and their claims stated, and the pretensions of Pope will be no more disputed" (*LP* 251).

What Johnson finds offensive about Pope is his refusal to recognize that he, like all other men, is subject to the limitations of the physical universe and the events of history. In Imlac's words, he is only one atom in the mass of humanity, and the fact that he could create brilliantly by appropriating material for his art from his own physical and historical situation does not make him immune from the trials and tribulations of all mortals. The difference between life and literature is, for Johnson, at its base religious. Pride prevents man from seeing that literature is encompassed by history and that the writer, like any other person, is subject to the limitations of his physical body. We come then again to the thesis of *The Vanity of Human Wishes,* appropriately enough, since here we first saw how literary understanding was successfully employed. Pope's less vain alternative would have entailed the recognition that he had been his own historical dupe in complaining of stolen papers, thus suggesting the idea to his enemies, and to have accepted that his sadly deformed body could never be wholly compensated for by poetic success. Johnson is particularly severe in his judgment here because Pope's great poetry displayed the alternatives to his own foibles. For Johnson, Pope's satire showed the means by which the satire undermined the satirist.

Pope's pride blinded him to the fact that literary understanding applies not merely to the poet but also to the man. If he had been a character in *Rasselas*, Imlac might have said to him that in applying poetic principles to life he neglected to live. At the end of his tale, the prince of Abyssinia is pointed in a direction opposite to that of Pope. Now that he realizes that his wishes cannot be obtained, Rasselas turns not to the happy valley, a literary realm, but to Abyssinia, which in containing but not being contained by the happy valley, represents the border between the literary and the extraliterary. Abyssinia reminds us of the happy valley and was for many years seen as synonymous with it because the paradise-on-earth wishes nurtured by it are never sated. Johnson deliberately avoids a religious conclusion in *Rasselas* to emphasize that literature, unlike faith, never satisfies the desires it evokes. Pope is severely criticized for not recognizing the boundaries of literature: writing, however accomplished, cannot disguise our limitations as human beings. On the contrary, Pope's genius manifested his vanity. From that awareness to religious faith is a vast step, one that Johnson believes Pope never made.

My own analysis of the *Life of Pope* has violated one of Johnson's cardinal precepts, and it is in that respect that my concept of literary understanding is to be distinguished from that of Johnson. In comparing the *Life of Pope* to *Rasselas*, I have treated biography as literature, subjecting a factual work to the same kind of analysis as a fictional one. My purpose is to demonstrate that the double perspective of literary understanding operates in the biographical section and not in certain parts of the critical section of the *Pope*. Although I believe a case can be made for the historical significance of the *Pope,* that task would involve a lengthy digression from the present purpose. I also believe that an equally good case can be made for an approach to Pope that demonstrates how he accommodated his satiric structures to his life. This fictive formal aspect is slighted by Johnson, who believes that truth always predominates over artifice. The decision about which predominates, an inner, formal view or an outer, mimetic one, is the choice of interpretation. In my view, literature is subsumed by history, but that procedure, if it is to do justice to literature, must reappropriate both the facts and the literary structure, the formalistic as well as the mimetic. A new kind of literary history, this goal can only be achieved by establishing that literary understanding rests not upon reified themes or objective facts but on the act of interpretation.

9

Theoretical Conclusion

THE APPROACH developed in this study has application beyond the realm of Johnson. One need only think of the axis of perspectives apparent in the first two books of *Gulliver's Travels,* the literary process essential to most fictional works of the period, and the referential element of formal verse satire, not to mention modern works in which the literary boundary is deliberately flouted to create verbal collages. The present study, however, focused on *Rasselas* because, having been the subject of a critical controversy for over two centuries, it raised the problem to the level of methodology. I began with a history of *Rasselas* criticism that posed one main question, why there is still disagreement about the genre and whether or not the story of the prince of Abyssinia ends in religious resolution. My answer is that critics sought a product in a book about process. The problem is that the methods of approach are based on the assumption that the tale can be understood in either mimetic or formalistic terms, an assumption rendering them incapable of accommodating a process that encompasses both poles of literature. But in the past twenty years we have experienced the rise of literary theory; during this period, both the formal and the mimetic approaches to literature have been examined and found wanting. How then do we explain the fact that the problems inherent in *Rasselas* and Johnson's other literary writings have not been resolved by recent innovations in theory?

My comments on this question will have to be speculative, since I believe that the present study is part of a new movement in literary criticism that is still unfolding, a movement aptly named by the journal seminal to it, *New Literary History.*[1] The reader of this periodical or any other devoted to literary theory can see that two kinds of methods seem to predominate at present, one deriving from the philosophy of phenomenology, usually referred to as reader-response criticism, and the other based upon structuralism, which has now evolved toward various deconstructive or poststructuralist positions. The difference between the two is essentially that the former focuses on the manipulation of reader expectation while the latter emphasizes the place of the text within the system or matrix of written discourse. Johnson's literary works raise two kinds of problems for these literary approaches. First, they refer to history or the life of events, not merely to historical discourse or the reader's perceptions of history. That realm where history happens, the world that Johnson believes Pope tried futilely to evade by way of poetry, is not susceptible to analysis by either of these theories. Second, *Rasselas* and Johnson's other literary writings contextualize, frame, and manipulate the ideas at the heart of both of these literary methods. In *Rasselas*, for instance, the reader's responses evoked by the happy valley become in the course of the journey immersed in the web of discourse. The principle of literary understanding must be seen on the level of theory as combining in a dialectical relationship phenomenological and poststructuralist conceptions in order to make the literary process applicable to the extraliterary.

Here my literary theory diverges from that of Johnson, who, as a mimeticist in an age of mimeticism, never articulated such a position. My claim is that Johnson's work embodies a literary approach the theoretical implications of which were beyond the capacity of mimeticism to articulate. My own method, of course, is also subject to personal and historical limitations. But how, it may be asked, do I justify the use of my literary theory on the work of an eighteenth-century writer who did not share this method? My own hermeneutic circle, my analysis, begins and ends with the belief that literary criticism is a distinct discipline with a methodology worthy of separate study. No attempt has been made to define literature or literary criticism because, in my view, both are procedural in nature, redefining themselves in history, and as Johnson said at the end of the *Life of Pope,* "to circumscribe poetry by a definition will only shew the narrowness of the definer" (*LP* 251). But it is important to recognize that the enabling conception of this study is contained within a hermeneutic circle. Perspectivism cannot be proffered as scientific knowledge. It is a form of communication distinctively human, a discipline of the humanities, limited like other humanities by its ultimate subjectivity. Its only claim to our time and interest lies in its ability to help solve human problems. Literary criticism is representative in this respect because great literature always poses new questions and highlights new problems.

My own approach to certain of Johnson's writings rests on its ability to help solve problems in literary criticism and literary theory. With regard to the former, the present analysis explains why *Rasselas* has been under attack for over two centuries and why *A Journey to the Western Islands of Scotland* has until recently been neglected as a literary work. With regard to the latter, I present my approach as one that, while giving full weight to the fictive nature of literature, explains how the literary has application to the extraliterary. Perspectivism enables us to understand why literature, like other forms of writing, has from the times of the earliest civilizations through the eighteenth century been related to conduct. For most of human history, writing has been considered an act, often a dangerous one, if we can judge from the fate of writers in history. Only in the last two centuries has language been placed in a realm apart. Nonetheless, the insight of recent history should no more be slighted than those insights preceding it. My approach combines ancient mimeticism with recent formalism by showing how the structures of writing, fictive forms, affect both our literary discourse and how we conduct our lives.

Notes

1. A History of *Rasselas* Criticism

Most of the notes for this chapter are presented in an abbreviated form; for complete information concerning these references, see the Checklist, pages 194-202.

    1. The most complete critical bibliography on Johnson is edited by James L. Clifford and Donald J. Greene, *Samuel Johnson: A Survey and Bibliography of Critical Studies* (Minneapolis: U of Minnesota P, 1970), which has been updated by John Vance and Donald J. Greene in *A Bibliography of Johnsonian Studies* (Vancouver: Univ. of British Columbia, 1987). Any material not found in this bibliography is marked with an asterisk in the checklist.   2. Owen Ruffhead, *Monthly Review* 7 (April 1759): 142; and P. O'Flaherty, "Dr. Johnson as Equivocator," *MLQ* 31 (1970).   3. G.J. Kolb, "The Early Reception of *Rasselas,* 1759-1800," *Greene Centennial Studies,* ed. P.J. Korshin and R.R. Allen (Charlottesville: Univ. Press of Virginia, 1984) 218-24. Helen Louise McGuffie in *Samuel Johnson in the British Press, 1749-1784: A Chronological Checklist* (New York: Garland, 1976) 20-21, indicates that a number of other periodicals reproduced synopses or summaries of one or more of these five reviews.   4. *Gentleman's Magazine* 29 (1759):186.   5. *London Magazine* 28 (1759): 258.

    6. *Critical Review* 7 (1759): 372-73.   7. *Monthly Review* 20 (1759): 428-29. See note 2, above.   8. See *Rambler* 3: 19-25.   9. *Annual Register* 2: 477.   10. T.R. Preston, "The Biblical Context," *PMLA* 84 (1969): 274-81.

    11. See my checklist, p. 195.   12. T. Tyers, "A Biographical Sketch," *Gentleman's Magazine* 1784: 18.   13. *Rasselas* (Dublin, 1787) 6.
14. Sir J. Hawkins, *The Works of Samuel Johnson* (London, 1787) 1:371, 366.
15. E.C. Knight, *Dinarbas* (London, 1790). C.J. Rawson in "The Continuation of *Rasselas,*" *Bicentenary Essays* (1959), claims that Dinarbas fails as a sequel because as a sentimental novel it cannot refute the pessimism of *Rasselas* (pp. 92-94).

    16. J. Boswell, *The Life of Samuel Johnson* 1: 343.   17. Ibid. 342-44. A year after Boswell's *Life,* Arthur Murphy, in *An Essay on the Life and Genius of Samuel Johnson,* 1792 (see *Johnsonian Miscellanies,* ed. G.B. Hill [Oxford: Clarendon Press, 1897] 472) also defended *Rasselas* against the claim that it was inordinately gloomy. Murphy was the first to associate Johnson with the astronomer, an association converted by nineteenth-century critics into a means of attack. Specifically, Johnson was seen to share the dementia of the astrono-

mer.   18. W. Mudford, *A Critical Enquiry* 80-105.   19. L. Hunt, *Classic Tales* 3: 7. Hunt was the first to employ Murphy's defense (see note 17 above) as a means of attack.   20. A.L. Barbauld, *The British Novelists* 26: iii-iv.

21. W. Hazlitt, *Lectures on the Comic Writers* 201.   22. *Rasselas*, ed. Sir W. Scott, *Ballantyne's Novelist's Library* (London: Hurst, Robinson, 1823) 5: xlv.   23. Robert F. Metzdorf, "The Second Sequel to *Rasselas*," *New Rambler* 16 (January 1950): 5-7.   24. *Rasselas* (London, 1823) vii.   25. *Rasselas* (Edinburgh, 1824) 216.

26. *Rasselas* (London, 1843) iii.   27. *Rasselas*, ed. Rev. John Hunter (London, 1860) xx.   28. *Rasselas,* ed. Rev. W. West (London, 1869) xxvii, xlii. Because Johnson used the exotic trappings of romance to demonstrate the vanity of human wishes, T.B. Macaulay, who is famous for his attack upon Johnson, approved of *Rasselas* (see Boswell's "Life of Johnson" [London, 1878], 21, which first appeared in *Edinburgh Review* 54 (1831): 1-38).   29. *Johnson: Selected Works,* ed. A. Milnes (Oxford, 1879) xxix, xxxii. A year earlier, Leslie Stephen had praised Johnson in *Samuel Johnson* (London, 1878) for being content, in *Rasselas,* "to state the fact of human misery without perplexing himself with the resulting problem as to the final course of human existence" (p. 178).   30. See Clifford and Greene, 225-27, and my Checklist.

31. "Johnson's *Rasselas*," *Bibliographer* 3 (May 1883): 173-75.

32. "The Story of 'Rasselas,'" *Book-Lore* 1 (December 1884): 5-11.

33. Walter Raleigh, *The English Novel* (1894) 204, 206. Wilbur Cross also attempted to integrate the religious element of *Rasselas* within the confines of the novel, asserting in *The Development of the English Novel* (1899) that "the novel of Richardson has thus been turned to the purpose of an eloquent funeral sermon" (p. 78).   34. See note 3 above.   35. O.F. Emerson, "The Text of Johnson's *Rasselas*," *Anglia* 22 (December 1899): 499-509.

36. C.S. Fearenside, *Classic Tales* (1906) vii-x. During this period, two other critics attempted to account for what they believed was the pessimistic form of Christianity in *Rasselas*. Justin Hannaford, in his London edition of 1900, advised his reader to make allowances for Johnson's "puritanical perversity and the possession of a very limited humour in himself" (p. xxiv). Charles Whittuck, in *The Good Man of the XVIIIth Century* (1901) offered a cultural explanation: the eighteenth-century man was seen to have been confronted with an "absence of ideals"; Voltaire and Johnson were "good men" whose pessimism was the result of a deep but unavailing search for happiness (p. 147).   37. M. Conant, *The Oriental Tale* (1908) 144, 149.   38. *Rasselas,* ed. A.J.F. Collins (1910) xv.   39. G. Saintsbury, *The English Novel* (1913) 34-35.   40. W.D. Howells, "Editor's Easy Chair," *Harper's* 131 (July 1915): 310.

41. P.H. Houston, *Doctor Johnson* (1923) 196.   42. R. Markland, "Dr. Johnson and Shelley," *N&Q* 9 (Nov. 5, 1921): 368, and P.T. Armstrong, "Emerson and Dr. Johnson," *N&Q* 10 (Mar. 4, 1922): 124.   43. C.B. Tinker, "*Rasselas* in the New World," *Yale Review* 14 (Oct. 1924): 99.   44. L.F. Powell, "*Rasselas*," *TLS* Feb. 22, 1923: 124. During this same period Hilaire Belloc, in "On *Rasselas*," *New Statesman* 25 (September 5, 1925), went a step further, asserting that *Rasselas* was now considered a staple of the British diet, "a good British meal, solid stuff; beef, good beef with Yorkshire pudding" (p. 572).   45. E.M. Palser, *A Commentary and Questionnaire on the History of Rasselas* (1927) 17-18. See also P. Henderson, *The Shorter Novels of the Eighteenth Century* (1930) xii, vii. Also writing in the same year, Oliver Warner, in "*Rasselas*: The Testament of a Romantic," *Bookman* (June 1932), characterized *Rasselas* as more than a novel— "a complete exposition of a man's personal discoveries in life"—and less than a novel because "all is subservient to ideas" (p. 147).

46. N. Collins, *Facts of Fiction* (1932) 83-84.   47. E. Baker, *The History of the English Novel* (1934) 5: 56.   48. H.D. Jenkins, "Some Aspects of the Background of *Rasselas*," *Studies in English in Honor of R.D. O'Leary and S.L. Whitcomb* (1940) 13. Five years earlier, Geoffrey Tillotson, in *"Rasselas* and the *Persian Tales*," TLS August 19, 1935: 534, made some interesting suggestions concerning the influence of the exotic on *Rasselas*. For careful research on Johnson's translation of Lobo's Voyage, see Joel Gold, "Johnson's Translation of Lobo," *PMLA* 80 (March 1965): 51-61, and his introduction to *A Voyage to Abyssinia: The Yale Edition of the Works of Samuel Johnson*, 15: xxiii-lviii. For a view during this same period that the oriental aspect of *Rasselas* was "thin" and being overemphasized by others, see E. Wagenknecht, *Cavalcade of the English Novel* (1943) 130.   49. J.W. Krutch, *Samuel Johnson* (1944) 174, 176, 183. For a different attempt to document the "modern" quality of *Rasselas*, see K.N. Cameron, "A New Source for Shelley's *A Defense of Poetry*," *SP* 38 (Oct. 1941): 629-44, and *"Rasselas* and *Alastor:* A Study in Transmutation," *SP* 40 (Jan. 1943): 58-78.   50. Previous to Krutch, G.K. Chesterton, in his edition of *Rasselas* (London, 1926) had mentioned the humor in *Rasselas,* suggesting the narrative was a "sort of philosophical satire on philosophy" (p. viii).

51. See note 23 above.   52. C.L. Tracy, "Democritus Arise!" *Yale Review* 39 (1950): 303, 306, 308.   53. M. Lascelles, *"Rasselas* Reconsidered," *Essays and Studies by Members of the English Association* ns 4 (1951) 51.   54. G.J. Kolb, "The Structure of *Rasselas*," *PMLA* 64 (1951): 702.   55. F.R. Leavis in *The Common Pursuit* (1952) 115.

56. J.R. Moore, in two articles, "Conan Doyle, Tennyson and *Rasselas*," *N&Q* 7 (1952-53): 221, and *"Rasselas* and the Early Travelers to Abyssinia," *MLN* 15 (1954): 36-42, further attempted to place the narrative in the tradition of the novel by showing that its exotic element was semirealistic. E. Leyburn, however, disagreed, believing that the main source for the oriental was Johnson's translation of Lobo. For Leyburn, *Rasselas* was a moral tale with exotic trappings that Moore had taken too literally. See, E.D. Leyburn, " 'No Romantick Absurdities or Incredible Fictions,'" *PMLA* 70 (1955): 1060.   57. R.B. Hovey, "Dr. Samuel Johnson, Psychiatrist," *MLQ* 15 (1954): 321.   58. A Whitley, "The Comedy of *Rasselas*," *ELH* 23 (1956): 51, 65, 70.   59. W. Kenney, "Johnson's *Rasselas* after Two Centuries," *Boston University Studies in English* 3 (1957): 94-95. For two other religious readings, see N. Joost, "Whispers of Fancy," *Modern Age* 1 (1957): 171, and F.M. Link, *"Rasselas* and the Quest for Happiness," *Boston University Studies in English* 3 (1957): 123. For two readings that attempt to avoid the religious question, see N. Frye, *Anatomy of Criticism* (1957) 200, and F.L. Lucas, *The Search for Good Sense* (London, 1958) 115.   60. A. Lombardo, "The Importance of Imlac," *Bicentenary Essays* 47, 49.

61. W. Kenney, *"Rasselas* and the Theme of Diversification," *PQ* 38 (1959): 89, and B. Bronson, ed., *Samuel Johnson: Rasselas, Poems and Selected Prose* (1958) xvi.   62. G. Sherburn, "Rasselas Returns—To What?", *PQ* 38 (1959): 383-84. Although a number of critics agreed with Sherburn that the end of *Rasselas* was to be regarded as pessimistic, there was some disagreement about the precise formulation of the nature of the pessimism. Lionel Stevenson, in *The English Novel* (London, 1960), used the term "Christian stoicism" (p. 124), while Paul West, in "Rasselas: The Humanist as Stoic," *English* 13 (1961), resorted merely to "stoic" (p. 182). But R.K. Kaul, in "The Philosopher of Nature in *Rasselas* XXII," *Indian Journal of English Studies* 3 (1962), demonstrated convincingly that one of the doctrines being satirized in chapter XXII was that of stoicism (pp. 116-20).   63. J.M. Aden, *"Rasselas* and *The Vanity of Human*

Wishes," Criticism 3 (1961): 298, 300, 303.   64. R. Voitle, *Samuel Johnson the Moralist* (Cambridge, Mass., 1961) 40.   65. E.D. Leyburn, "Two Allegorical Treatments of Man: *Rasselas* and *La Peste," Criticism* 4 (1962): 205, 209.

66. K.M. Grange, "Dr. Samuel Johnson's Account of a Schizophrenic Illness," *Medical History* 6 (1962): 166. For Hovey's position, see note 57 above.

67. D.M. Lockhart, "'The Fourth Son of the Mighty Emperor'" *PMLA* 78 (1963): 516-28. For the Egyptian background, see A.M. Weitzman, "More Light on *Rasselas," PQ* 48 (1969): 42-58.   68. W.K. Wimsatt, Jr., "In Praise of *Rasselas," Imagined Worlds,* ed. Maynard Mack (London, 1968) 134.

69. F.W. Hilles, *"Rasselas,* An 'Uninstructive Tale,'" *Johnson, Boswell and Their Circle* (Oxford, 1965) 119. That the controversy continued is evidenced by the difference between S. Sacks, who, in *Fiction and the Shape of Belief* (1964), maintained that *Rasselas* was a "representative apologue" (p. 50) and M. Price, who, in *To the Palace of Wisdom* (1964), believed that such a view overlooked "the comedy of misdirected effort and undeserved luck" (p. 320). The somber reading still predominated because it was generally believed that Johnson's writing rarely evidenced humor. S.T. Fisher pointed out, for example, in "Johnson on Flying," *TLS* (Nov. 4, 1965) that the "Dissertation on Flying" of *Rasselas* was included in Stephen Potter's *The Sense of Humour* (first published in 1954 and reissued in 1964) as an illustration of the "unintentionally funny" (p. 988). But that Hilles' article had raised an issue that could not be avoided is evidenced by W.O.S. Sutherland, Jr.'s argument in his chapter entitled "The Plot of *Rasselas"* in *The Art of the Satirist* (1965). Sutherland argues that "the satirist is not bound to the conventions of either completion or climax, yet they are so ingrained in author and reader that he often makes a gesture toward both" (p. 94). We are left in doubt, however, as to how to interpret the final gesture of Imlac. During this period of debate about the form of *Rasselas,* some critics felt free to extract parts of the content of the tale without considering it in relation to form. Martin Kallich, in "Samuel Johnson's Principles of Criticism," *JAAC* 25 (1966): 71-82, treated Imlac's "Dissertation on Poetry" as an extractable entity, as did Geoffrey Tillotson in "Imlac and the Business of the Poet," *Studies in Criticism and Aesthetics* (1967) 296-314.   70. E. Jones, "The Artistic Form of *Rasselas" RES* ns 18 (1967): 401.

71. W.K. Wimsatt, Jr., "In Praise of *Rasselas,"* pp. 115, 116-7, 124, 126, 128, 130. For a more recent version of this position, see Charles E. Pierce, Jr., "The Conflict of Faith and Fear in Johnson's Moral Writing," *ECS* 15 (1982): 334.   72. *Rasselas,* ed. J. Hardy (1968) xii, xvi, xxiv. Further evidence of the difficulties that arise from not fully appreciating the nature of the breakthrough involved in Jones' coda is provided by Hugo Reichard's essay "The Pessimist's Helpers in *Rasselas," TSLL* 10 (1968). Reichard argues that "the search for happiness, unwittingly sabotaged by the inquisitors, the yesmen, the proxies, comes to seem as preposterous as the boobies who prosecute it" (p. 63). The problem here is the same one encountered by any claim for total satire based on formalist grounds—how the form of the satire escapes being satirized.   73. T.R. Preston, "The Biblical Context of Johnson's *Rasselas,"* PMLA 84 (1969): 274-81. See also D.M. Korte's response to Preston in *PMLA* 87 (1972): 100, and Preston's reply to Korte in the same issue of *PMLA* 87 (1972): 312-14.   74. P. O'Flaherty, "Dr. Johnson as Equivocator," *MLQ* 31 (1970): 203, 205, 207, 208. Also see note 2 above.   75. M. Lascelles, *"Rasselas:* A Rejoinder," *Notions and Facts* (1970) 121, 126, 128, 129.

76. D.J. Greene, *Samuel Johnson* (1970) 133-39, and "Voltaire and Johnson,"

in *Enlightenment Studies in Honour of Lester G. Crocker,* ed. Alfred J. Bingham and Virgil W. Topazio (Oxford: Voltaire Foundation, 1979) 130-31. Although Greene and Lascelles are both influenced by Sherburn and Jones, some critics refused to acknowledge their findings. L.A. Landa, in "Johnson's Feathered Man," *18th Century Studies* (1970), argued that *Rasselas* is typified by the flying episode, "a story of failure" that represents the philosophic substance of the entire tale, "man's delusive hopes, the discrepancy between human pretensions and human achievements" (p. 163).   77. G. Tillotson, "Time in *Rasselas,*" *Cairo Studies* (1959) 97-103.   78. H.E. Pagliaro, "Structural Patterns of Control in *Rasselas,*" in *English Writers of the Eighteenth Century,* ed. J.H. Middendorf (1971), 214, 219, 229 and *Rasselas,* ed. G. Tillotson and B. Jenkins (London: Oxford UP, 1971), xi-xix. For another attempt to incorporate comedy within a religious reading, see P. Fussell, *Samuel Johnson and the Life of Writing* (1971) 243.   79. H. Weinbrot, "The Reader, the General and the Particular," *ECS* 5 (1971): 80-96. See responses by A. Scouten in *ECS* 1973: 506-8, and D.T. Siebert, Jr., *ECS* 1974: 350-52, and R. Folkenflik, "The Tulip and Its Streaks," *Ariel* 9 (1978): 57-71.   80. I. White, "On *Rasselas,*" *Cambridge Quarterly* 6 (1973): 24-30.

81. T. Curley, "The Spiritual Journey," *Anglia* 91 (1973): 36, and chapter 5 of *Samuel Johnson and the Age of Travel* (1976) 147-82.   82. C. McIntosh, *The Choice of Life* (1973) 193.   83. W. Holtz, "We Didn't Mind His Saying So," *American Scholar* 1974: 271-73. Gwin Kolb, however, believed that the text itself gave certain direction to the reader. In "The Intellectual Background of the Discourse on the Soul in *Rasselas,*" *PQ* 54 (1975), Kolb argued that the discussion about the soul at the catacombs directed the reader's attention "to the certain prospect of eternity" (p. 357). This assertion was based upon historical material, but the question remained what sort of transformation the material Kolb had unearthed underwent when it entered the context of *Rasselas.* See note 49 above.   84. E. Wasserman, "Johnson's *Rasselas:* Implicit Contexts," *JEGP* 74 (1975): 5, 25. Wasserman had earlier discussed these two motifs in "The Inherent Values of Eighteenth Century Personification," *PMLA* 65 (1950): 435-63.   85. R.G. Walker, *Eighteenth-Century Arguments for Immortality* (1977) 153.

86. W. Vesterman, *The Stylistic Life of Samuel Johnson* (1977) 104.   87. W.J. Bate, *Samuel Johnson* (1978) 338. During this time a similar difference of opinion can be seen in the views of D.J. Enright and W.B. Carnochan. Both agreed that the body of narrative was about the learning procedure. Enright, in the introduction to his 1976 edition of *Rasselas* (New York: Penguin), describes the conclusion as a return to a world of action, to Abyssinia, which is a realm of participation, not merely of observation (p. 12). Carnochan, on the other hand, in *Confinement and Flight* (Berkeley: U of Calif. P, 1977), characterizes the end as a state of confinement that inhibits learning (p. 170).   88. *The Mid-Eighteenth Century,* ed. J. Butt, completed by G. Carnall (1979) 36-37.   89. I. Ehrenpreis, "Rasselas and Some Meanings of 'Structure' in Literary Criticism," *Novel* 14 (1981): 108, 110, 113, 117. For a richly suggestive essay respectfully calling into question many of the assumptions in Ehrenpreis' analysis, see Leopold Damrosch, Jr., "Johnson's *Rasselas:* Limits of Wisdom, Limits of Art," *Augustan Studies,* ed. Douglas Patey and Timothy Keegan (Newark: U of Delaware P, 1985) 205-14. A number of the insights in the essay are close to those pursued in this study, particularly the concept of education on p. 207 and the analysis of the flying episode on p. 208.   90. A. Liu, "Beckford's *Vathek* and Johnson's *Rasselas,*" *TSLL* 26 (1984): 202, 204, 205.

2. Prison-Paradise

1. Arthur J. Weitzman, "More Light on *Rasselas*: The Background of the Egyptian Episodes," *PQ* 48 (Jan. 1969): 42-56. The fullest treatment of the background to the happy valley is Lockhart's essay cited in chapter 1, note 67 above.   2. *Milton: Poetical Works,* ed. Douglas Bush (London: Oxford UP, 1966) 281.   3. Maren-Sofie Røstvig, *The Happy Man: Studies in the Metamorphoses of a Classical Ideal* (Oslo: Norwegian Univ. Press, 1962) 1: 194. For a more recent article on the cult of retirement, see A.S. Knowles, Jr., "Defoe, Swift and Fielding: Notes on the Retirement Theme," *Quick Springs of Sense,* ed. L.S. Champion (Athens: U of Georgia P, 1974) 121-36.   4. *A Voyage to Abyssinia, by Father Jerome Lobo with a Continuation by Mr. Legrand* (London, 1735) viii. I have decided to use this first edition for citations since the new Yale version, with vol. 15 edited by Joel Gold, does not preserve the capitalization of the original.   5. *A Voyage to Abyssinia* x.   6. Joel J. Gold, "Johnson's Translation of Lobo," *PMLA* 80 (March 1965): 51-61. See also Gold's introduction to his edition of the translation of Lobo, *Samuel Johnson: A Voyage to Abyssinia* (trans. from the French) (New Haven: Yale UP, 1985) xv, xlvii-lvi, and his useful account of the transformations of the Abyssinian story in "The Voyages of Jeronomo Lobo, Joachim Le Grand and Samuel Johnson," *Prose Studies* 5 (1982): 20-41.   7. *A Voyage to Abyssinia* 99-100.
8. Ibid., 39-40.   9. See chapter 1, note 67 above.   10. Morris R. Brownell, *Alexander Pope & the Arts of Georgian England* (Oxford: Clarendon Press, 1970) 122, 134.

11. See Kenneth Woodbridge, *Landscape and Antiquity* (Oxford: Clarendon Press, 1970).   12. Frère Jean Denis Attiret, *A Particular Account of the Emperor of China's Gardens Near Pekin,* trans. Sir Henry Beaumont (London, 1752) 44.   13. Sir William Chambers, *Dissertation on Oriental Gardening* (London, 1757) 12-13.   14. *The Genius of the Place: The English Landscape Garden, 1620-1820,* ed. John Dixon Hunt and Peter Willis (London: Paul Elek, 1974) 265.   15. *The Genius of the Place* 274-75.

16. Ibid., 276. For a recent attempt to establish a relationship between eighteenth-century literature and the garden, see John Dixon Hunt, *The Figure in the Landscape: Poetry, Painting and Gardening during the Eighteenth Century* (Baltimore: Johns Hopkins UP, 1976).   17. Boswell's *Life,* 5: 457.
18. Røstvig, 2: 109-10.   19. Joseph Addison, *The Spectator,* ed. Donald F. Bond (Oxford: Clarendon Press, 1965), 2: 126-27.   20. Oliver Goldsmith, *The Collected Works,* ed. Arthur Friedman, (Oxford: Clarendon Press, 1966) 2: 157.

21. Ibid. 157-58.   22. Ibid. 161. For an alternative reading of the Valley of Ignorance, see Douglas Lane Patey, *Probability and Literary Form: Philosophic Theory and Literary Practice in the Augustan Age* (Cambridge: Cambridge UP, 1984) 177-79.   22. Goldsmith, 2: 145.   23. For evidence that Johnson did not see *Candide* before he completed *Rasselas,* see Boswell, *Life* 1: 342, and James L. Clifford, *"Candide* and *Rasselas," New York Times Book Review* Apr. 19, 1959: 4. For background on the flying incident, see Kolb, "Johnson's Dissertation," *MP* 47 (1949): 24-31, reprinted in *New Light on Dr. Johnson: Essays on the Occasion of His 250th Birthday,* ed. Frederick W. Hilles (New Haven: Yale UP, 1959).   24. See *Rasselas,* G.B. Hill (Oxford: Clarendon Press, 1960), 165.   25. F.M.A. Voltaire, *Candide,* ed. and trans. Robert M. Adams (New York: Norton, 1966), 75.

26. For an alternative view of this episode, see Louis Landa, "Johnson's Feathered Man," 161-78. For Johnson's attitudes on flying, see S.T. Fisher,

"Johnson on Flying," *TLS* Nov. 4, 1965: 988, and A.J. Meadows, *TLS* Dec. 2, 1965: 1112. For an earlier version of my own reading of the happy valley, see "Prison-Paradise: A Point of Departure in *Rasselas*," in *Gefängnis and Paradies,* ed. Gerhard Charles Rump (Bonn, West Germany, 1982) 1-17.

3. The History of Imlac

1. A. Lombardo 47.   2. R. Walker 42-47.   3. Boswell, *Life* 3: 6.   4. M-S. Røstvig 1: 72-73.   5. Ibid. 2: 7. 6. Ibid. 81.   7. Ibid. 148.   8. J.D. Fleeman, *The Poems of Samuel Johnson* (Harmondsworth, Middx.: Penguin Books, 1971) 183.   9. The term "axis" is derived from H. Pagliaro, "Structural Patterns," 213, whose position is discussed in chapter 1 (see note 78). Pagliaro employs the notion of an axis for a formal analysis of *Rasselas* as a novel. For me, it forms part of the learning procedure that has reference beyond the limits of literary form.   10. W. Wimsatt, "The General and the Particular," *PQ* 22 (Jan. 1943): 76. For a measured and intelligent discussion of this issue throughout all of Johnson, see Isobel Grundy, *Samuel Johnson and the Scale of Greatness* (Leicester: Leicester UP, 1986) 155-70. It seems to me that in the end Grundy comes to see greatness and littleness or pettiness as of equal weight for Johnson (see pp. 233-39); she does not, however, see them as dialectically related. For me, the connection of viewpoints is an interpretive device. For a helpful and stimulating discussion of the background of this speech, see Richard Eversole, "Imlac and the Poets of Persia and Arabia," *PQ* 58 (1974): 155-70.

11. A. Friedman, *PQ* 21 (Apr. 1942): 211-13.   12. W. Bate, *The Achievement of Samuel Johnson* 200. See also Jean Hagstrum's 1967 preface to *Samuel Johnson's Literary Criticism* (Chicago: U of Chicago P, 1967, originally published in 1952) vii-ix. For a recent view in essential agreement with Hagstrum, see William Edinger, *Samuel Johnson and Poetic Style* (Chicago: U of Chicago P, 1977) 199-207.   13. M. Kallich 71-82.   14. G. Tillotson, "Imlac and the Business of the Poet," 296-314.   15. H. Weinbrot, "The Reader, the General, and the Particular," 80-96. Arthur Scouten reinforced Weinbrot's view in "Dr. Johnson and Imlac," *ECS*, Forum, 6 (1973): 506-8.

16. D. Siebert, Jr., "The Reliability of Imlac," 352. See chapter 1, note 79 above.   17. For consideration of Johnson's manner of proceeding in the periodical essays, see A.T. Elder, "Irony and Humour in the *Rambler*," *UTQ* 30 (1960): 57-71, and "Thematic Patterning and Development in Johnson's Essays," *SP* 62 (1965): 610-32, and Leopold Damrosch, Jr., "Johnson's Manner of Proceeding in the *Rambler*," *ELH* 40 (1973): 70-89.   18. Wolfgang Iser, *The Act of Reading: A Theory of Aesthetic Response* (Baltimore: Johns Hopkins UP, 1978) 164-70.   19. Lucien Dällenbach, "Reflexivity and Reading," trans. Annette Tomarken, *NLH* 9 (Spring 1980): 441.   20. Gérard Genette, *Narrative Discourse: An Essay in Method,* trans. Jane E. Lewin (Ithaca: Cornell UP, 1980) 233.

21. M.M. Bakhtin, *The Dialogic Imagination,* trans. Caryl Emerson and Michael Holquist (Austin: U of Texas P, 1981) 263.   22. Iser 159.   23. Dällenbach 445.   24. Genette 27.   25. Bakhtin 84-85, 257-58. It might be helpful to point out that for Bakhtin the chronotope enters the novel by way of a voice that is then subject to the dialogic process. Voice is a term that only has meaning within discourse; my term, perspective, is both linguistic and behavioral. For an earlier version of chapter 3, see Edward Tomarken, "Perspectivism: The Methodological Implications of 'The history of Imlac' in *Rasselas*," *Age of Johnson* 2 (1989): 264-92.

4. A Journey to Understanding

1. For the most recent and most comprehensive discussion of Johnson's general attitude toward stoicism, see Donald Greene, "Johnson, Stoicism, and the Good Life," in *The Unknown Samuel Johnson,* ed. John Burke, Jr., and Donald Kay (Madison: U of Wisconsin P, 1983) 17-38. For an alternative position, see Robert Voitle, "Stoicism and Samuel Johnson," in *Essays in English Literature of the Classical Period Presented to Dougald Macmillan,* ed. P.W. Patterson and A.B. Strauss, *SP,* Extra Series no. 4 (1967): 107-27.   2. For discussion of the specific relationship between stoicism and this episode, as opposed to the general ones in note 1 above, see G.J. Kolb, "The Use of Stoical Doctrines in *Rasselas,* Chapter XVIII," *MLN* 68 (1953): 374-76.   3. I am indebted for this suggestion to Leopold Damrosch, Jr.   4. For a discussion of the background and references to this episode, see R.K. Kaul, "The Philosopher of Nature in *Rasselas* XXII," *Indian Journal of English Studies* 3 (1962): 116-20. For a more recent discussion, see Richard Schwartz, "Johnson's Philosopher of Nature: *Rasselas,* Chapter 22," *MP* 74 (1976): 196-200.   5. In chapter 1, pp. 25-28, it was demonstrated that this fact attained general acceptance in the 1960s.

6. Ernest Lee Tuveson, *The Imagination as a Means of Grace* (Berkeley: U of California P, 1960) 301.   7. Tuveson 319.   8. M. Lascelles, in *"Rasselas: A Rejoinder,"* 123, is one of the critics most troubled by this episode.   9. See chapter 1, p. 22 above.   10. *Lives of the English Poets,* ed. G.B. Hill (Oxford: Clarendon Press, 1905), 3: 438.

11. D. Patey, *Probability*; for his discussion of character, see pp. 122-24. For the discussion of mimesis and the novel, see pp. 145-54. For an application of Locke's concept of probability to Johnson's *Preface to Shakespeare,* see Hoyt Trowbridge, "Scattered Atoms of Probability," *ECS* 5 (1971-72): 1-38.   12. Eric Rothstein, *Systems of Order in Late Eighteenth Century Fiction* (Berkeley: U of California P, 1975), 35.   13. E. Wasserman, 7, 10, and M-S. Røstvig, "Tom Jones and the Choice of Hercules," in *Fair Forum: Essays in English Literature from Spenser to Jane Austen,* ed. M-S. Røstvig (Cambridge: D.S. Brewer, 1975) 151.   14. E. Wasserman 12.

5. Trial and Error

1. Northrop Frye, *Anatomy of Criticism* (Princeton: Princeton UP, 1957) 246-47.   2. David Nichol Smith and Edward L. McAdam, *The Poems of Samuel Johnson* (Oxford: Clarendon Press, 1974) 275-76.   3. See Clifford and Greene, 205-7.   4. Smith 275-77.   5. Bertrand H. Bronson, *Johnson Agonistes and Other Essays* (Berkeley: U of California P, 1965) 100-153. For interesting but somewhat disconnected comments on the failure of *Irene,* see Leopold Damrosch, Jr., *Samuel Johnson and the Tragic Sense* (Princeton: Princeton UP, 1972) 109-38.

6. Donald J. Greene, *Samuel Johnson* (New York: Twayne, 1970) 67.   7. Marshall Waingrow, "The Mighty Moral of Irene," in *From Sensibility to Romanticism; Essays Presented to Frederick A. Pottle,* ed. F. W. Hilles and H. Bloom (New York: Oxford UP, 1965) 91.   8. Philip T. Clayton, "Samuel Johnson's *Irene:* 'An Elaborate Curiosity' " *Tennessee Studies in Literature* 19 (1974): 122. For information concerning Johnson's attitude toward the theater, see Roy S. Wolper, "Johnson's Neglected Muse: The Drama," in *Studies in the Eighteenth Century,* ed. R.F. Brissenden (Toronto: U of Toronto P, 1968), 109-17.   9. James Gray, *"Mohamet and Irene:* More Tragedy than Triumph,

Part II," *Humanities Association Review* 28 (1977): 87.   10. Arthur H. Scouten, in *The London Stage: 1660-1800* (Carbondale: Southern Illinois UP, 1961), lists May 29, 1735, as the date of the premiere of Hill's *Zara* and indicates that it was performed at Drury Lane in 1736 (3: xxxiii). Subsequent volumes of *The London Stage* list the dates of the revival. Johnson's *Irene,* according to this record, was presented at Drury Lane in 1749.

11. Eric Rothstein, *Restoration Tragedy: Form and the Process of Change* (Madison: U of Wisconsin P, 1967) 141-44, points out that in the Restoration two heroines became fashionable because of the actresses, Mrs. Bracegirdle and Mrs. Barry, but that even then the dramatist was responsible for any theme or structure resulting from this dualism.   12. Aaron Hill, *The Tragedy of Zara* (London, 1736) 12. Future references to *Zara* will provide act and scene numbers from this edition. For an account of Hill's translation of Voltaire's "Alzire," see *Studies on Voltaire in the Eighteenth Century* 68 (1969): 45-57.   13. F.M.A. de Voltaire, *Zaïre* (Paris: Librarie Larousse, 1934). All further references to the French version give the act, scene, and line numbers from this text. Voltaire did write a play entitled *Irène,* but that heroine is a different person from Johnson's Irene, and the action takes place in another historical situation.   14. Boswell's *Life* 4: 5.   15. M. Lascelles, "Johnson and Juvenal," *New Light on Dr. Johnson,* ed. Frederick W. Hilles (New Haven: Yale UP, 1959) 42-44. For evidence of the influence of both Oldham and Dryden on *London,* see E. and L. Bloom, "Johnson's London and the Tools of Scholarship," *Huntington Library Quarterly* 34 (1971): 115-39.

16. H. Weinbrot, *The Formal Strain* 165-91. For a response to those who questioned Weinbrot's reading of Juvenal, see "Johnson's *London* and Juvenal's *Third Satire:* The Country as 'Ironic' Norm," *MP* 74 (1976): S56.   17. D.V. Boyd, "Vanity and Vacuity: A Reading of Johnson's Verse Satires," *ELH* 39 (1972): 391-96. For an interesting theoretical essay that employs *London* to distinguish between Hirsch's and Gadamer's concepts of interpretation, see Joel Weinsheimer, " 'London' and Hermeneutics," *Critical Inquiry* 9 (1982): 303-22.   18. For a discussion of the textual problems of Johnson's last line, see H. Weinbrot, *The Formal Strain,* who points out that the lines are "extremely assertive" (p. 179). The most recent essay on the relationship between Thales and Savage is Thomas Kaminski's "Was Savage 'Thales'?: Johnson's *London* and Biographical Speculation," *Bulletin of Research in the Humanities* 85 (1982): 322-35.   19. For a discussion of how the historical and political situation surrounding *London* adds further unresolved complications, see Weinbrot, 186-88.

6. Form and Reference

1. Howard D. Weinbrot, *The Formal Strain: Studies in Augustan Imitation and Satire* (Chicago: U of Chicago P, 1969). For information concerning Johnson's knowledge of Juvenal and the edition he consulted, see Edward A. Bloom and Lillian D. Bloom, "Johnson's *London* and Its Juvenalian Texts," *Huntington Library Quarterly* 34 (1970-71): 1-24; and 34 (1971): 115-39. For a general study of imitation, see Joel Weinsheimer, *Imitation* (London: Routledge and Kegan Paul, 1984) and, more recently, " 'Give Me Something to Desire' " *PQ* 64 (1985): 211-23.   2. R.G. Peterson, "Johnson at War with the Classics," *ECS* 9 (1975): 69-86.   3. William Kupersmith, "More Like an Orator than a Philosopher: Rhetorical Structure in *The Vanity of Human Wishes,*" *SP* 72 (1975): 454-72. For a comparison of Juvenal to Johnson, see Kupersmith's "Declamatory Grandeur: Johnson and Juvenal," *Arion* 9 (1970): 52-72. See also Walter J. Bate, "Johnson

and Satire Manqué," in *Eighteenth Century Essays in Honor of Danald F. Hyde,* ed. W.H. Bond (New York: 1970) 145-60.   4. Paul D. McGlynn, "Rhetoric as Metaphor in *The Vanity of Human Wishes,*" *SEL* 15 (1975): 473-82.   5. Lawrence Lipking, "Learning to Read Johnson: *The Vision of Theodore* and *The Vanity of Human Wishes,*" *ELH* 43 (1976): 517-37. For an attempt to mediate between the opposition of the satiric and religious readings by way of the tragic tone, see Michael M. Cohen, "Johnson's Tragedy of Human Wishes," *English Studies* 63 (1982): 410-17.

6. John E. Sitter, in "To *The Vanity of Human Wishes* through the 1740s," *SP* 74 (1977): 447-57, develops a similar notion about the point of view of Observation. Sitter's point, however, is historical, having to do with the "voice" of poetry in the 1740s, and he agrees with McGlynn's formalist view that the poem "catalogs" rather than suggests alternatives to vanity (see p. 463). For Sitter's general consideration of this thesis, see "Mother, Memory, Muse and Poetry after Pope," *ELH* 44 (1977): 312-36, and *Literary Loneliness in Mid-Eighteenth-Century England* (Ithaca: Cornell UP, 1982).   7. For a full discussion of the role of the *kataskopos* and the *episkopos* as satiric observers, see Douglas Duncan, *Ben Jonson and the Lucianic Tradition* (Cambridge: Cambridge UP, 1979) 236, note 7. For an informed discussion of Johnson's general position on observation, see Isobel Grundy, *Samuel Johnson and the Scale of Greatness,* 154-75.   8. See Smith and McAdam, 115, note.   9. Ibid., 416.   10. R. Selden, in "Dr. Johnson and Juvenal: A Problem in Critical Method," *Comparative Literature* 22 (1970): 297, makes a similar point, asserting that "the empty-handed, unencumbered traveler is no longer simply a carefree vagrant." Selden's careful comparison is for the purpose of describing Johnson's poem in purely literary terms, in reaction to the moral tradition exemplified by Edward A. Bloom, "*The Vanity of Human Wishes:* Reason's Images," *Essays in Criticism* 15 (1965): 182-92. But in my view, the *Vanity* is at once literary and extraliterary; that the literary image has a moral purpose need not detract from either function.

11. For an intelligent if brief comparison of Juvenal's and Johnson's Democritus, see R. Selden, "Dr. Johnson and the Tears of Heraclitus," *New Rambler* 12 (1972): 51-54, who suggests that Johnson "regarded Democritan mirth as a limited response to human folly" (p. 54). It seems to me that Johnson uses Democritus to go beyond the ancient philosopher's traditional posture. His mirth reveals alternatives to vanity.   12. See Smith and McAdam, 119, note.   13. For a general consideration of Johnson's revisions of *London* and *The Vanity of Human Wishes,* see A.D. Moody, "The Creative Critic: Johnson's Revisions of *London* and *The Vanity of Human Wishes,*" *RES* 22 (1971): 137-50. My own consideration of this particular alteration suggests that Johnson as reviser was more "immersed in the destructive element" than Moody assumes (p. 149).   14. D.V. Boyd, in "Vanity and Vacuity: A Reading of Johnson's Verse Satires," *ELH* 39 (1972): 387-403, develops the thesis that in the *Vanity* "ethical decision is not solved, but dissolved" (p. 403). Wolsey is therefore seen as a case of the "evaporation of a subjective ordering of the world" (p. 399). But attention to Wolsey in retirement suggests that he did have a subjective decision. Moreover, awareness of the alternatives, the less vain possibility, provides an answer to Patrick O'Flaherty, "Johnson as Satirist: A New Look at *The Vanity of Human Wishes,*" *ELH* 34 (1967): 78-90, who believes Johnson fails because his satire is cynical and bitter. Johnson, in my view, does not regard the specific vanities of the poem as inevitable; his poem is for the purpose of pointing to more hopeful alternatives. For an attack on the portraits in the poem, see Graham Cullum, "Dr. Johnson and Human Wishing," *Neophilologus* 67 (1983): 315-17.   15. Mary Lascelles, "Johnson and Juvenal," *New Light on Dr. Johnson,* ed. F.W. Hilles (New

Haven: Yale UP, 1959) 49. For other comparisons of these texts, see Francis G. Schoff, "Johnson and Juvenal," *N&Q* 198 (1953): 293-96; Henry Gifford, *"The Vanity of Human Wishes," RES* ns 6 (1955): 157-65; and R. Voitle, *Samuel Johnson the Moralist* 40-45.

16. Ian Jack, *Augustan Satire* (Oxford: Clarendon Press, 1952) 143.   17. Marjorie Nicolson, *Mountain Gloom and Mountain Glory* (Ithaca: Cornell UP, 1959) 323.   18. Samuel Monk, *The Sublime* (New York: Modern Language Association of America, 1935) 63, 236. David Morris, in *The Religious Sublime* (Lexington: Univ. Press of Kentucky, 1973), accepts Monk's distinction between the two sublimes but refines somewhat their progression.   19. Smith and McAdam, 121, note.   20. Ibid., 124, note. For a view of the conclusion as unconvincing, see Charles E. Pierce, Jr., "The Conflict of Faith and Fear," *ECS* 15 (1982): 320.

21. M.F.A. Voltaire, *Historic de Charles XII* (Paris: Garnier-Flammarion, 1968) 238. See also Donald Greene, "Voltaire and Johnson," *Enlightenment Studies* 130-31.   22. M. Lascelles 52; E. Bloom 182-92.   23. Voltaire 237.   24. For a suggestion about the relationship between this poem and *Rasselas*, see John Vance, "A Poem of Joy: Johnson's *On the Death of Dr. Robert Levet*," *PLL* 20 (1984): 392-95.

7. Historical Understanding

1. Jeffrey Hart, "Johnson's *A Journey to the Western Islands:* History as Art," *ES* 10 (1960): 57.   2. Francis R. Hart, "Johnson's Journey," *ELH* 36 (1969): 690.   3. R.B. Schwartz, in "Johnson's Journey," *JEGP* 69 (1970): 292-303, which is first suggested by Donald Greene, in "Johnsonian Critics," *ES* 10 (1960): 394.   4. Thomas Curley, "Johnson and the Geographical Revolution: *A Journey to the Western Islands of Scotland*," *SBHT* 17 (1976): 194. See also his *Samuel Johnson and the Age of Travel* (Athens: U of Georgia P, 1976) 183-219. For an alternative view of eighteenth-century travel literature, see Charles Batten, Jr., *Pleasurable Instruction: Form and Convention in Eighteenth Century Travel Literature* (Berkeley: U of California P, 197. In contrast to Batten's historical approach, see George H. Savage, " 'Roving among the Hebrides': The Odyssey of Samuel Johnson," *SEL* 17 (1977): 494-501, for a metaphoric view of the *Journey* that completely separates the form from that serving a historical purpose. For a fine scholarly account of travel literature during this period, see Percy G. Adams, *Travel Literature and the Evolution of the Novel* (Lexington: Univ. Press of Kentucky, 1983). Adams, however, believes that Johnson's *Journey* is "not a travel book but historical autobiography" (p. 165).   5. André Perraux, "Samuel Johnson en Ecosse," *Regards sur L'Ecosse au XVIII siècle* (Publications de L'Université de Lille III, 1977) 71.

6. M. Martin, *A Description of the Western Islands of Scotland* (London, 1703) 264.   7. T. Pennant, *A Tour in Scotland and Voyage to the Hebrides* (Chester: John Monk, 1774) 247, 259.   8. Ibid., 248-50.   9. See, for example, *Weekly Magazine* 17 (1774-75): 204-6, 257-60, 189-92, 350-55, and Donald Mac-Nicol, *Remarks on Dr. Samuel Johnson's Journey to the Hebrides* (London, 1779) 371.   10. See note 9 above. For a provocative essay on trees, see John B. Radner, "The Significance of Johnson's Changing Views of the Hebrides," in *The Unknown Samuel Johnson* (Madison: U of Wisconsin P, 1983) 131-49. Radner, it seems to me, is one of the few critics to locate the complex historical-literary problem in the *Journey*. He concludes, however, by focusing on the autobiographical and historical aspect. My own interpretation combines this element with the

literary aspect. For previous versions of my own attempts to come to terms with this complex problem, see " 'The Fictions of Romantic Chivalry': Samuel Johnson's Attitudes to the Middle Ages," *Studies in Medievalism* 1 (1979): 5-13, and "Travels into the Unknown: *Rasselas* and *A Journey to the Western Islands of Scotland*," in *The Unknown Samuel Johnson* 150-67. Donald Greene makes a suggestion about the political significance of trees in *Samuel Johnson: Political Writings* (New Haven: Yale UP, 1977) 125, and Robert G. Walker presents a religious view in "Johnson and the Trees of Scotland," *PQ* 61 (1982): 98-101.

11. For a welcome reassessment of Johnson's understanding of and commitment to history, see John Vance, *Samuel Johnson and the Sense of History* (Athens: U of Georgia P, 1984). Eithne Henson presents a sensitive reading of Johnson's attitude toward ancient Highland life in "Johnson's Quest for 'the Fictions of Romantic Chivalry' in Scotland," *Prose Studies* 7 (1984): 97-128.   12. For Johnson's "prejudice" against the Scots, see Boswell, *Life* 2: 121, 236; 4: 169.

8. The Limitations of Perspectivism

1. See M. Brownell 132. On the process of composing the *Pope,* see F.W. Hilles, "The Making of *The Life of Pope*," in *New Light on Dr. Johnson,* ed. F.W. Hilles (New Haven: Yale UP, 1959) 257-84. For an intelligent, if brief, view of the grotto similar to mine, see Harriet Kirkley, "Johnson's *Life of Pope:* Fact as Fiction," *Wascana Review* (Spring 1980): 74-76. Kirkley, however, does not pursue the difference between Johnson's assessment of Pope as poet and as man. For a more sympathetic reading of the grotto, see Maynard Mack, " 'The Shadowy Cave': Some Speculations on a Twickenham Grotto," in *Restoration and Eighteenth Century: Essays in Honor of Alan Dugald McKillop* (Chicago: U of Chicago P, 1963) 69-88; *The Garden and the City,* (Toronto: U of Toronto P, 1968) 61; and *Alexander Pope: A Life* (New York: Norton, 1985) 365, 446. For a general discussion of Johnson as biographer, see Robert Folkenflik, *Samuel Johnson, Biographer* (Ithaca: Cornell UP, 1978).

9. Theoretical Conclusion

1. For a statement of the editorial policy of New Literary History, see Ralph Cohen, "A Note on *New Literary History*," *NLH* 1 (1969): 3-6, 168-70, 172, 174, and "The First Decade: Some Editorial Remarks," 10 (1978): 417-21. For an application of the concept of Johnsonian perspectives in a literary-critical context, see my work in progress, entitled *The Discipline of Criticism,* which will be the first full-length work on the critical method inherent in Johnson's *Notes to Shakespeare.*

A Chronological Checklist
of *Rasselas* Criticism
1759-1986

Note: Asterisks indicate material found in neither *Samuel Johnson: A Survey and Bibliography of Critical Studies,* ed. James Clifford and Donald J. Greene (Minneapolis: U of Minnesota P, 1970), nor *A Bibliography of Johnsonian Studies,* ed. John Vance and Donald J. Greene (Vancouver: U of British Columbia, 1987).

Critical Review Apr. 1759:372-75.
*Gentleman's Magazine Apr. 1759:184-86.
*London Magazine May 1759:258-62.
[Owen Ruffhead] *Monthly Review* May 1759:428-37.
Annual Register Dec. 1759:477-98.
*Tyers, Thomas. *A Biographical Sketch of Dr. Samuel Johnson.* London, 1784.
*Hawkins, Sir John. *The Life of Samuel Johnson.* London, 1787. 154-57.
Rasselas. Dublin, 1787. 4-6.
Knight, Ellis Cornelia. *Dinarbas: A Tale, Being a Continuation of Rasselas, Prince of Abyssinia.* London, 1790.
*Boswell, James. *Boswell's Life of Johnson.* London, 1791. 340-44.
*Mudford, William. *Critical Enquiry into the Moral Writings of Dr. Samuel Johnson.* London, 1802. 80-85.
*Murphy, Arthur. "An Essay on the Life and Genius of Samuel Johnson, LL.D." *Johnsonian Miscellanies.* London, 1792. 472.
*Rasselas. Dublin, 1803. 3-39.
*Rasselas. London, 1805. i-ii.
More, Hannah. *Hints Towards Forming the Character of a Young Princess* in *Works of Hannah More.* London, 1805.
*Hunt, Leigh. *Rasselas.* In *Classic Tales Serious and Lively, with Critical Essays on the Merits and Reputations of the Authors,* 3:1-13. London, 1807.
*Rasselas. London, 1809. i-xx.
Barbauld, Anna Letitia. "Johnson." *British Novelists, with . . . prefaces, biographical and critical.* London: Rivington, 1810. 26:i-viii.
*Rasselas. Edinburgh, 1812. v-xii.
*Rasselas. London, 1815. i-xx.
*Hazlitt, W. *Lectures on the Comic Writers.* London, 1819. 102-3.
*Rasselas. Ed. Sir Walter Scott. London, 1823. xl-xlvi.
*Rasselas. London, 1823. iii-viii.
Rasselas. Edinburgh, 1824. iii-v.

*Macaulay, Thomas Babington. "Boswell's Life Of Johnson." *The Six Chief Lives from Johnson's Lives of the Poets,* ed. M. Arnold. London: Macmillan, 1878. 21-22. [First appeared in *Edinburgh Review* 54 (1831): 1-38.]

*Whately, Elizabeth Pope. *The Second Part of Rasselas, Prince of Abyssinia.* London, 1835.

Rasselas. London: Charles Till, 1838. iii-v.

M., J. [John Mitford]. [Letter attributing to Johnson Book IX, Chapter XI, of Charlotte Lennox's *The Female Quixote.*] *GM* ns 20 (Aug. 1843): 132.

Rasselas. London, 1843. iii-viii.

Rasselas. Philadelphia: Hogan and Thompson, 1850. xv-xxii.

Rasselas. London: Longmans, 1860. xi-xxiii.

Eirionnach. "*Rasselas* and the Happy Valley." *N&Q* 4th ser. 2 (July 4, 1868): 1-2.

Rasselas. Ed. Rev. William West. London, 1869. xiii-xlv.

Rasselas. Philadelphia: Yale University, 1873. vii-x.

*Stephen, Leslie. *Samuel Johnson.* London: Macmillan, 1878. 173-82.

Rasselas. Ed. Alfred Milnes. Oxford: Clarendon Press, 1879. v-xxxii.

Rasselas. London: Whittaker & Co., 1879. v-vi.

"Johnson's *Rasselas.*" *Bibliographer* 3 (May 1883): 173-75.

"The Story of 'Rasselas.' " *Book-Lore* 1 (Dec. 1884): 5-11.

Rasselas. Ed. Henry Morley. London: George Routledge & Son, 1884. 5-8.

Rasselas. Ed. Dr. James Macaulay. London: Elliot Stock, 1884. iii-xvii.

Rasselas. Ed. George B. Hill. London: Oxford UP, 1887. 20-32.

Rasselas. Ed. Henry Morley. London: Cassell & Co., 1888. 7-8.

*Cross, W.L. In *The Development of the English Novel.* New York: Macmillan, 1889. 77-78.

[The publisher of *Rasselas*]. *Critic* ns 14 (Aug. 16, 1890): 85.

Rasselas. Ed. Fred N. Scott. Boston and New York: Leach, Shewell and Sanborn, 1891. 1-24.

Raleigh, Walter A. "Rasselas." *The English Novel.* London: John Murray, 1894. 203-6.

Rasselas. Ed. Oliver F. Emerson. New York: Henry Holt, 1895. 18-53.

Emerson, Oliver F. "The Text of Johnson's *Rasselas.*" *Anglia* 22 (Dec. 1899): 499-509.

Rasselas. Ed. Justin Hannaford. London, 1900. xvi-xxiv.

Whittuck, Charles. "Anti-Cant: Candide; Rasselas." *The "Good Man" of the XVIIIth Century.* London: George Allen, 1901.

Rasselas. Ed. Hannaford Bennett. London: John Lang, 1905. i-iv.

Rasselas. Ed. C.S. Fearenside. London, 1906. vii-xx.

Conant, Martha P. *The Oriental Tale in England in the Eighteenth Century.* New York: Columbia UP, 1908, 140-54.

Rasselas. Ed. A.J.F. Collins. London: W.B. Cline, 1910. ix-xxix.

*Raleigh, Walter A. *Six Essays on Johnson.* Oxford: Clarendon Press, 1910. 33.

Collison-Morley, Lacy. " 'Rasselas': The First Italian Translation." *N&Q* 11th ser. 1 (May 21, 1910): 404.

*Bailey, John. *Dr. Johnson and His Circle.* London: Williams & Norgate, 1913. 196-201.

Saintsbury, George. *The English Novel.* London: Dent & Sons, 1913. 34-35.

Howells, W.D. "Editor's Easy Chair." *Harper's* 131 (July 1915): 310-13.

Markland, Russell. "Dr. Johnson and Shelley." *N&Q* 12th ser. 9 (Nov. 5, 1921): 368.

Armstrong, T. Percy. "Emerson and Dr. Johnson." *N&Q* 12th ser. 10 (Mar. 4, 1922): 167.

*Houston, Percy H. *Doctor Johnson: A Study in 18th-Century Humanism.* Cambridge: Harvard UP, 1923.

Powell, Lawrence F. "Rasselas." *TLS* Feb. 22, 1923:124.

Tinker, Chauncey B. "Rasselas in the New World." *Yale Review* 14 (Oct. 1924): 95-107.

Belloc, Hilaire. "Mrs. Piozzi's *Rasselas.*" *SRL* 2 (Aug. 15, 1925): 37-38.

Belloc, Hilaire. "On *Rasselas.*" *New Statesman* 25 (Sept. 5, 1925): 571-72.

Rasselas. Ed. G.K. Chesterton. London: J.M. Dent & Sons, 1926. vii-x.

Palser, Ernest M. *A Commentary & Questionnaire on the History of Rasselas.* London: Sir Isaac Pitman & Sons, 1927.

Rassleas. Ed. R.W. Chapman. Oxford: Clarendon Press, 1927. ix-xxi.

Rasselas. Ed. Philip Henderson. *Shorter Novels of the 18th Century.* New York: E.P. Dutton & Co., 1930. vii-xii.

Collins, Norman. *Facts of Fiction.* London: Victor Gollancz, 1932. 82-84.

Warner, Oliver. "*Rasselas:* The Testament of a Romantic." *Bookman* (London) 82 (June 1932): 147-48.

*Kingsmill, Hugh [Hugh Dobbs]. *Samuel Johnson.* London: Arthur Barker, 1933. 108-14.

Baker, Ernest A. "The Oriental Story from *Rasselas* to *Vathek.*" *The History of the English Novel.* London: H.F. & G. Witherby, 1934. 5:55-76.

Barnouw, A.J. "*Rasselas* in Dutch." *TLS* Apr. 11, 1935: 244.

Tillotson, Geoffrey. "*Rasselas* and the *Persian Tales.*" *TLS* Aug. 29, 1935: 534.

Squire, Sir John C. "Johnson and Abyssinia." *Lichfield Mercury* Sept. 27, 1935.

Sewall, Richard B. "Rousseau's Second Discourse in England from 1755 to 1762." *PQ* 17 (Apr. 1938): 97-114.

Jenkins, Harold D. "Some Aspects of the Background of *Rasselas.*" *Studies in English in Honor of R.D. O'Leary and S.L. Whitcomb.* U of Kansas, 1940. 8-14.

Cameron, Kenneth N. "A New Source for Shelley's *A Defense of Poetry.*" *SP* 38 (Oct. 1941): 629-44.

Cameron, Kenneth N. "*Rasselas* and *Alastor:* A Study in Transmutation." *SP* 40 (Jan. 1943): 58-78.

*Wagenknecht, Edward. *Cavalcade of the English Novel.* New York: Henry Holt, 1943. 130.

*Krutch, Joseph Wood. *Samuel Johnson.* New York: Henry Holt & Co., 1944. 174-84.

Kolb, Gwin J. "Johnson's 'Dissertation on Flying' and John Wilkins' *Mathematical Magick.*" *MP* 47 (Aug. 1949): 24-31.

Metzdorf, Robert F. "The Second Sequel to *Rasselas.*" *New Rambler* 16 (Jan. 1950): 5-7.

*Tracy, Clarence R. "Democritus, Arise." *Yale Review* 39 (1950): 294-310.

*Church, Richard. *The Growth of the English Novel.* London, 1951. 77-80.

*Neill, S. Diana. *A Short History of the English Novel.* London, 1951. 77-80.

Lascelles, Mary. "*Rasselas* Reconsidered." *Essays and Studies by Members of the English Association* ns 4 (1951): 37-52.

Kolb, Gwin J. "The Structure of *Rasselas.*" *PMLA* 66 (Sept. 1951): 698-717.

*Leavis, F.R. *The Common Pursuit.* New York: New York UP, 1952. 115.

Moore, John Robert. "Conan Doyle, Tennyson, and *Rasselas.*" *Nineteenth Century Fiction* 7 (Dec. 1952): 221-23.

Kolb, Gwin J. "The Use of Stoical Doctrines in *Rasselas,* Chapter XVIII." *MLN* 58 (Nov. 1953): 439-47.

Metzdorf, Robert F. "The First American 'Rasselas' and Its Imprint." *PBSA* 47 (4th quarter, 1953): 374-76.

Moore, John Robert. "*Rasselas* and the Early Travelers to Abyssinia." *MLQ* 15 (Mar. 1954): 36-41.

Osgood, C.G. "Johnson and Macrobius." MLN 59 (Apr. 1954): 246.

Hovey, Richard B. "Dr. Samuel Johnson, Psychiatrist." *MLQ* 15 (Dec. 1954): 321-35.

*Bate, Walter Jackson. *The Achievement of Samuel Johnson*. New York: Oxford UP, 1955. Passim.

Leyburn, Ellen D. " 'No Romantic Absurdities or Incredible Fictions': The Relation of Johnson's *Rasselas* to Lobo's *Voyage to Abyssinia*." *PMLA* 70 (Dec. 1955): 1059-67.

Bredvold, Louis I. "*Rasselas* and the *Miscellanies* of John Morris." *JNL* 16. 1 (Mar. 1956): 3-4.

Whitley, Alvin. "The Comedy of *Rasselas*." *ELH* 23 (Mar. 1956): 48-70.

Barnett, George L. "*Rasselas* and *De Senectute*," *N&Q* Nov. 1956: 485-86.

*Frye, Northrop. *Anatomy of Criticism: Four Essays*. Princeton UP, 1957. 200.

Pakenham, Thomas. "Gondar and the Mountain." *History Today* 7 (Mar. 1957): 172-81.

Barnett, George L. "*Rasselas* and *The Vicar of Wakefield*," *N&Q* July 1957: 303-5.

Kenney, William. "Johnson's *Rasselas* after Two Centuries." *Boston University Studies in English* 3 (Summer 1957): 88-96.

Link, Frederick M. "Rasselas and the Quest for Happiness." *Boston University Studies in English* 3 (Summer 1957): 121-23.

Joost, Nicholas. "Whispers of Fancy; or, the Meaning of *Rasselas*." *Modern Age* 1 (Fall 1957): 166-73.

*Lucas, F.L. *The Search for Good Sense: Four 18th Century Characters*. London: Cassell & Co., 1958. 115-20.

*Bronson, Bertrand. *Samuel Johnson: Poems and Selected Prose*. New York: Holt, Rinehart and Winston, 1958. xv-xvi.

Fisher, Marvin. "The Pattern of Conservatism in Johnson's *Rasselas* and Hawthorne's *Tales*." *JHI* 19 (Apr. 1958): 173-96.

Kolb, Gwin J. "The 'Paradise' in Abyssinia and the 'Happy Valley' in *Rasselas*." *MP* 56 (Aug. 1958): 10-16.

Clifford, James L. "Some Remarks on *Candide* and *Rasselas*." *Cairo Studies in English* (1959), 7-14.

Mahmound, Fatma Moussa. "*Rasselas* and *Vathek*." Cairo Studies in English (1959), 51-57.

Goodyear, Louis E. "*Rasselas*' Journey from Amhara to Cairo Viewed from Arabia." *Cairo Studies in English* (1959), 21-29.

Lombardo, Agostino. "The Importance of Imlac." *Cairo Studies in English* (1959), 31-49.

Dina Abdul-Hamid Al Aoun. "Some Remarks on a Sacred Reading of *Rasselas*." *Cairo Studies in English* (1959), 15-20.

Manzalaoui, Mahmoud. "*Rasselas* and Some Mediaeval Ancillaries." *Cairo Studies in English* (1959), 59-73.

Metzdorf, Robert F. "Grand Cairo and Philadelphia: The Frontispiece to the 1768 Edition of Johnson's *Rasselas*." *Cairo Studies in English* (1959), 75-80.

Moore, John Robert. "*Rasselas* in Retrospect." *Cairo Studies in English* (1959), 81-84.

Rawson, C.J. "The Continuation of *Rasselas*." *Cairo Studies in English* (1959), 85-95.

Tillotson, G. "Time in *Rasselas*." *Cairo Studies in English* (1959), 97-103.

Wahba, Magdi. "A Note on the Manner of Concluding in *Rasselas*." *Cairo Studies in English* (1959), 105-10.

Willard, Nedd. "*Zadig* and *Rasselas* Considered." *Cairo Studies in English* (1959), 111-23.

Kenney, William. "*Rasselas* and the Theme of Diversification." *PQ* 38 (Jan. 1959): 84-89.

Duncan-Jones, E.E. "Marvell, Johnson, and the First Sunset." *TLS* Apr. 3, 1959: 193.

Clifford, James L. "*Candide* and *Rasselas*." *New York Times Book Review* Apr. 19, 1959: 4, 14.

Johnson, J.W. "Rasselas and His Ancestors." *N&Q* May 1959: 185-88.

Sherburn, George. "Rasselas Returns—to What?" *PQ* 38 (July 1959: 383-84.

*Stevenson, Lionel. *The English Novel: A Panorama*. London: Constable & Co., 1960.12-24.

West, Paul. "Rasselas: The Humanist as Stoic." *English* 13 (Summer 1961): 181-85.

Tillotson, Geoffrey. "Time in *Rasselas*." *Augustan Studies*. London: Athlone Press, 1961. 229-48. [First published in *Bicentenary Essays,* ed. M. Wahba, 1959.]

Aden, John M. "*Rasselas* and *The Vanity of Human Wishes*." *Criticism* 3 (Fall 1961): 295-303.

*Voitle, Robert. *Samuel Johnson the Moralist*. Cambridge, Mass.: Harvard UP, 1961. 37-46.

Kaul, R.K. "The Philosopher of Nature in *Rasselas* XXII." *Indian Journal of English Studies* 3 (1962): 116-20.

Rasselas. Ed. Warren L. Fleischauer. Great Neck, N.Y.: Barron's Educational Series, 1962, 1-12.

Kolb, Gwin J. "Textual Cruxes in Rasselas." *Johnsonian Studies,* ed. Magdi Wahba. Cairo, U.A.R.: privately printed, 1962.

Rasselas. Ed. Gwin J. Kolb. New York: Appleton-Century-Crofts, 1962. v-xii.

Eddy, Donald D. "The Publication Date of the First Edition of *Rasselas*." *N&Q* Jan. 1962: 21-22.

Grange, Kathleen M. "Dr. Samuel Johnson's Account of a Schizophrenic Illness in *Rasselas* (1759)." *Medical History* 6 (Apr. 1962): 162-69.

Leyburn, Ellen Douglass. "Two Allegorical Treatments of Man: *Rasselas* and *La Peste*." *Criticism* 4 (Summary 1962): 197-209.

Halsband, Robert. "*Rasselas:* An Early Allusion." *N&Q* Dec. 1962: 459.

Powell, L.F. "For Johnsonian Collectors." *TLS* Sept. 20, 1963: 712.

Lockhart, Donald M. " 'The Fourth Son of the Mighty Emperor': The Ethiopian Background of Johnson's *Rasselas*." *PMLA* 78 (Dec. 1963): 516-28.

Price, Martin. *To the Palace of Wisdom*. Garden City, N.Y.: Doubleday, 1964. 316-19.

Sacks, Sheldon. *Fiction and the Shape of Belief: A Study of Henry Fielding, With Glances at . . . Johnson*. Berkeley: U of Calif. P, 1964. 49-60.

Fisher, S.T. "Johnson on Flying." *TLS* Nov. 4, 1965: 988.

Hilles, F.W. "*Rasselas*, an 'Uninstructive Tale.' " *Johnson, Boswell and Their Circle: Essays Presented to Lawrence Fitzroy Powell*. Ed. Mary M. Lascelles, James L. Clifford, J.D. Fleeman, and John P. Hardy. Oxford: Clarendon Press, 1965. 111-21.

Steeves, Harrison R. *Oriental Romance: Johnson and Beckford, before Jane Austen*. New York: Holt, Rinehart and Winston, 1965. 226-33.

Sutherland, W.O.S., Jr. "The Plot of *Rasselas*." *The Art of the Satirist*. Austin: U of Texas P, 1965. 92-104.

Manzalaoui, Mahmoud. "A Textual Crux in the Concluding Chapter of *Rasselas*." *Cairo Studies in English* (1966), 213-16.

Suderman, Elmer F. "*Candide, Rasselas* and Optimism." *Iowa English Yearbook* 11 (1966): 37-43.

Baker, Sheridan. "*Rasselas:* Psychological Irony and Romance." *Essays in English Neoclassicism in Memory of Charles B. Woods. PQ* 45 (Jan. 1966): 249-61.

Kallich, Martin. "Samuel Johnson's Principles of Criticism and Imlac's 'Dissertation upon Poetry.' " *Journal of Aesthetics and Art Criticism* 25 (Fall 1966): 71-82.

Tillotson, Geoffrey. "Imlac and the Business of a Poet." *Studies in Criticism and Aesthetics. 1660-1800: Essays in Honor of Samuel Holt Monk.* ed. Howard Anderson and John S. Shea. Minneapolis: U of Minnesota P, 1967. 296-314.

Jones, Emrys. "The Artistic Form of *Rasselas.*" *RES,* ns 18 (Nov. 1967): 387-401.

*Alkon, Paul. *Samuel Johnson and Moral Discipline.* Evanston, Ill.: Northwestern UP, 1967.

*Sachs, Arieh. *Passionate Intelligence: Imagination and Reason in The Works of Samuel Johnson.* Baltimore: Johns Hopkins Press, 1967.

Wimsatt, W.K. "In Praise of *Rasselas:* Four Notes (Converging)." *Imagined Worlds: Essays on Some English Novels and Novelists in Honor of John Butt,* ed. Maynard Mack and Ian Gregor. London: Methuen, 1968. 111-36.

Rasselas. Ed. John Hardy. New York: Oxford UP 1968. viii-xxiv.

Bernard, F.V. "The Hermit of Paris and the Astronomer in *Rasselas.*" *JEGP* 67 (Apr. 1968): 272-78.

Reichard, Hugo M. "The Pessimist's Helpers in *Rasselas.*" *Texas Studies in Literature and Language* 10 (Spring 1968): 57-64.

Weitzman, Arthur J. "More Light on *Rasselas:* The Background of the Egyptian Episodes." *PQ* 48 (Jan. 1969): 42-58.

Preston, Thomas R. "The Biblical Context of Johnson's *Rasselas.*" *PMLA* 84 (Mar. 1969): 274-81.

Reed, Kenneth T. " 'This Tasteless Tranquility': A Freudian Note on Johnson's *Rasselas.*" *Literature and Psychology* 19. 1 (1969): 61-62.

Lascelles, Mary. "*Rasselas:* A Rejoinder." *Notions and Facts: Collected Criticism and Research.* Oxford: Clarendon Press, 1970. 120-29.

*Greene, Donald. *Samuel Johnson.* New York: Twayne Publishing Co., 1970. 133-39.

Landa, Louis A. "Johnson's Featured Man: 'A Dissertation in the Art of Flying' Considered." *19th Century Studies in Honor of Donald F. Hyde,* ed. W.H. Bond. New York: Grolier Club, 1970. 161-78.

O'Flaherty, Patrick. "Dr. Johnson as Equivocator: The Meaning of *Rasselas.*" *MLQ* 31 (1970): 195-208.

Weinbrot, Howard. "The Reader, the General and the Particular." *ECS* 5 (Fall 1971): 80-96.

*Schwartz, Richard B. *Samuel Johnson and the New Science.* Madison: U of Wisconsin P 1971. 155-56.

Pagliaro, Harold E. "Structural Patterns of Control in *Rasselas.*" *English Writers of the 18th Century,* ed. John H. Middendorf. New York: Columbia UP, 1971. 208-29.

Rasselas. Ed. Geoffrey Tillotson. New York: Oxford UP, 1971. xi-xix.

*Fussell, Paul. *Samuel Johnson and the Life of Writing.* New York: Harcourt, Brace, Javanovich, 1971. 216-48.

*Damrosch, Leopold, Jr. *Samuel Johnson and the Tragic Sense.* Princeton: Princeton UP, 1972. 152-53.

Kearney, Anthony. "Johnson's *Rasselas* and the Poets." *English Studies* 53 (1972): 514-18.

Brinton, George. "*Rasselas* and the Problem of Evil." *PLL* 8 (1972): 92-96.

Margolis, John D. "Pekuah and the Theme of Imprisonment in Johnson's *Rasselas.*" *English Studies* (1972): 339-443.

Scouten, Arthur. "Dr. Johnson and Imlac." *ECS* 6 (Summer 1973): 506-8.

Curley, Thomas. "The Spiritual Journey Moralized in *Rasselas.*" *Anglia* 91 (1973): 35-55.

Hansen, Marlene. "The Happy Valley: A Version of Hell and a Version of Pastoral." *New Rambler* 14 (1973): 24-30.

White, Ian. "On *Rasselas.*" *Cambridge Quarterly* 6 (1973): 6-31.

*Price, Martin. *The Restoration and 18th Century* in *The Oxford Anthology of English Literature,* ed. Frank Kermode and John Hollander. New York: Oxford UP, 1973. 3: 543.

McIntosh, Carey. *The Choice of Life: Samuel Johnson and the World of Fiction.* New Haven: Yale UP, 1973. Passim.

*Rogers, Pat. *The Augustan Vision.* London: Methuen, 1974. 237-38.

Siebert, Donald T., Jr. "The Reliability of Imlac." *ECS* 7 (Spring 1974): 350-52.

*Wain, John. "A Death and a Journey in the Mind." *Samuel Johnson.* London: Macmillan, 1974. 206-15.

*Holtz, William. "We Didn't Mind His Saying So: Homage to Joseph Wood Krutch: Tragedy and the Ecological Imperative." *American Scholar* (1974): 267-79.

*Lipking, Lawrence. *Norton Anthology of English Literature,* 3rd ed. New York: W.W. Norton, 1974. 42-46.

Kolb, Gwin, "The Intellectual Background of the Discourse on the Soul in *Rasselas.*" *PQ* 54 (1975): 357-67.

Wasserman, Earl R. "Johnson's *Rasselas:* Implicit Contexts." *JEGP* 74 (1975): 1-25.

Rasselas. Ed. Gilbert Phelps. Edinburgh: Folio Society, 1975.

Rothstein, Eric. *Systems of Order and Inquiry in Later 18th Century Fiction.* Berkeley: U of Calif. P, 1975. 23-61.

*Røstvig, Moren-Sofie. "*Tom Jones* and the Choice of Hercules." *Fair Forms: Essays in English Literature from Spenser to Jane Austen.* Cambridge: D.S. Brewer, 1975. 147-77.

Rasselas. Ed. D.J. Enright. Baltimore: Penguin Co., 1976. 13-34.

Schwartz, Richard. "Johnson's Philosopher of Nature in *Rasselas,* Chapter 22." *MP* 74 (1976):196-200.

Monie, Willis J. "Samuel Johnson's Contribution to the Novel." *NR* 17 (1976): 39-44.

Carnochan, W.B. *Confinement and Flight: An Essay on English Literature of the 18th Century.* Berkeley: U of Calif. P, 1977.

Rasselas. Ed. R.W. Desai. Delhi: Doaba House, 1977.

Lerner, Laurence. "Literature and Social Change." *JES* 7 (1977): 231-52.

Gaba, Phylis. "'A Succession of Amusements': The Moralization in *Rasselas* of Locke's Account of Time." *ECS* 10 (1977): 451-63.

Walker, Robert G. *Eighteenth Century Arguments for Immortality and Johnson's Rasselas.* Victoria, B.C.: U of Victoria, 1977. Passim.

*Vesterman, William. *The Stylistic Life of Samuel Johnson.* New Brunswick, N.J.: Rutgers UP, 1977. 69-104.

Gross, Gloria Sybil. "Sanity, Madness and the Family in Samuel Johnson's *Rasselas.*" *Psychocultural Review* 1 (1977): 152-60.

*Bate, W. Jackson. *Samuel Johnson.* London: Chatto and Windus, 1978. 336-39.

Folkenflik, Robert. "The Tulip and Its Streaks: Contexts of *Rasselas* X." *Ariel* 9 (1978): 57-71.

The Mid-Eighteenth Century. Ed. John Butt, completed by Geoffrey Carnall. Oxford: Clarendon Press, 1979. 35-37.

*Greene, Donald. "Voltaire and Johnson." *Enlightenment Studies in Honour of Lester G. Crocker,* ed. Alfred J. Bingham. Oxford: Voltaire Foundation, 1979. 111-31.

Medina, Angel. *Reflection, Time and the Novel.* London: Routledge, Kegan Paul, 1979. 55-64.

*Hardy, John P. *Samuel Johnson: a Critical Study.* London: Routledge, Kegan & Paul, 1979.

Hansen, Marlene R. "*Rasselas,* Milton, and Humanism." *ES* 60 (1979): 14-22.

Sklenicka, Carol J. "Samuel Johnson and the Fiction of Activity." *SAQ* 78 (1979): 214-23.

Broadhead, Glenn J. "The Journey and the Stream: Space and Time Imagery in Johnson's *Rasselas.*" *Exploration* 8 (1979): 15-24.

Eversole, Richard. "Imlac and the Poets of Persia and Arabia." *PQ* 58 (1979): 155-70.

Arieti, James A. "A Herodotean Source for *Rasselas,* Chapter 6." *N&Q* 28 (June 1981): 241.

Ehrenpreis, Irvin. "*Rasselas* and Some Meanings of 'Structure' in Literary Criticism." *Novel* 14 (1981): 101-17.

Orr, Leonard. "The Structural and Thematic Importance of the Astronomer in *Rasselas.*" *Recovering Literature* 9 (1981): 15-21.

Temmer, Mark J. "*Candide* and *Rasselas* Reconsidered." *RLC* 56 (1982): 176-93.

*Pierce, Charles S., Jr. "The Conflict of Faith and Fear in Johnson's Moral Writings." *ECS* 15 (1982): 332-37.

Johnson and Juvenal. Ed. Niall Rudd. Bristol: U of Bristol, 1981.

*J.S. Cunningham. *Samuel Johnson: The Vanity of Human Wishes and Rasselas.* London: Edward Arnold, 1982. 37-61.

Tomarken, Edward. "Prison-Paradise: A Point of Departure in *Rasselas.*" *Gefängnis und Paradies: Momente in der Geschichte eines Motivs,* ed. Gerhard Charles Rump. Bonn: Dr. Rudolf Habelt, 1982. 1-17.

Tomarken, Edward. "Travels into the Unknown: *Rasselas* and *A Journey to the Western Islands of Scotland.*" *The Unknown Samuel Johnson,* ed. John J. Burke, Jr., and Donald Kay. Madison: U of Wisconsin P, 1983, 150-67.

*Collum, Graham. "Dr. Johnson and Human Wishes." *Neophilologus* 67 (1983): 305-19.

Bentley, G.E., Jr. "*Rasselas* and *Guadentio di Lucca* in the Mountains of the Moon." *Revista Canaria de Estudios Ingleses* 9 (1984):1-11.

*Bronson, Bertrand H. "Johnson, Travelling Companion, in Fancy and Fact." *Johnson and His Age,* ed. James Engell. Cambridge: Harvard UP, 1984. 163-87.

Liu, Alan. "Toward a Theory of Common Sense: Beckford's *Vathek* and Johnson's *Rasselas.*" *TSLL* 26 (Sept. 1984): 183-217.

*Wharton, T.F. *Samuel Johnson and the Theme of Hope.* New York: St. Martin's Press, 1984.

Politi, Jina. "The Hell of Paradise: A propos of *Rasselas.*" *Espaces et représentations dans le monde anglo-américain aux XVIIe et XVIIIe siècles.* Paris: P U de Paris-Sorbonne, 1984. 115-28.

Alkon, Paul. "Illustrations of *Rasselas* and Reader-Response Criticism." *Samuel Johnson: Pictures and Words.* Los Angeles: U of Calif. P, 1984. 3-62.

Kolb, G.J. "The Early Reception of *Rasselas.*" *Greene Centennial Studies,* ed. P.J. Korshin and R.R. Allen. Charlottesville: Univ. of Virginia Press, 1984. 217-49.

Damrosch, Leopold, Jr. "Johnson's *Rasselas:* Limits of Wisdom, Limits of Art." *Augustan Studies: Essays in Honor of Irvin Ehrenpreis,* ed. Douglas Lane Patey and Timothy Keegan. Newark: U of Delaware P, 1985. 205-14.

Hansen, Marlene. "Sex and Love, Marriage and Friendship: A Feminist Reading of the Quest for Happiness in *Rasselas*." *ES* 66 (1985): 513-25.

*Grundy, Isobel. *Samuel Johnson and the Scale of Greatness*. Leicester: Leicester UP, 1986.

Index

Addison, Joseph: garden designer, 42; "The Vision of Mirza," 47-48 (*see also* happy valley); and Pope, 167, 169-70 (*see also Life of Pope*; perspective[s])

Aden, John, 23, 184 n 63

Adventurer, The (no. 120), 75, 82, 87, 90

aesthetic: separation from knowledge not accepted in 18th C., 55; procedure as preparation for educational travels, 57; procedure alters concept of dissertation on poetry, 62-70; of understanding provided in dissertation on poetry, 68; formalistic, not formulated for over a century, 104

Armstrong, Percy, 16

Attiret, Frère Jean Denis, 43, 187 n 12

Baker, Ernest, 17, 184 n 47

Bakhtin, M.M., 70, 71, 188 n 21, 25. *See also* perspective(s): axis of

Barbauld, Anna Letitia, 10-11, 183 n 20

Bate, Walter Jackson, 33-34, 63, 186 n 87, 188 n 12. *See also* religion

biography: criticism of *Rasselas*, 8; in prefaces to *Rasselas*, 12 (*see also Rasselas*); relationship of Johnson and astronomer, 24; psychoanalytic reading of *Rasselas*, 24; psychological tradition, 35-36. *See also* Grange, K.; Hovey, R.B.; Liu, A.

Blount, Martha, 167

Bolingbroke, Henry St. John, 167, 169. *See also Life of Pope*

Boswell, James:

—*Life of Johnson*: on *Rasselas*, 9-10; position on *Rasselas* used by O'Flaherty, 28-29; identified Johnson and Imlac, 53; Xerxes passage is

Johnson's favorite, 145; taunts at Scotsmen, 161

—*Tour of the Hebrides*: encouraged Johnson to become part of Scottish history, 150; autobiography bordering on biography, 153; "coquetry" of woman, 158. *See also* history

Boyd, D.V., 118-19, 190 n 17. *See also* religion

Bronson, Bertrand, 22, 110, 184 n 61, 189 n 5

Brownell, Morris, 42-43, 187 n 10

Burney, Frances, 104

Chambers, Sir William, 43-44, 187 n 13

Chesterton, G.K., 184 n 50

Cibber, Colley, 167, 171-73

Clayton, Philip, 111, 189 n 8

Clifford, James, 6, 182 n 1, 183 n 30

Cohen, Ralph, 193 n 1

Collins, A.J.C., 15, 183 n 38

Collins, Norman, 17, 184 n 46

Conant, Martha, 15, 183 n 37. *See also* genre

contingency/contingent: move from "supposed True Paradise," 36; nature of man's educational procedure in flying episode, 49. *See also Rasselas*

Cumberland, Richard, 104

Curley, Thomas, 31-32, 151, 186 n 81, 192 n 4

Dällenbach, Lucien, 70, 71. *See also* hermeneutics; structuralism

Defoe, Daniel: *Moll Flanders*, 38, 73

Dennis, John, 167, 175. *See also Life of Pope*

dialectic: concept that avoids quarrel of